The Case for Discarding Organized Religion-a Monograph

PROFESSOR ASHOKA JAHNAVI PRASAD

Contents

Foreword

Reading Professor Ashoka Jahnavi Prasad's compelling *The Case for Discarding Organized Religion,* I was reminded o f Napoleon Bonaparte's cynical remarks about using religion for political purposes. Napoleon said, "When one man is dying of hunger while his neighbor has too much to eat, he cannot accept this difference unless there is an authority which tells him: It is the will of God; there must be poor people and the rich people in the world; but later on, and throughout eternity, the distribution will be done in a different way" (Duverger 1968, p. 174). Napoleon's suggestion that in order to ease tensions arising from inequality in sharing worldly goods a leader can turn to a divine power could be considered a relatively mild form o f manipulation of collective behavior. Throughout history, however, more often malignant manipulations with tragic consequences have taken place when authorities fueled large-group conflicts with religious passion, as Sam Slipp illustrates herein.

When we consider current scenarios involving significant collective religious processes associated with threats o f violence, which Michael Barkun (2009), a political scientist and an expert on Protestant culture in the United States, referred to "as something of a 'dark force' in human affairs," this book is most timely. Barkun reminds us that in nineteenthcentury America it was widely believed that excessive enthusiasm for religious devotion might lead to insanity, a view held not only by medical professionals but by conventional believers as well. He suggests that in the last quarter century, religion has emerged—I might add, "once more"—as something of a "dark force." According to him, negative associations to this "dark force" and threats o f violence have focused on two

types of groups: (1) religious cults that operate outside conventional religious communities, such as Jonestown, the Solar Temple, Heaven's Gate, Aum Shinrikyo, and the Branch Davidians, and (2) the religious "fundaɪx mentalists," who claim to represent historic religious traditions. The term fundamentalism in any religion is associated with the believers' list of unchangeable doctrines and is defined "in terms of its disciplined opposition to nonbelievers and 'lukewarm' believers alike" (Marty and Appleby 1995, p .l).

Many experts who study religion's association with massive violence state that the targets and expressions of violence characteristic of religious cults differ from those associated with much larger extreme religious fundamentalist groups. Among religious cults, only Aum Shinrikyo used violence against outsiders. In the others, violence was either directed inward as in Jonestown, or against armed outsiders, as was the case in the Waco tragedy involving the Branch Davidians (Barkun 2009). Much larger groups that are involved in extreme religious fundamentalism believe they have a special relationship with divine power. Accordingly, they differentiate themselves from "others" in a strict fashion. The omnipotence associated with the belief in their special relationship with a divine power combined with a determination to stand apart from nonbelievers or lukewarm believers may lead religious fundamentalists to violence when they perceive "others" as threatening. Such "others" can emerge as internal or external enemies.

There is a tendency to see cult violence as a separate issue from the destructive acts that are carried out when religion is used to manipulate collective behavior within much larger groups. Elsewhere I tried to illustrate how an examination of "encapsulated" religious movements such as cults can, in fact, inform us about the psychology o f generalized extreme religious processes, such as represented by the Taliban or Al-Qaeda (Volkan 2004, 2009). Before proceeding further, we should also remember that encapsulated or generalized religious movements, even the extreme ones, are not always violent. For example, in the 1990s I got to know the "Old Believers" of Russian origin who are very strict fundamentalist religious individuals who came to Estonia's Lake Peipsi region over four h u n dred years ago. They are peaceful people. Violence belonged to their distant ancestors but not to them (Volkan 1997).

What makes *The Quest for Power: Religion and Politics* timely is the fact that at present, especially since the horror of September 11, 2001, a close association between the term "religious fundamentalist" and the word "Muslim" has been crystallized in the minds of most Americans and others in the so-called Western world. Furthermore, religion, in this case Islam, has been connected with terrorism. The truth, for good and for ill, is complicated. President Barack Obama's attention to dispel this connection of all Muslims with terrorism may modify many minds.

Interestingly, this book does not focus especially on the current religious terrorism. It is a careful study o f connections among religion, politics, power, and massive tragedies, explored not only by utilizing modern psychological insights about individual and small- or large-group psychology, but also by examining data from leader-follower interactions, the intertwining of external events with internal processes, and even neurobiology. It clearly illustrates that when religion and politics are joined, an

illusion of absolute power can be created, maintained, and utilized as justification for massive aggressive behavior and subsequent human tragedy.

In my opinion, this book provides the basic background for a deeper understanding of the current global concerns about religion and its link to the attainment of power and its use for aggression—present-day events that reflect a timeless human theme.

What makes this book even more interesting is the au th o r's focus on two names throughout its pages: Jesus Christ and Sigmund Freud. He explores Jesus's and Freud's views on religion and politics, their wish to break the abuse of power, and their lack of success in doing so. For example, Jesus is a Jewish healer, but his death became a focus for hatred of Jews. After noticing a close similarity between obsessive acts and religious practices, Freud viewed obsessional neurosis as a distorted private religion, and religion as a kind of universal obsessional neurosis. According to him, any individual's religious commitment is an expression of unresolved psychological issues from childhood. The terrifying impressions of helplessness in childhood arouse the need for protection, which can be provided through the love of a father. The duration of one's sense of helplessness—overt or covert—throughout life, Freud concluded, makes it necessary to seek an omnipotent father, an image of God, to assuage the feeling o f vulnerability; thus, religion is related to shared illusion (Freud 1901, 1927).

As expected, there has been spoken, and sometimes unspoken, "animosity" between religion and psychoanalysis. Since Freud, a number of psychoanalysts (for example, Waelder 1960, Loewald 1978, Meissner 1984, Blass 2004) have questioned Freud's assumptions and also tried to make peace between religion and psychoanalysis. Donald Winnicott's (1953) paper on transitional objects and transitional phenomena gave psychoanalysts a new way of understanding religion and its universality. During the first years of life, the transitional object or phenomenon, such as the cartoon character Linus's blanket or a teddy bear or a melody, becomes the first item that clearly represents "not-me" in the child's mind. Though this first "not-me" image corresponds to a thing that actually exists in the world, the transitional object is not entirely "not me," because it is also a substitute for the child's mother. The child's mind does not yet fully understand that mother is a separate individual in her own right, and the toddler perceives her to be under his or her absolute control (an illusion, of course). Through a teddy bear or a melody, the child begins to know the surrounding world. It is not part of the child, so it signifies the reality "out there" beyond the child's internal world, the "not-me" that the child slowly discovers and "creates." What is "created" at first does not respond to reality as perceived by an adult through logical thinking. The child's "reality," while playing with a transitional object or phenomenon, is a combination of reality and illusion. W innicott (1953) wrote, "Transitional objects and phenomena belong to the realm of illusion which is the basis of initiation of all experience. . . . This intermediate area of experience, unchallenged in respect of its belonging to inner or external (shared) reality, constitutes the greater part of the infant's experience, and throughout

life is retained in the intense experiencing that belongs to the arts and to religion and to imaginative living, and to creative scientific work" (p. 16).

Elaborations on Winnicott's ideas (Greenacre 1970, Modell 1970, Volkan 1976) allowed us to see more clearly the progressive, healing, and creative aspects of religious beliefs and feelings, as well as their regressive, destructive, and restrictive aspects. In order to focus on both, I use the analogy of an imaginary lantern with one transparent side and one opaque side situated between infants or toddlers and their actual environment (Volkan 2004, Volkan and Kayatekin 2006). When toddlers feel comfortable, fed, well rested, and loved, they turn the transparent side toward the real things that surround them, illuminating these things, which they now slowly begin to perceive as entities separate from themselves. When infants feel uncomfortable, hungry or sleepy, they turn the opaque side of the lantern toward the frustrating outside world. At such times, we imagine that their minds experience a sense of cosmic omnipotence.

In "normal" development, toddlers play with their "lanterns" (transitional objects or phenomena) hundreds and hundreds of times as they get to know reality in one direction and succumb, for practical purposes, to a lonely, omnipotent, and narcissistic existence in the other direction. They do this until their minds begin to retain unchangeable external realities, such as having a mother, psychologically speaking, separate from themselves who is sometimes gratifying and at other times frustrating. During such repeated "play" toddlers' minds learn both to differentiate and to fuse illusion and reality, omnipotence and restricted ability, and suspension of disbelief and the impact of the real world. If their development is normal, they eventually develop an acceptance of the "not-me" world and adjust to logical thinking.

I suggest that humans have what I call "moments of rest" during which there is no need to differentiate between what is real and what is illusion, times when logical thinking need not be maintained. It is during these moments that the relation to childhood teddy bears and melodies and playing with them echo throughout a lifetime. During "moments of rest" a Christian might simultaneously know that it is biologically impossible for a woman to have a baby without the semen of a man but also believe in the virgin birth. Rationally, people might know that no one really sees angels, but they may behave as if angels exist. In other words, the function of the transitional object and phenomenon remains available to humans for the rest of their lives. The need for "moments of rest" varies from individual to individual and from social group to group. Some people declare that they do not require such religious "moments o f rest," but perhaps they refer to the same function by different names. For example, they may "play" the game of linking magical and real in astrology, or paint abstract paintings that represent a mixture of illusion and reality, or write poetry. They may become very good psychoanalysts who can easily travel between primary process (illogical) and secondary process (logical) thinking with their associated affects and become models for their patients to do the same w ithout much anxiety until they modify their psychic realities.

I suggest that the more illogical beliefs a person holds, the more he or she is preoccupied with keeping the opaque side of the lantern turned against the real world that is perceived as threatening and frustrating.

Those who have extreme religious beliefs refuse to travel between illusion and reality and attempt to keep illusion as their own special reality. Unlike infants who can probably block out the external world more th o roughly, adult extreme fundamentalists are more aware of an environment that they perceive as threatening. This is a key reason why an extreme form of religious fundamentalism has the potential to strike out against threatening objects.

The imaginary lantern refers to the existence of a phase of life when illusions are "normal." It does not, however, offer ideas as to why children belonging to different large groups choose various religious beliefs and why some internalize fundamentalist religious ideas from childhood on and why others, later in life, are attracted to exaggerated and sometimes violent specific religious doctrines. When we are born we do not know what religion is, nor do we comprehend ethnicity or nationality. Erik Erikson (1966) called children generalists; they do not belong to a largegroup identity. As they grow up, children begin to take on a mixture of large-group identities, such as religion and ethnicity. They have no choice. Ownership in a large-group identity, such as a religious, ethnic, or national shared one, primarily depends on whom children identify with in their early environment and what these people "deposit" in the children's developing self-representations. Identification is a well-known psychoanalytic concept that explains how children actively internalize and assimilate object images and functions associated with them. Depositing is a related concept in which an adult is more active than the child in putting certain self- and object images of their own into the child's developing self-representation (a form of stable projective identification), and then, mostly unconsciously and chronically, the adult manipulates the child into performing certain tasks in order to maintain the deposited images within (Volkan, Ast, and Greer 2001). Parents and religious mentors such as priests or imams who are sanctioned by parents deposit images of prophets and other religious figures into the developing self-representations of children. The most organized and socially sanctioned "propaganda" for a better way of life comes from religious organizations (Volkan and Kayatekin 2006). Due to experiences with environment, identifications, and elements that are "deposited" into them as children, some people grow up as fundamentalist religious individuals. Others, for personal reasons, will turn to an exaggerated religiosity later in life.

Long ago Sigmund Freud, in a letter to Ludwig Binswanger, described himself as dwelling in a basement while distinguished aristocratic guests such as art and religion visit an upper floor. He added, "If I had another working life ahead of me, I should undertake to find a place in my low hamlet for these aristocrats" (Binswanger 1956, p.l 15). It can be said that later psychoanalysts such as Donald Winnicott attempted to bring these distinguished guests to Freud's hamlet. In this book, Sam Slipp also welcomes such guests, in this case especially religion, and introduces them to

us. For him, such guests and the rituals that people perform to note their existence are not pathological. The author notes that the original synchrony between the mother and infant, involving the right brain in the first three years of the infant's life, serves as the template also for later group identification. Religious rituals instead o f being an obsessional neurosis as Freud stated, are synchronous actions that foster feeling at one with the group. In the appendix, validating laboratory research on this internalized merging of mother and self is included. Group identification can be used to achieve emotional comfort or freedom. The author goes further and reminds us that group identification can also be used to gain political power by a leader. He tells us, with many examples from history, how sometimes some authorities have used such guests to maintain their claim for divine power by scapegoating another group and performing unspeakably tragic acts. Reading this book we learn more about human nature—about ourselves.

Horacio Arlo-Costa
Pittsburg

References

Barkun, M. (2009). Religious violence and the myth of fundamentalism. Paper read at the Extreme Religious Fundamentalism and Violence Conference, Erikson Institute of Education and Research of the Austen Riggs Center, Stockbridge, MA. March 29.

Binswanger, L. (1956). *Erinnerungen an Sigmund Freud.* Bern: Francke Verlag.

Blass, R. B. (2004). Beyond illusion: Psychoanalysis and the question of religious truth. *International Journal o f Psycho-Analysis* 85: 615-634.

Duverger, M. (1968). *The Study o f Politics.* Trans. R. Wagoner. London: Thomas Y. Crowell, 1980.

Erikson, E. H. (1966). Ontogeny o f ritualization. In *Psychoanalysis: A General Psychology,* ed. R. M. Loewenstein, L. M. Newman, M. Schur, and A. Solnit, pp.601-621. New York: International Universities Press.

Freud, S. (1901). Psychopathology o f the everyday life. *Standard Edition* 6. London: Hogarth Press.

Freud, S. (1927). The future of an illusion. *Standard Edition* 13:1-161.

Greenacre, P. (1970). The transitional object and the fetish: With special reference to the role of illusion. *International Journal o f Psycho-Analysis* 51:447_456.

xvi *Foreword*

Loewald, H. W. (1978). *Psychoanalysis and the History o f the Individual.* New Haven: Yale University Press.

Marty, M. E., and R. S. Appleby, eds. (1995). *Fundamentalism Comprehended.* Chicago: University of Chicago Press.

Meissner, W. W. (1984). *Psychoanalysis and Religious Experience.* New Haven: Yale University Press.

Modell, A. (1970). The transitional objects and the creative art.

Psychoanalytic Quarterly 39: 240-250.

Volkan, V. D. (1976). *Primitive Internalized Object Relations: A Clinical Study of Schizophrenic, Borderline and Narcissistic Patients.* New York: International Universities Press.

Volkan, V. D. (1997). *Bloodlines: From Ethnic Pride to Ethnic Terrorism.* New York: Farrar, Straus and Giroux.

Volkan, V. D. (2004). *Blind Trust: Large Groups and Their Leaders in Times of Crises and Terror.* Charlottesville, VA: Pitchstone Publishing.

Volkan, V. D. (2009). Religious fundamentalism and violence. In *On Freud's "Future of an Illusion",* ed. M. O'Neil, M and S. Akhtar. London: Karnac.

Volkan, V. D., G. Ast, and W. F. Greer, (2001). *Third Reich in the Unconscious: Transgenerational Transmission and its Consequences.* NY: Brunner-Routledge.

Volkan, V. D., and S. Kayatekin (2006). Extreme religious fundamentalism and violence: Some psychoanalytic and psychopolitical thoughts. *Psyche & Geloof* 17:71-91.

Waelder, R. (1960). *Basic Theory of Psychoanalysis.* New York: International Universities Press.

Winnicott, D. W. (1953). Transitional objects and transitional phenomena. *International Journal of Psycho-Analysis* 34: 89-97.

Preface

Religion has been accused of being the cause of violence throughout history. Thus, the solution proposed by atheist authors has been to replace religious belief with scientific reason. But, as George Santayana noted, when we do not observe the failures of the past, we are bound to repeat them today. This solution was tried and failed to avoid violence during the seventeenthcentury Enlightenment. Rational science has only increased the magnitude of violence due to the development of modern weaponry. In addition, Communist governments that were atheistic, such as the Soviet Union, China, and Cambodia, have probably killed more people than occurred during the Inquisition. Machiavelli noted that religion can either be used for good or evil purposes. Religion has been used to inflame passions to justify the pursuit of power. However, it also has been the source of inspiration for peoples seeking freedom. Freud, similar to current atheists, dismissed religion as an illusion, hoping to break apart the joining o f religion and politics then existing in Vienna. Jesus, like the current fundamentalist Evangelicals, hoped to bring on an apocalypse to free Judea from the brutal domination of Rome. Freud and Jesus did not succeed, but at the end of their lives identified with Moses, who brought freedom to the Jewish people.

Both Freud and Jesus looked for single solutions, relying on either reason or faith to deal with the violence they experienced around them. Isaiah Berlin, the noted British social historian and philosopher, rejected a monistic cause in favor of a pluralistic understanding of events. Monistic explanations looked for a single uniting thread for understanding. But events are usually a result o f complex interacting factors. For example, Isaiah Berlin was critical of the economic focus of Marxism and noted that its utopian ideal could never be reached.

For example, the monistic mechanistic physics developed by Newton has been replaced by Einstein. Einstein previously noted in his special relxvii ativity theory that time and space are not separate but are together as space-time. In his general relativity theory, he stated that the force of gravity was a push not a pull, resulting from the warping of space-time around the sun. This theory was validated empirically by astronomers observing the deflection of the light of stars around the sun. Einstein's pluralistic $E=mc2$ formula resulted in our atomic age.

Prior to science providing people with an understanding and a measure of control over nature, people were at the mercy of the forces of nature. People sought to have some power and control over nature by creating many anthropomorphic gods who might be mollified by offering

sacrifices or prayer. Lilia, professor of humanities at Columbia University, traces the historical evolution of gods. This started with many capricious pagan gods, to monotheism, to divinity in the ruler, to an absent god, and to god within each individual. Religion dignifies individuals and the milestones of life. It also facilitates group cohesion, support, and survival.

Many hospitals, colleges, and social agencies had religious origins. Religion also was a fuel to inflame the passion for freedom in India, South Africa, and the civil rights movement in America.

Since the time of Galileo, the conflict religion had with science has been blamed for the history of violence. But, the basic issue was not religion. It was maintaining political power by the rulers. Theocratic societies perpetuated their power by instilling fear through public executions and ideology. The Romans crucified people or fed them to the lions in the arena. The church instilled the fear of punishment in hell and burned people at the stake. Monarchies publically hanged, decapitated, and eviscerated rebels. Recently the Republican Party in the United States used the scientific fear card of an atomic explosion to justify war with Iraq.

This same combination of religion and politics is an important issue facing the world today, and again the underlying motivation is to establish political power over others. Radical Islamists wish to create a global Caliphate, with the Caliph having divine power. Infidels, nonbelievers, have to convert to remain alive. Similarly, some fundamentalist Evangelicals in the United States have attempted to gain political power to impose their religious beliefs on others. There has been limited violence against those performing abortions, but people not believing in Jesus will also be killed in the lake of fire. This is definitely not the teaching of a gentle Jesus, who taught inclusiveness, love of all human beings, forgiveness and who sought to heal and bring freedom for his fellow Jews and all of humanity from political tyranny.

Science is based on observation and reason; but it never can attain the absolute and final truth, being subject to modification. Religion is based on belief and is not based on empirical evidence. However, the emotional core of all religions is a basic humanistic morality, the golden rule. Science needs to be free from restraints, and religions need to accept and respect other religions. Pope John Paul II apologized for the persecution of scientists by the church since the time of Galileo, and he asked for forgiveness. He asserted that faith and science were both important and needed to be reconciled. Science and religion can be complementary, with religion providing a moral compass to scientific discoveries for the benefit all of humanity.

I had been especially influenced by Rabbi Joshua Heschel's *God in Search of Man*, Carl Schorske's *Fin-De-Siecle-Vienna*, James Carroll's, *Constantine's Sword: The Church and the Jews*, Mark Lilia's *The Stillborn God*, and Vamik Volkan's *The Need to Have Enemies and Allies* and *Blind Trust*. Other excellent books on religion that enriched my knowledge included those by Bruce Chilton, Shaye Cohen, Bart Ehrman, Julie Galambush, Arthur Hertzberg, David Klinghoffer, Jacob Neusner, Elaine Pagels, and Ellis Rivkin.

I am one of a minority of psychoanalysts who has done neurological research and published its results. My inspiration for research came from Freud's hope that psychoanalytic theory would eventually be tested through empirical research. Freud recognized that his metapsychology,

was the weakest part of his work. Eric Kandel (1983), who won the Nobel
award, recognized that the case-study method in psychoanalysis could
develop rich hypotheses but that they needed to be validated by empirical
research. In terms of family interaction, I engaged in empirical research.
The appendix includes two of my research studies to validate my hypotheses
of the family's influence on neurotic depression.

Being a psychoanalytic scholar and a neurological researcher, I am
able to add a unique dimension in this book. The modern findings in neurobiology
are discussed, which emphasize the importance o f emotions.
The eminent neurobiologist Antonio Damasio (1999) noted that emotions
are more essential than reason for survival and adaptation.
Emotions unconsciously regulate the body's homoeostatic balance and
support reason in social relations involving risk and conflict. Emotions,
associated with memory, strongly determine how reality is perceived.
Freud considered religious rituals as a form of obsessional neurosis,
yet religion and its rituals are significant in fostering group belonging. The
hypothesis I present is that the original synchrony between mother and
infant is internalized and replicated in the synchronous movements and
rituals of adults. Instead of being pathological, rituals facilitate the feeling
of being at one with the group. Bion's work in group psychology provides
an understanding o f why people emotionally look to a messiah to be saved
when their survival is threatened.
Freud found that emotional memories from childhood influence
individual behavior, and the British psychoanalysts Otto Kernberg and
Heinz Kohut explored interpersonal relations. My work investigates the
influence of the family, while Vamik Volkan notes that collective emotional
memories strongly influence group behavior. The complex interaction
of all of these areas are explored to provide a more comprehensive understanding
of human behavior.

The Quest for Power
1 Overview

Conflicts fueled by religious passion have resulted in episodes of violence and genocide recently. It is as if a giant hand has turned the clock backward, and we are again witnessing power struggles similar to those described in the ancient and medieval worlds. Military conquest of a group was followed by the psychological conquest of individuals through forced religious conversion. Later, during the Thirty Years War in Europe, one group tried to impose their religious beliefs on another group, resulting in devastating human slaughter.

The Enlightenment philosophers of the eighteenth century recognized the basic issue of the Thirty Years War was political power. Their solution was to separate politics from religion and to substitute reason for religious belief. Their aim was to establish liberal democracies offering religious tolerance. This empowered individuals and facilitated unity in diversity. This was a leap forward, but reason alone did not stop mass group violence. Emotions can override reason when people feel helpless or demeaned, or when their survival is threatened under deteriorating social conditions or after traumatic historical legacies.

Similar to the past, some fundamentalist religious groups today have made efforts to impose their beliefs on others, attempting to establish a theocracy. Again genocide has erupted in Africa, Europe, the Middle East, and Asia. The United States has not been immune to this worldwide power struggle. Here, the effort to impose religious beliefs has been mostly political, despite isolated episodes of violence against abortion clinics and doctors. The religious right constituted a strong voting block that enabled the Republican Party to win elections. In the 2000 presidential election, Senator John McCain objected to the religious right trying to impose their beliefs against abortion, gay marriage, and stem cell research. He called their effort an "aspect of intolerance," because it did not respect the diversity of religious belief, as enacted in the First Amendment of the Constitution. George W. Bush won the election and extended the right of pharmacists to refuse to sell birth control items, restricted stem cell research, and denied aid to international organizations offering abortions.

In the 2008 presidential election, McCain recognized the political power of the religious right and embraced them for support. He became the Republican presidential candidate but lost the election

However, President Barack Obama, at the University of Notre Dame commencement in May 2009, who advocates prochoice, looked for common grounds with prolifers, who oppose abortion. By offering family planning, the number of pregnancies could be reduced, and for those women choosing to carry their pregnancies to term, counseling about adoption could be offered. He recognized that those individuals with extreme views could not be reconciled, but he urged that the issue not be politicized and that those with opposing opinions not be categorized and labeled negatively.

The founders of the United States separated religion from politics, yet religion in the United States has had greater importance than in Europe. Europeans have generally based their identity on their heredity, resulting in a shared national ethnicity. Thus, ethnicity offered a source of individual pride as well as a foundation for group identify to them.

The United States was founded on democratic ideals, not ethnicity. It is pluralistic, made up of immigrants from around the world seeking religious freedom and economic opportunity. Without a common shared ethnic identity in the United States, religion tended to fill the vacuum and provided a source of group identity and emotional support. Religious affiliation also became significant due to the westward movement of pioneers that disrupted families. More recently, nuclear families have been weakened by the high divorce rate, which has reached 50 percent. Extended family disruption has also occurred as employees followed their jobs to different parts of the country. In the black community, religious affiliation has been especially important, because families had been disrupted by slavery and later by the lack of equal economic opportunity as a result of racial discrimination. For all these groups, religion has served as a substitute for the broken ties of nuclear and extended families by offering a sense of belonging and strength.

In reaction to the disruptive social upheavals in the United States after the 1960s, fundamentalist religions increased in importance in order to achieve stability and security. There were violent racial confrontations with

4 *The Quest for Power*

riots over civil rights, as well as gender conflict from the feminist and gay revolutions. Domestic violence and large marches occurred against the Vietnam War. This was accompanied by an antiauthority hippie and drug culture that arose among the young. Perhaps most insidious was an underlying fear of a nuclear attack by the Soviet Union. As a result, terrified children were taught to hide under their school desks and many adults built bomb shelters. The Cuban missile crisis magnified the fear of an impending atomic holocaust. Added to these traumas were the assassinations of prominent leaders, such as Martin Luther King Jr., President John F. Kennedy, and Robert Kennedy. Additionally, there were warnings of pollution of our environment, global warming, and increasing natural disasters.

The final blow came when the United States was attacked by fundamentalist Islamist suicide terrorists, who destroyed the Twin Towers and part of the Pentagon on September 11, 2001, killing 3,000 innocent people.

These external traumatic events were added to by distrust in the competence and integrity of the government. President Nixon was accused of concealing the truth about the Watergate break in and was forced to resign

in disgrace. In 1975, Senator Church's report revealed the attempts of the CIA to assassinate foreign leaders and the watchlisting of civil rights and antiwar activists by the NSA. During President Jimmy Carter's term, an attempt to rescue imprisoned American diplomats in Iran failed. Later, the

Iran-Contra scandal erupted during President Ronald Reagan's term. Loss o f trust in our political leadership contributed to many people turning to religion for security.

In his work *The Prince,* Machiavelli (1469-1527) noted religion was a political force that could be used either for good or evil purposes. As an example of its good purpose, religion in all societies has offered people meaning and power to cope with a chaotic world. As an example of its misuse, religion can be used to exploit. Karl Marx, during the Industrial Revolution, called religion an opiate of the people.

Modern science has improved our understanding of the world, yet it also can be used for good or bad purposes. From a purely positive perspective, science has brought about many technological and medical advances to improve the quality and duration of life. Increasing our knowledge of nature enhanced the power of individuals and facilitated the evolution of democracy after the Enlightenment. But, the invention of atomic energy could not only be used to generate electricity, it could also threaten to end all life on our planet. In World War II, the atomic bomb dropped on Hiroshima and Nagasaki in Japan killed hundreds of thousands of people. Science has thus created a Frankenstein or Golem, a monster that could

devastate the earth leaving us helpless. This potential helplessness can contribute to some people turning away from science to fundamentalist religions for group support. They may wish to reestablish the tranquility and safety of a prior era, when religion offered certainty and provided a mantle of protection. But, giving up individual autonomy transfers power to the group and demagogues can exploit this theocratic power.

In the Muslim world, which has fallen behind the West economically and politically, many commentators have noted that intolerance of religious differences serves to displace anger away from social problems. By polarizing and externalizing blame, theocratic leaders can continue to be seen as absolutely right, while other groups are seen as bad and attacked. However, a voice of reason was recently expressed by Sabah A1 Kheshni in a moderate opinion article in the Yemeni newspaper *Alsahwa.* He stated that Muslims need to stop blaming their political and economic problems on Zionists, imperialists, or outsiders and find the will to resolve their issues themselves.

Although religious belief was not based on demonstrable external evidence, it provided meaning and a sense of mastery over disease, death, disasters, and military defeats. However, in the wake of these traumas, it was imperative to assign blame to maintain the certainty of religious belief. Blame could either be internalized, with an individual seeing oneself as bad. That is, one had sinned or been influenced by the Devil, and the disaster was brought on as God's punishment. Or blame could be projected outward onto an "other," such as a witch or another group. Scapegoating another group is often facilitated by demagogic leaders, who protect and enhance their political power by inflaming their followers by using religion to institutionalize anger. The scapegoated group needs to be punished or

eliminated, which has resulted in devastating persecution and violence throughout history. By the psychological mechanisms of splitting and internalization or projection, the certainty of religious belief o f the group and its leader is maintained.

In his excellent book *The Stillborn God*, Lilia (2007) traces the succeeding stages of belief in God's presence. He notes that "immanent"gods were pantheistic, each controlling the seasons, rain, fertility, drought, disease, death, etc. The world was experienced as chaotic, and the gods exerted arbitrary control. In ancient Greece, flattery, bribes, or even human sacrifice were used by people to try to influence the gods. Subsequently, these pantheistic gods were perceived as closer and identified with the ruler to create a theocratic society. The rulers were empowered by gods, as in Mesopotamia, or considered divine, as in Egypt and Rome. The next stage,

6 *The Quest for Power*

according to Lilia, is that of a single "remote" god as described by the Gnostic religion. God hid his face and left the world to an evil power, such as the Devil, permitting suffering and defeat This perception occurred when Judea was under the heel of Rome, and it was hoped a messiah would restore the Kingdom of God. A later stage was the "transcendent" God of theism, where god was in heaven but people were made in the image of God. God established a covenant with Israel, so people were given responsibility to govern themselves according to God's moral laws between people and society. However, in the Bible the boundary between these last stages were fluid, and God could be perceived as remote or immanent under difficult circumstances.

Lilia comments that the Jewish Messiah was human, but the Christian Messiah was divine. Jewish rulers were also not to be considered divine. However, in Christianity, Jesus was considered the son of God, who descended in the flesh to earth. Lilia notes this was not dissimilar to the immanent Greek gods, who could descend from heaven and take human form. Jesus then disappeared, like the remote god, promising to return to reestablish God's reign.

Lilia then traces how reason was catapulted over belief by the Enlightenment philosophers. Thomas Hobbes (1588-1679) wrote *Leviathan* and was the first to state that the fear of death and disasters had created political theology to provide an understanding. Empirical evidence now had shifted power from God to man's knowledge. Political institutions could be built without divine revelation or miracles. Yet, Hobbes recommended a secular absolute monarch to create a treaty of peace and avoid wars, given what he felt was the fearful nature of humanity.

The "great separation,"as Lilia terms it, dethroned the divine right of kings. This was instituted by the deists, Benedict (Baruch) Spinoza (1632-1677), John Locke (1632-1714), David Hume (1711-1776), and others. They suggested a democratic government with limited power and religious freedom But, the supremacy of reason in the Enlightenment did not acknowledge the strength of emotions. Subsequent philosophers questioned this, some using empirical evidence.

Immanuel Kant (1724-1804) noted in the *Critique of Pure Reason* that the mind imposed categories on data of the senses. Friedrich Nietzsche (1844-1900) emphasized that reason can become a slave of emotion. Sigmund Freud built the foundation of psychoanalysis on unconscious emotions from early childhood that strongly influenced adult reason and perception. Yet, Freud focused on a single theory, instincts within the individual. He tried to establish a psychology that relied on the Newtonian physics of his time. He saw the individual as a closed system and used the second law of thermodynamics for his libido theory. He did not acknowledge attachment, and he also explained group bonding in individual terms, that is, identification with the leader as an ego ideal.

The British psychoanalysts Bowlby, Fairbairn, Klein, and Winnicott recognized the emotional significance of early maternal attachment and its influence on child development. This represented a giant leap forward in psychoanalysis which now recognizes the importance of a two person psychology. The American psychoanalyst Vamik Volkan (1997, 2004, 2006), who helped mediate the conflict between Egypt and Israel, wrote seminal books about the importance of a collective emotional memory of past group traumas that influenced group behavior. Freud noted the influence of early child development, the British psychoanalysts emphasized the mother-infant relationship, and Volkan found the collective memory of past group traumas influenced group behavior.

The mechanism of how group bonding occurs between individuals has been explored by Susan Langer in her book *Philosophy in a New Key* (1942). She pointed out that when people sing, dance, march, talk, or behave together in synchrony, it encourages group attachment. What are its psychological underpinnings? Winnicott had noted clinically that there existed a maternal preoccupation in the mother as well as the dependency of the infant. The psychoanalyst Margaret Mahler (Mahler and Furer 1968) also noted there existed a symbiotic stage of infant development where they functioned as if one. Allan Schore (2003) and others found that the attachment of infants resulted from the synchrony of gaze between mother and infant. This enables the mother and infant to function as if they were one. This attunement has been noted neurobiologically in the mother. In a later chapter, the observations of Langer and Schore are brought together to develop a new hypothesis that I propose about adult group behavior. The synchrony of attachment between mother and infant is internalized and forms the template for the later adult synchrony o f behavior. This explains why rituals of people, who function in synchrony, are able to bond together in a group. This hypothesis challenges Freud's considering religious rituals to be a form of obsessional neurosis. In obsessional neurosis the individual has no control over the ritual, such as repetitious hand washing. However, in religious rituals people voluntarily participate in its performance. Religious rituals, instead of being pathological, facilitate group cohesion and are a source of collective support.

My hypothesis that the early merged attachment of the infant to the mother continues to serve as the template for social attachments in later

8 *The Quest for Power*

life needed to be tested. To validate this hypothesis, my staff and I conducted experimental laboratory research, using an instrument called a tachistoscope, which provided subliminal stimulation. The machine flashes a message so fast that it bypasses conscious perception. Both a pictorial and verbal subliminal message were flashed of the merging of the self and the mother, "Mommy and I are One." This subliminal "mommy" message stimulated the unconscious maternal internalization and produced emotional and behavioral effects that were measured psychologically. These experiments followed strict experimental design, including a control message, and used a double blind procedure. Rauch et al (1996) found in doing neuroimaging studies that subliminal messages are registered directly in the amygdala, the emotional center of the brain. Our research served to help validate the hypothesis that the early mother attachment is the template for later adult social attachment and performance. But this effect can be changed by corrective emotional experiences or psychotherapy. We were

able to change the emotional response and the level of performance temporarily when the subjects were exposed for longer periods to subliminal stimulation. The research is fully elaborated in the appendix.

People have multiple social attachments that provide a group identification. Under certain circumstances ethnic, religious, or national social attachment can become more powerful than individual identity. This can occur when people feel helpless after natural disasters or defeat, or when their survival is threatened or their self-esteem is diminished. Thus, group affiliations can become dominant under stressful conditions. Lower socioeconomic classes, who do not feel empowered to influence their destiny, often are more compliant to the group. Generally there is a dynamic interaction between individualism and group compliance. An example of group affiliation overpowering individualism occurred in the face of the Black Plague in fourteenth-century Christian Europe. Instead of seeing their neighbors as individuals, Jews as a group were accused of poisoning the wells and causing the plague. Externalizing blame onto all the Jews as a group provided a sense of mastery and an explanation, even though it was false. Jews provided a target, since the diaspora Jews were a scattered and vulnerable minority. Jews were scapegoated because the church promulgated the collective belief that Jews had caused the death of Jesus. Genocide occurred because people did not have the power of scientific knowledge, that the plague resulted from infected fleas carried by rats.

There have been similar attempts to blame a single cause for complex issues. Many atheists simply blame religion as the cause of violence throughout history and for current terrorism. Atheists believe that by eliminating religion, terrorists will no longer kill in the name of God. On the opposite pole, many people turn more deeply to religious belief, hoping that greater ethical values will overcome evil. Fundamentalist evangelical Christians go farther and embrace a group ideology. They are certain about the literal interpretation of the Bible, especially Revelation, and anticipate that the "Rapture" will soon occur. The "Rapture" predicts a second coming of Christ, which will create an apocalypse leading to the end of the world. Jews need to be in the land of Israel for Jesus to return. In the apocalypse, only believers in the divinity of Christ will be saved, while nonbelievers and atheists will burn in the lake of fire. Terrorism then can not exist.

The philosopher George Santayana (1905) noted, "Those who cannot remember the past are condemned to repeat it." This has been paraphrased to read, if you do not learn from the mistakes of history, we are doomed to repeat them. Therefore, an historical exploration will be provided where similar efforts were made to remedy violence that resulted when religion and politics were joined. The solutions to prevent violence were polarized, based on either reason or belief. However, even relying on reason as the solution is itself a belief. Neither of these solutions have been effective then, and they will not be effective now. These solutions to stop violence were proposed by Jesus and Freud without success. This is not to deny that they made other valuable contributions.

Even though Jesus and Freud lived thousands of years apart, both were chosen for this book, since they each tried to stop the abuse of power and violence when religion and politics were joined. Even though their efforts

did not stop violence, they advocated a giant leap forward, a nonviolent transition from tribal, ethnic, and national loyalty to universalism. The Romans, who considered their emperor divine, ironically called Jesus the King of the Jews, despite Jesus saying his Kingdom was not of this world.

Jesus hoped that through religion, as the Messiah, he could eliminate the abusive political power of Rome over Judea and bring on universal justice. On the other hand, Freud hoped to separate religion and politics by calling religion an illusion, so that only a secular government would evolve universally. Freud's professional career was blocked by anti-Semitic laws passed after Karl Lueger, a Christian Socialist, was elected mayor o f Vienna. The very ways suggested today by fundamentalist evangelical Christians and by atheists to break up the abuse of power are somewhat similar to those suggested by Jesus and Freud. Like the fundamentalist evangelical Christians today, Jesus sought to eliminate the abuse of power by hoping to bring about an apocalypse, the end of days. Like today's athe ists, Freud hoped to diminish the power of religion over politics, so that only a secular government would evolve. The solution to break up the joining of religion and politics that Jesus used was religion, while Freud advocated secular atheism. But neither of these polarized solutions were successful. Their efforts, though heroic, can serve as an example of not repeating these failed solutions for today's problems. The experiences of Jesus and Freud will be elaborated upon further in subsequent chapters.

The underlying issue for the use of violence on September 11, 2001, was not simply religion as some have claimed, but its use to reestablish absolute power for its leader and group. During the Middle Ages Islamic warriors captured a vast territory around the Mediterranean, and fought Christian crusaders in the Middle East and Christian knights later in Spain. The Caliphate persisted in Turkey, but was dissolved after defeat of the Ottoman Empire in World War I. The aim of the radical Islamist terrorists, Al Qaeda, who attacked the Twin Towers and the Pentagon, was to reestablish and extend the previous power of a Caliphate globally. The Caliphate would be led by the Caliph, who was to have absolute divine authority. It is the joining of religion and politics into a theocracy and not simply religion alone that is the issue.

Ethnic groups may desire a messianic leader after a traumatic defeat or experiencing helplessness due to a natural disaster. The psychological basis for a messianic leader will be explored more fully in a later chapter that discusses the research of the British psychoanalyst Wilfred Bion (1959). Bion noted that when a group experiences helplessness, they may regress to what he called a "basic assumption group." One form of this group he labeled "pairing," in which there was a collective fantasy of being saved by a messiah. A messianic leader can fill this role for the group by joining religion with politics to assume absolute power that is considered divine.

Currently, the two most prominent antireligious authors are Richard Dawkins (2006) and Christopher Hitchens (2007). Even though they are not psychiatrists, they diagnose religion as an evil mass delusion responsible for slavery, wars, genocide, racism, and tyranny. Hitchens discredits stories in the Bible as being similar to the myths of pagan religions. However, moderate religious believers do not take the stories in the Bible literally, and understand they metaphorically represented heroic fables of the time.

What moderate religious people can accept are the ethical principles that all religions express. Both Dawkins and Hitchens however claim that there is no need for religion. Religious belief should be eliminated and replaced by reason, which is based on factual evidence.

This polarization is a repetition of what gave rise to the Enlightenment originally. After the Thirty Years War, the French philosopher Rene Descartes (1596-1621) recognized there was no absolute truth, which he felt was responsible for wars. The hope was to prevent wars, which was felt to result when one group tried to impose their absolute religious beliefs on others. Despite the important advances that occurred from the elevation of rationality over belief by the Enlightenment, reasoning was not sufficient to prevent war. In fact, war became more devastating due to advances in science and weaponry and genocide continued on an even greater scale in atheistic countries.

Dawkins and Hitchens enshrine reason as the solution to the world's problems. However, blaming religion for violence is like blaming gasoline for a car crash. Gasoline fuels the car to operate, but it is the driver and the car that cause the violent results. Religion can be used to inflame passions, but the ultimate goal is to gain power. Neither Dawkins nor Hitchens recognize the significance of emotions or the impact of group affiliation on behavior.

As mentioned, Volkan (1997), a psychiatrist and psychoanalyst, found that the collective emotional memory in groups affects group behavior. Volkan noted that some groups maintain a shared historical memory of a past trauma. This provokes an emotional need to restore self-esteem and group cohesion. Instead of mourning and working through the trauma and loss, the group often seeks retaliation against its former oppressor. Through identification with the aggressor, the group becomes the victimizer instead of the helpless victim. Volkan mentions a number of examples of conflict between ethnic and religious groups from a remembered collective historical trauma. One example is the killing of the Shia leader al-Husayn ibn Ali by the Sunnis in a battle to be the fourth Caliph after Mohammed. The Bosnian war occurred partly due to the defeat of the Christian Serbs by the Ottoman Muslim army at Kosovo 600 years ago, where the Serbian leader Prince Lazar was killed. Another example is the collective emotional memory of holding Jews responsible for the death of Jesus. This is despite the fact that Jesus and all his followers were Jews. This collective memory resulted in sustaining anti-Semitism, even paradoxically in France, the home of the Enlightenment. Anti-Semitic statements were made by the famous Enlightenment philosopher Voltaire (1694-1778) even though he criticized all religions in his novel *Candide*.

Dawkins claims there are "scientific" reasons for not needing religious morality, since he proposes the existence of selfish as well as altruistic genes. His "scientific" evidence employs simple genetic determinism, which is contradicted by psychological, developmental, and neurological research. First of all, no single gene can operate without the cooperation of other genes. It is not simple linear genetic determinism. Also, people's moral decisions are often made in response to the immediate situation

(Appiah 2007), and environmental learning influences and triggers gene expressions (Kandel 1983).

What is significant is the interaction of genes and interpersonal interaction, especially during infancy. Developmentally, in the first three years of life, the right brain (especially the orbitofrontal cortex) and the subcortical limbic system (also called the reptilian or emotional brain) are dominant. This is where attachment to the mother, the family, and the culture occurs and emotional regulation is established. The cultural values are internalized like mother's milk and serve to maintain social attachment. The left cortex of the brain only comes online later and is where language and conscious reason evolve. Normally there is a harmonious relationship between social attachment and autonomy. But during times of fear and helplessness, the limbic system is activated and social attachment may overwhelm autonomy and reason. This can result in being controlled by the group perception of seeing another group as threatening, which can result in violence against the other group. (This is the probable biological explanation of the inhuman genocide that occurred in World War II by an advanced civilized country, Germany, which Elie Wiesel, one of its victims, could not understand.)

Dawkins does attempt to include the influence of society by suggesting a "zeitgeist," which depicts a progressively evolving secular morality. This, he claims, makes religious morality unnecessary. This theory does include a dynamic interaction between individualism and social attachment.

Dawkins' arguments rest more on philosophy and not on science, and thus a brief history of the conflict between belief and reason as well as between autonomy and society in philosophy would be useful to provide a contextual background.

Jean Jacques Rousseau (1712-1778) presented an ideology that man was naturally good but society made man unhappy. On the other hand, Thomas Hobbes (1588-1679), a rationalist, considered self-preservation and self-assertion to be primary in man, and that society was beneficial by establishing a social contract for a treaty of peace. Immanuel Kant (1724-1804) wrote that people are inherently moral as a result of reason placed there by God. Adam Smith (1723-1790) and Arthur Schopenhauer (1788-1860) argued that people were naturally compassionate, while John Stewart Mill (1806-1873) considered the pursuit o f pleasure to be primary. Post-Enlightenment philosophers such as Soren Kierkegaard (1813-1855) stated that subjectivity, which included passion and commitment, was as important as rational objectivity. In addition, he considered that reason was limited and thus could not prove or disprove the existence of God. Friedrich Nietzsche (1844-1900), an atheist and a Darwinian, rejected theological explanations and considered that God was dead. He noted that most people feared being excluded and submitted to a herd mentality that maintained religion. But, the "superman," an autonomous individualist, was free to be creative. Nietzsche stressed that passion, the Dionysianinfluenced intellect, the Apollonian. Freud elaborated on this, noting that unconscious emotions influence conscious reason in individuals.

What is most striking is the similarity of Dawkins' "zeitgeist" to Herbert Spencer's concept of Social Darwinism. Spencer claimed that social evolution was parallel to Darwin's biological evolution, so that society

improved over time. However, Darwin never made such a claim, limiting his observations to biology and not to society. Jacoby (2008) found there is no scientific evidence for Social Darwinism, and that scientific language was simply used to mask unscientific belief. This seems to be the case for Dawkins. Social Darwinism advocated unrestricted capitalism and justified poverty as well as discrimination against foreigners. Jacoby notes this pseudoscientific belief was vigorously opposed as false by such thinkers as Ralph Waldo Emerson, William James, Theodore Roosevelt, and Thorstein Veblen.

Most early cultures, such as Egyptian, Babylonian, Persian, and Roman, believed their leaders to be divine and their decisions as the absolute truth. Similarly, in the modern era, some atheistic leaders have believed their assertions to be the absolute truth. Two such examples were the C ommunist parties in Russia and China, where leaders were worshiped as if they were gods and atheism became a fundamentalist religion. They denied people choice and demanded submission in thought, speech, literature, art, theater, and science. Nonconformists were humiliated, hospitalized as mentally ill, imprisoned, exiled to the work camps of the Gulag, or murdered. Atheism did not stop violence; in fact, it increased it. Stalin probably killed more people than during the religious persecution of the Inquisition.

Again, Dawkins' work is reductionistic, since behavior cannot be limited to a gene nor to simple linear concepts about society. Behavior results from the complex interaction of the bodily systems interacting with the environment. Kandel and others noted that genes are subject to the environment. Their DNA influences RNA to produce different proteins causing varying responses.

To summarize, learning is especially important in the early interactions of the mother and infant. The infant makes an attachment, which involves the synchrony of gaze and movement with the mother (Schore 2003). As adults, group identification is promoted when people's movements and sounds are also synchronous. This occurs in singing, dancing, or speaking together (Langer 1942). I have hypothesized that the early synchrony of the infant and mother is internalized by the infant as the model for later group attachment. On an individual level, lovers gaze into each other's eyes, which supports their attachment. These synchronous actions from infancy facilitate adult attachment (Slipp 2000). It is the synchronous behavior in religious rituals as well as the shared values that foster group belonging and identification. Singing together, reciting scripture together, moving together, and celebrating holidays together all enhance group affiliation.

These rituals are performed voluntarily in a group and are not an obsessional neurosis as Freud speculated. In obsessional neurosis, the repetitious actions are of an individual and are out of control.

The chapter on Constantine traces the establishment of the absolute power o f the Christian nobility and church. Carroll (2001) notes the divine right of Christian kings to rule was initiated by the Roman Emperor Constantine. Constantine legitimized Christianity and combined religion with politics. The divinity of the king to rule continued the belief in the divinity of the Roman emperor that had been initiated by Emperor Augustus. The church and the king both supported each other's power as being divinely appointed, although at times they were competitive. The divinity o f the king resulted in a theocratic society with a strict social hierarchy.

Carroll notes the power of the nobility and the church was maintained during the Middle Ages by instilling fear. Sinning would result in eternal punishment in hell after death. This terrified people into complying, needing the church to save their souls. Constantine enhanced his grip on power by creating divisiveness between Christians and Jews and fostered anti-Semitism. This will be covered more fully in a later chapter.

Interestingly, in the novel *The Brothers Karamasov* by Fyodor Dostoyevsky, the brother Ivan tells a parable of the Grand Inquisitor that is relevant here. Jesus returns to earth in the sixteenth century to Seville, Spain, during the Inquisition. He proceeds to heal the sick but is arrested as a heretic and condemned. Just before, there had been a hundred heretics burnt in the *auto de fe* by the cardinal in front of the king, the court, and the knights, because of their complicity. The Grand Inquisitor asks Jesus why he refused the three temptations offered him by the Devil. The first temptation was to turn stone into bread, the second to jump from the Temple and be rescued by angels, and the third to rule the world. Jesus rejected all of them so that people would have freedom. But the Grand Inquisitor states people are weak and prefer security to freedom. Had Jesus accepted the three temptations, he could have provided bread, proven his divinity, and had absolute power. The Grand Inquisitor states that since the time the church and the Roman Empire combined, it secretly preferred the three temptations of the Devil. It provided security, the rulers were considered divine, and they became powerful. Jesus is not executed. He kisses the lips of the Grand Inquisitor and is set free with a warning not ever to return again.

There were distinct differences between the Judaism practiced by Jesus and the Christian church that evolved after his death. The church developed a hierarchical structure in the first two centuries and later Constantine joined it with the political elite to enhance his power. Prior to the destruction of the Temple by the Babylonians in 586 BCE, the Jewish religion itself had been hierarchical. The priests in the Temple, who were descendants of Aaron the brother o f Moses, were the most powerful. After the destruction of the second Temple by the Romans in 70 CE, the rabbinic movement and synagogues gained greater transcendence. Reading the Bible was prescribed for all Jewish males, so a society based on meritocracy and not heredity evolved. The famous historian Josephus compared the facility of the Jews to be able to read to that of lawyers in Rome. The ability of Jews to read and discuss the Bible added to the greater autonomy of individuals. It changed the structure of Jewish society from a hereditary hierarchy to an egalitarian structure based on knowledge. Since the Sadducee high priests could no longer sacrifice in the Temple, the Pharisees gained prominence and reading the Torah, the five books of Moses, became the most important part of Judaism.

However, reading the Bible in the Roman Catholic church during the Middle Ages was restricted to priests. Since knowledge was power, it served to guarantee the political power of the church hierarchy. Most people were illiterate anyway and complied, since they felt protected and secure by a powerful leadership. The breakdown of the joining of religion and politics started after the printing of the Bible, followed by the Protestant Reformation, and then the Enlightenment. Martin Luther encouraged Protestants to read the Bible for themselves, and challenged the centralized powerful hierarchy of the church. Luther especially was critical of the sale

of indulgences by the church. Money was given to the church to wipe out sins so people's souls would not go to hell after death. Today the Catholic church no longer focuses on sin, is ecumenical, and emphasizes the b rotherhood of humanity and twentieth-century global concerns.

The conflict between subjective religious belief and objective scientific observation is not new, and has threatened the power of religious and political leaders. It began when Copernicus and Galileo challenged the biblical belief that the earth was the center of the universe. This view was in the Bible and had been upheld by the Egyptian Ptolomy. They held that the earth was stationary with the sun rotating around it from east to west. Galileo observed through his telescope that the earth was not the center, and that it moved around the sun. Galileo's discovery undermined the political power base of the church, since his findings contradicted the certainty of belief in the Bible. To prevent Galileo from disseminating his findings, he was called to appear before the Inquisition and was forced to recant his findings at the Minerva Church in Rome. Although he was not burned at the stake, he was forced to spend the rest of his life under house arrest at his home in Arcetri to keep him silent.

The Enlightenment severed the connection between church and state, and resulted in the American and French Revolutions. The brilliant founding fathers of the United States sought to prevent the tyranny that had existed in Europe for centuries by the power of the church and nobility. The founding fathers established a secular government, separating church and state, and offered religious freedom without establishing any national religion. This was to prevent one group from imposing their religious views on others. Although the advances of the Enlightenment emphasized reason, the founding fathers of the United States also recognized the limitations of reason. The abuse of power could also occur even by secular rational individuals. Thus, they built a system of checks and balances into the structure of the government, by dividing it into three branches. They created a democratic government with representatives elected by its citizens and responsive to the needs of the people. They saw the United States as a shining city on a hill, to be seen by the world.

Many of the founding fathers of the United States were Deists, who believed in a God who did not perform miracles, as described by Hobbes and Spinoza. They deliberately created a government that separated church and state and that saw all men as created equal. The First Amendment to the Constitution advocated there was to be no national religion but that religious freedom should prevail. Essentially, the fathers of the United States built in the values of religious tolerance, respect, and protection for differences. To confirm this, George Washington wrote a letter to the Truro Jewish Synagogue in Newport, Rhode Island. Washington wrote that the government of the United States would protects all religions against bigotry, so that all could feel safe, protected, and unafraid.

However, despite the wishes of the founding fathers, conflict between religion and politics was not put to rest, but continued. This time it was not like Galileo's trial about the sun and the earth but about the origin of human beings as described in the Bible and by Charles Darwin (1809-1882). A conflict between the literal interpretation of the Bible and science occurred in the Scopes Monkey Trial of 1925. John Scopes was

arrested for teaching Darwin's theory of evolution, which went against the literal belief in the biblical account of the origin of man. The Bible stated God created man in six days. The famous lawyer, Clarence Darrow, defended Scopes and the powerful politician, William Jennings Bryant, was the prosecutor. Scopes was found guilty and fined $100, and evolution was removed from the textbooks used in the classroom.

Charles Darwin, the English naturalist, created the theory of evolution, which was published in his book *The Origin of Species* in 1859. On his voyage on the ship the HMS *Beagle*, he observed that birds, animals, and plants gradually changed physical form in different environments. Those that were more adaptive to the specific environment survived and passed the physical change onto future generations. In his next book, *The Descent of Man,* published in 1871, he traced the ancestry of m an to a primitive apelike ancestor. Darwin's work built on the foundation of his grandfather, Erasmus Darwin, and he graciously credited the work of fellow naturalist Wallace, the demographer Malthus, and Lamarck.

Today, Darwin's theory of evolution is understood as occurring after many generations of genetic mutations and by the way genes are switched on and off. This is an example of what Wilson (1998) termed consilience, where knowledge from different levels come together. Other examples are Einstein integrating physics with e=mc2, and Kandel showing that the environment affects gene protein expression. Wilson considers that although separate, both religion and science have a unity of purpose, to explain the universe and the role of people in it.

An effort to resolve the conflict between religion and science even dates back to the twelfth century. The great Jewish physician and philosopher Moses Maimonides (1135-1204) combined the thoughts of Aristotle with Jewish ethical values to reconcile faith and reason. He stated that knowledge of the world increased our knowing God (Ausubel 1961). For more sophisticated individuals, he considered that nature and God were one, a position later taken by the philosopher Spinoza. For less sophisticated individuals an anthropomorphic god was needed.

Despite these efforts to reconcile difference, some fundamentalist Evangelical Christians again recently tried to inject their religious beliefs

into the politics of the United States. They desired Creationism to be taught in the classroom. They wanted their religious values to be imposed on others, since it would validate the authenticity of their beliefs. However, in 1987 the Supreme Court of the United States decided that the teaching of Creationism violated the separation of church and state and infringed on the religious freedom of the First Amendment.

More recently, another trial occurred about evolution being taught in the classroom. The school board of Dover, Pennsylvania, voted to have "intelligent design" taught in the classroom. They claimed evolution had unexplained gaps making it just another theory. The school teachers there legally challenged this as a religious belief, and a trial occurred in 2005 that lasted six weeks, fudge Jones had been appointed by President George W. Bush, who favored teaching intelligent design. Thus, many were concerned about the judge not being impartial. Intelligent design denied Darwin's evolution and claimed that all organisms were created fully formed at one time by a godlike figure. They quoted from the book *Of Pandas and People*,

which claimed there was a designer that created all life. However, evidence showed this book was originally w ritten about Creationism and only later changed to intelligent design following the negative Supreme Court decision of 1987.

As evidence at this trial for Darwin's theory, scientists demonstrated transitional fossils that showed the evolution of animals from the sea to the land. In addition, we now know humans have a similar genetic makeup as apes, especially chimpanzees. Apes have 24 chromosomes and humans have 23, with one of the chromosomes (#2) a fusion of two chromosomes. Scientific facts can be tested, falsified, and revised, but intelligent design is a fixed belief that can not be tested. The decision of Judge Jones was that intelligent design was not a science but a belief and that it was unconstitutional to teach it in the classroom.

Gary Wills (2007), the eminent social historian, lists who of the founding fathers of the United States were Deists. They included John Adams, Franklin, Hamilton, Jefferson, Madison, Paine, and Washington. As mentioned, Deists did not believe that God performed miracles and did not control the behavior of each individual. In addition, Wills points out that Karl Rove, the strategist for the Republican party, who is not religious himself, used the religious controversy to gain political votes. Wills noted that Rove used religious values as a political tool and was a master of electoral technology. Rove made abortion the "linchpin" of his strategy, which brought together Catholics and Evangelical Protestants. These values were used to emotionally distract citizens from voting on issues that would rationally have been in their own interest. Wills points out that abortion is not in the Ten Commandments, not in any Jewish Scripture, not in Jesus's Sermon on the Mount, nor anywhere in the New Testament. Also, St. Thomas Aquinas did not consider life to begin when the semen fertilized the egg, but only at birth. Wills states that there is no theological basis at all for condemning abortion or stem cell research, as if it is killing life. Other issues that some fundamentalist religious groups tried to oppose included homosexuality, gay marriage, and Darwin's theory of evolution.

However, Jesus did not seek to gain political power to impose his views on others. He preached to the poor about the values of tolerance, acceptance of differences, and nonviolence. Interestingly, the United States Conference of Roman Catholic bishops in Baltimore on November 14, 2007, issued a document titled "Forming Consciences for Faithful Citizenship." Catholics could vote for candidates they considered best qualified, even those who supported abortion rights or stem cell research.

Moderate Evangelicals, Catholics, Protestants, Jews, Muslims, Buddhists, and other religions would agree that the best qualified candidate, concerned about the citizens' needs, should be elected.

An important development in the United States has accentuated the conflict between religion and politics. In recent years there has been an exponential expansion o f scientific knowledge and its application. Scientific discoveries have threatened some of the basic concepts of the Bible about the origins of humankind and our knowledge of the world. Gene mutations can facilitate better adaptation to the environment as Darwin noted, but it also can predispose us to certain illnesses. Mutation is a double-edged sword, being both beneficial and pathogenic. But genes alone do not predict health, since other factors, such as food, sunlight, exercise, smoking, stress, etc., have an effect. Research on a molecular level

has demonstrated how the environment affected a number of protein expressions by genes. We may soon understand the causes and devise more specific treatment for many abnormalities, illnesses, and cancers. Some examples of current research are gene therapy and the use of stem cells to correct illnesses and deformities.

A modern miracle is the ability to look directly into the brain through the use of neuroimaging and to see the brain functioning under many circumstances. In addition, anthropology, archaeology, astronomy, and other sciences have made important discoveries that better help us understand the world we live in. All these scientific advances present a threat to the religious explanations that were considered absolute truths and unchangeable.

Some biblical stories have been found to be historically accurate, while o th20

ers are probably fables passed down through oral traditions. The scientific discoveries confirm or negate some biblical statements. For example, the earth was not created 6,000 years ago; scientific dating reveals the earth to be 4.5 billion years old. The advances in medicine may eventually eliminate faith healing, which believes that diseases are due to God's punishment for sins or from evil spirits entering the body. Also, our ability to explore the depths of the earth and travel in space has challenged the collective religious belief that hell is below and heaven is above the earth. The core of many religious beliefs that offered security and facilitated group affiliation have been challenged by science.

It is understandable why some fundamentalist religions have attempted to gain political power to negate these scientific advances, so as to confirm the certainty of their religious beliefs. They experience science as an assault on the dignity of the individual and as something that damages group identity and security. As an added assault, to accept that there may be no life after death as some claim, that one will not be reunited with one's loved ones, delivers a painful blow.

Science needs to be free and not shackled by religion, to advance our knowledge of the world. Science provides objective knowledge o f the n a tural world, but it is neutral concerning human values. The best aspect of every religion can offer a moral compass on how scientific discoveries can be used to benefit of all of humanity. The humanistic values of all religions interacting with the objectivity of natural science can lead to belief and reason freely complementing each other.

2 The Impact of Social Context on Belief

The social context of a particular time is the lens through which we need to view people and events that occurred in history. Hitchens and Dawkins blame religion as the cause for all the violence, and they diagnose religion as a form of mental illness, a delusion. However, blaming a single linear cause and effect for misfortunes befalling a society is only a step away from blaming the devil, witches, or another religious group. Religion has been misused to gain and maintain political power, but it also brought benefits. Without the scientific knowledge we have today, religion provided an explanation of the world that offered a sense o f mastery. It facilitated group support and diminished fear and despair by instilling hope to face the existential tragedies of life.

An interesting comment, concerning mental illness and religion and its relation to history, was expressed by the famous German physician, philosopher, musician, and theologian, Dr. Albert Schweitzer. Schweitzer (1948) wrote his doctoral thesis in 1913 contradicting the diagnosis of three psychiatrists, who considered Jesus to be emotionally disturbed. Brilliantly, Schweitzer took them to task, since they did not take into account the social context in which Jesus lived. These psychiatrists were judging Jesus by the standard of modern society, which is not applicable. The same error is true of Hitchens and Dawkins, who make simple judgements from a modern perspective. In addition, they offer a diagnosis about religion, when they are not psychiatrists.

Schweitzer stated that the beliefs of Jesus were not delusional; they were part of the normal social context in which he lived. During the time that Jesus lived people absolutely believed in miracles and magic. They saw or heard visions, and strongly relied on religion to cope with the vicissi22 tudes of life. Religious belief sustained hope against overwhelming circumstances. First, psychiatrists do not attempt to make an accurate psychiatric diagnosis without directly interviewing an individual. Second, the individual needs to be seen in the context of the family and culture in which he or she lived. Even today some people believe in spiritismo, zombies, and miracles that are part and parcel of their culture. These individuals cannot be diagnosed as mentally ill when they are brought up in a culture where such beliefs are normal.

Most of all, there is no indication that Jesus was at all mentally deranged. He was not a political creature who compromised his ideals for power. In fact, he spoke to power for an ethical and moral society. Through

his religious belief, he hoped to relieve the suffering o f his fellow Jews. Jews were being persecuted by the theocratic Roman Empire, the emperor of which was considered divine. Jews would not submit to accepting the

Roman belief that the Roman emperor was a god nor to their pantheistic beliefs. The Jews upheld the Ten Commandments, which mandated that there was only one God. Jesus was clearly influenced by the society in which he lived. This involved maintaining its cultural integrity and beliefs. There was a widespread Jewish belief that a messiah would arise, who would miraculously rescue the Jews from Roman oppression. The Messiah would bring on the Kingdom of God and eliminate Roman rule. This hope for a messiah is mentioned in the Bible and in the Dead Sea Scrolls, which were discovered in 1947. W hen this occurred, only God would rule instead of the "divine" Roman emperor. Jesus both was influenced by the society in which he lived and attempted to change it to bring about greater freedom. Although he was not successful, his sincere belief and effort was normal, seen in the context of the time in which he lived.

A great deal changed in the way people perceived and experienced their existence from the time Jesus lived up to the time when Freud lived. Even though both Jesus and Freud were not successful in their heroic efforts to break up the abuse of power when politics and religion are joined, they made other lasting contributions. The humanistic teachings of Jesus and Freud about personal integrity were not only applicable to their time but have also continued to have an impact that is timeless. Both Jesus and Freud were healers and tried to relieve the suffering of individuals. Both bravely attempted to improve relationships between people and to create conditions for greater personal freedom, honesty, and gender equality.

Jesus opposed the patriarchal and hierarchical Jewish society that existed, and he advocated equality for social classes and for women. However, the sect of Jesus was only one of a number of other social divi*Samuel Slipp 23*

sions in Jewish society. The most powerful group in Judea were the Sadducees. They were all men, who through heredity were the priests in the Temple and rich land owners. The other group were the Pharisees, who held that reading the Torah (the five books of Moses) was of prime importance. The sect of Jesus was distinctly humanistic and egalitarian. Jesus advocated equality between social classes and genders. The concept of social equality may have come from the Pharisees, who had a meritorious concept of the culture. The Pharisees emphasized that knowledge of the Torah had priority over the hereditary Sadducees' sacrifice in the Temple. The faith preached by Jesus also may have been derived from the moral and social teachings advocated by the academies of learning run by the sages Hillel and Shammai, who lived at the same time. Hillel taught, "What is hateful to you do not do unto your fellow man: that is the whole Law, the rest is commentary" and "Do not condemn your friend: you do not know what you would have done in his place." In the academy of Hillel, both the teachings of Shammai and those of Hillel were presented, so that one did not have to believe in one absolute truth. Jesus similarly preached love of God and one's neighbor, and do not judge lest you be judged.

It is interesting that after the Christian religion became institutionalized in the first few centuries after the death of Jesus, women were again put into an inferior position and denied the right to be leaders. This helped

to consolidate the hierarchical power position of men, who became the political and religious leaders. This was opposite to the beliefs o f Jesus, who accepted women as equals and was not involved in establishing a hierarchical social structure. Women belonged to the Jewish sect of Jesus, and there is evidence that Mary Magdalene may have even been preferred by him among his disciples. He hoped that after the apocalypse, the poor would be elevated to equality with the rich.

Freud has been accused of being a misogynist because of his biological theory of female development. Freud clearly was influenced by his culture, which was patriarchal and strongly influenced by advances in biological knowledge. In my book, *The Freudian Mystique: Freud, Women, and Feminism* (Slipp 1991), I point out that Freud was basically not prejudiced against all women; but he was prejudiced against mothers. Freud had a conflicted relationship with his own mother, which undoubtedly influenced his theory of female development. However, his mother was a victim o f the patriarchal and anti-Semitic culture in which she lived. Most women were denied an education, were limited to being housewives and mothers, and were prevented from having an independent identity of their own. Freud's theory used a biological perspective, penis envy, to explain female

24 *The Quest for Power*

development. Other psychoanalysts, especially Karen Horney (1950), objected to this theory and identified the effect of a biased culture on the identity of women. Like other women in that culture, Freud's mother's identity was a reflection of her husband's status. If that failed, she could identify with her son. This was the case for Freud. Since his father was considered a failure; his m other lived vicariously through Freud's achievement. Freud resented this, which was expressed by keeping her waiting when he visited and not attending her funeral.

However, Freud also challenged the Victorian culture that denied that both boys and girls in early childhood had sexual impulses. But he overlooked the important interaction of infants with their mother and the culture on female development. However, Freud admitted many bright, educated career-oriented women into the psychoanalytic movement. They were more interested in their careers than in motherhood, and here he advocated gender equality. In particular, his relationship with Lou Andreas-Salome, one of his disciples, was very special. She was a brilliant emancipated woman whom Freud often consulted for advice on his literary work. He respected her comments, which he sought before publication of many of his writings. Andreas-Salome made significant contributions of her own to psychoanalysis, which are now recognized as very relevant. She acknowledged the role of the mother in the preoedipal period of child development.

Freud never analyzed his ambivalent relationship with his mother, and he began his analysis of the relationship with his father after the father's death. Besides being influenced by the patriarchal culture, Freud's own ambivalence toward his mother was unconsciously reflected in his theory of female development. As a consequence, Freud focused both his male and female developmental theory on the oedipal conflict with the father and not on the early relationship with the mother. In his theory, the mother was seen almost as a passive inanimate object, toward whom the child satisfied its oral or sexual needs.

Lou Andreas-Salome also wrote on female personality development and had the courage to criticize the theory that Freud formulated. She also objected to the mechanistic instinct theory developed by Freud, which he erroneously thought would make psychoanalysis scientific. The work of Andreas-Salome has stood the test of time, and is more acceptable in modern psychoanalysis than some of Freud's work.

Freud's theory of female development was undoubtedly influenced by the patriarchal society, but even more so by his troubled relationship with his mother. She was unable to provide him with the nurturing that he

Samuel Slipp 25

needed during infancy and early childhood. As evidence of this, in the summer of 1872 Freud accompanied two of his friends from the Sperlgymnasium, where he was a student, back to his birthplace of Freiberg, Moravia (Gay 1988). He stayed at the Fluss home, and later wrote a letter about his time there to his friend Silberstein. In the letter Freud acknowledged that his mother only satisfied his physical needs. This was unlike Frau Fluss, who was sensitive to and responded to the emotional needs of her children. However, had Freud had Frau Fluss as his mother, in all likelihood his theories about child development would have been different.

Freud's developmental theory considered that both boys and girls were originally bisexual and that the m other was the first love object for both. But he did not mention the emotional responsiveness of the mother, let alone an attuned relationship between both infant and mother. In his theory, he stated the girl turns to the father in order to separate from the mother. Femininity then is seen by Freud as a retreat from masculinity. He stated the girl becomes aware she does not have a penis, feels castrated, and suffers penis envy. Freud said that at puberty the girl identifies with the mother and changes from clitoral to vaginal sensations. She is attracted to men and hopes to have a male child to seek the penis that she does not have.

Karen Horney (1950) strongly disagreed with Freud and considered that femininity was inborn and not the product of such a complicated and tortuous masculine analogy. Horney considered the concept of penis envy, advocated in Freud's theory, as not biological but a direct product of the cultural bias against women. Penis envy was only a biological symbol Freud used to explain the envy of women who were denied the empowerment society gave to men. As mentioned, except for some exceptionally gifted women, most women were denied an independent identity. Men held onto their power both at home and in the hierarchical structure of the culture.

Simone de Beauvoir (1961) in *The Second Sex* and Betty Friedan (1963) in *The Feminine Mystique* both opposed Freud's view that anatomy is destiny. They also emphasized that it was not biology but society that imposed an inferior role on women. They advocated gender equality, giving women choices and empowerment by society. Friedan compared women's role to that of being constricted by a social corset, since society limited a woman's freedom.

The inferior role for women in society was derived from the institutionalized Christian religions, since it enhanced men's hierarchical political power. This was rationalized as natural, since the Bible stated Eve was born out of Adam's side, so that Adam was created first. This implied that men should be first, the master, and women second. Eve was also held responsible for the original sin and their being rejected by God from the Garden of

Eden. As a result of stereotyped thinking, all women were then blamed as a group for original sin and put into an inferior position.

There are a number o f theories concerning the Bible story about Adam and Eve. It may have arisen out o f rebellion against the pagan religions that worshiped the great mother goddess, who controlled creation and destruction. She was responsible for fertility, life, death, and rebirth. In Mesopotamia she was called Ishtar, among Semitic tribes Astarte or Ashtoreth, in Greece Rhea or Gaea, in Egypt Isis, in Asia Minor Cybele, in Persia Anaitis, and in India Shakti or Kali. This was later reflected in the Greek goddess Demeter, mother earth, and her daughter Persephone who controlled the seasons and judged souls in the underworld. The suppression and control of women probably thus had to do with this fear of women who represented nature. Women were seen as closer to nature, since they menstruated monthly and were able to create life. Women were associated with the animal part of humanity, thus Cybele was associated with lions, Syrian Dea with serpents, the Greek Artemis with her deer, and Eve with her snake. Previously, in order not to feel helpless by seeing nature as impersonal, nature was anthropomorphized into these female goddesses, who might be influenced by penance or sacrifice.

Rabbi Reuven Kimelman of Brandeis University offers another explanation for the Adam and Eve story. He calls it a fable, which cannot be proven historically, as can later sections of the Bible. There were no apple trees in the Garden of Eden and perhaps not even a snake. He postulates that the snake was a metaphor for Eve's inner desire to have power like God by gaining his knowledge. Diminishing women by literally understanding the story of Adam and Even has little validity.

Freudian psychoanalysis has also questioned the absolute "truths" of society and given people greater freedom, understanding, and empathy for the motivation and dynamics o f individual behavior. Essentially, both Jesus and Freud helped individuals and followed the Jewish dictum that to save one individual is to save the world. The Hebrew term for improving the world is *tikkun olum.* Both offered a humanistic understanding that was inclusive of individuals and not exclusive or hierarchical. Both had female associates who were respected and treated as equal, and in some instances, considered even superior to their male disciples. As mentioned, this apparently was the case of Mary Magdalene for Jesus and definitely of Lou Anreas-Salome for Freud.

The social world in which Jesus and Freud lived affected how they dealt with the domination of Jews, resulting from the abuse of power when religion and politics were joined. As mentioned, Jesus was born at a time when people relied on religion to understand the universe and on miracles to achieve a sense of meaning and mastery over their life. They did not have the findings of modern science to understand nor the m ethods to cope with disease and natural disasters. In the time of Jesus, people believed disease resulted from evil demons entering the body or as punishment by God for sinful acts. People hoped that a rabbi, like a shaman, could exorcize the demons and restore health. This gave them a modicum of a sense of control.

In the ancient world, people believed that the earth was the center of the universe and that the sun rotated around the earth from east to west. The ancient Greeks anthropomorphized this, believing Apollo, the Sun God, rode his chariot from east to west every day. Religion was not a delusion but provided people with answers that offered certainty and emotional

security. We now know that their anthropomorphic projections and beliefs were incorrect even though they were helpful at the time. By incorporating religion into politics, there was an illusion that instilled divine power into its leader. People accepted this illusion of a powerful leader, since it offered a sense of mastery over their world. Being part of a group that believed in this illusion increased their sense of safety and security. It was adaptive given the circumstances of their lives.

The experimental study of Solomon Asch (1956) tested whether people's perception could be pressured to conform to group pressure. Three quarters of the subjects revised their perception when pressured, while only one fourth remained independent. This psychological test showed that the majority of people were obedient to the group's perception and influenced by external pressure. The majority did not wish to be the o u tsider but wished to be part of the group.

The geocentric view of the universe, developed by Ptolomy around 130 CE, was considered scientific proof that the earth was the center o f the universe. This was accepted in the culture and considered an absolute truth.

The Catholic church opposed the subsequent scientific evidence found in the Middle Ages by Copernicus (1473-1543) and Galileo (1564-1642). These findings contradicted the Bible and represented a threat to church authority. The Bible taught that the earth was the center of the universe, and the sun moved around it from east to west. This seemed to agree to what people perceived. The certainty of religious belief held by the church was the source of its political power, and it was now shaken. As a result, Galileo needed to be silenced to maintain the obedience of the populace and maintain political power o f the church. Galileo was forced to recant his findings in the Minerva Church in Rome and then sentenced to house arrest for the remainder of his life in Arcetri. It was as late as the seventeenth century that Kepler defined the movement of the planets around the sun, which eventually lead to our scientific understanding of the universe.

Why is understanding the cultural context of a society so important, and how did it arise? The ancient Jewish nation was small and vulnerable, surrounded by large, powerful military states. The invaders included the Assyrians, Babylonians, Egyptians, Philistines, Greeks, and Romans. Jews needed their religion for survival against these odds. Their strong religious belief gave them hope and courage, and they continued to rely on miracles performed by God to survive. Their covenant with God helped them feel secure and protected. The religion was not an opiate, as Marx declared, but a source of emotional nourishment that helped the Jews survive originally as a nation and later as an ethnic group. Group solidarity provided the Jews with strength and hope and prevented their being swallowed up by despair. The external circumstances they faced were out of their control, yet they could rise up again like a Phoenix after each defeat. The one miracle is that the Jews as a distinct group have survived at all despite their repeated history of oppression.

To facilitate the survival of this vulnerable community, they believed in miracles, which also influenced the absolute belief of Jesus. As mentioned, each Jewish holiday commemorates a past miraculous occurrence. Now, although people rely on scientific reason and do not depend on miracles,

most Jews still observe holidays based on past miracles. These holidays support group identity by glorifying the ancient collective history of the Jews.

The greatest miracle in the Bible was the liberation of the Jews from Egyptian slavery. On the instructions of God, Moses, with his brother

Aaron, confronted the Pharaoh Ramses II of Egypt (1292-1225 BCE). When the Pharaoh refused to free the Jews, God sent ten plagues, with nine of them defeating the power of a particular Egyptian god. The plagues ended with the death of Pharaoh's first born son. This was the same sentence decreed by the Pharaoh earlier against all Jewish firstborns. The Pharaoh was seen as the divine god Horus when he was alive. After death, his body needed to be preserved, the Ra, and his soul, the Ba, became the god Osiris, his father. (This triad unified their human and divine god and has similarities to the Christian father, son, and holy ghost.) The authority of the Pharaoh was threatened, since he and his gods were shown to be less powerful than the God of Moses. To protect his illusion of divine power, the Pharaoh agreed to the exodus around 1250 BCE. Another miracle reported in the Bible was the parting of the Red Sea. This enabled the Jews to escape the pursuing army of Ramses II, who relented after freeing the Jewish slaves. Freedom from Egyptian slavery is celebrated each year by the Jewish holiday of Passover with a festive meal, the Seder. This was the last meal Jesus had with his disciples, hoping for another miracle that would free his fellow Jews from Roman oppression. Interestingly, the son of Ramses II, Merneptah, later invaded Israel, and erected a stele to celebrate his victory.

The Bible recounts another great miracle when God gave Moses the Ten Commandments on Mount Sinai and the belief in a monotheistic God. God established a covenant with the Israelites which they needed to observe. The Prophets Amos, Hosea, and Mica criticized the social injustices later existing in Israel and warned that not adhering to the Covenant with God would bring about disaster. The Assyrians conquered the upper part, Israel, and ten tribes were lost. Then the Babylonians conquered the lower part, Judah, in 586 BCE. This again reinforced the belief that the prophets had miraculously predicted the disasters as God's punishment for sinning.

During the captivity of Judah in Babylonia, the book of Daniel 4 describes the miracle of the fiery furnace. King Nebuchadnezzar made an image of gold and when people heard music they were ordered to fall down and worship this idol. Those who did not fall down would be thrown into the fiery furnace. The king commanded three Jews, Shad'rach, Me'shach, and A-bed'ne-go, to fall down and worship the idol. They refused and said that the Jewish God would deliver them. The furnace was superheated, and they were thrown into it. But the Bible says an angel of God protected them, and they came out unharmed. It was another miracle and the power of the Jewish God was acknowledged. The king promoted the three men, since the political legitimacy of the king was threatened, as the Jewish God was more powerful than his gods.

Another miracle was said to have occurred around 167 BCE with the victory of Judah Maccabee's Jewish army over the powerful Syrian part of Alexander the Great's army. The Syrian army, under the Seleucid emperor, Antiochus Epiphanes IV, had conquered Judah, plundered the Holy Temple in Jerusalem, and imposed the pagan religion. Judah Maccabee assembled an army and fought and defeated the Syrian army. After the

Jewish victory over the Syrian army, a single cruse of unprofaned oil was found in the Temple. The oil was enough for only one day, however a miracle by God was proclaimed for this victory when the oil lighted up the

Temple for eight days. The Temple was cleaned and restored as the center of the Jewish religion. Judah Maccabee then decreed the holiday of Hannukah. Eight candles are lit to celebrate the miraculous military victo30

ry over such a powerful foe and the restoration of the Temple. The Maccabees set up a political family hierarchy that ruled Judah for nearly 100 years.

All these holidays celebrated in the culture reinforced the belief in miracles by God that had saved the Jewish people. But why did these miracles not continue to save Judah from Roman conquest and oppression, especially when the Jews did observe the covenant? Jesus believed that God, who had lost supremacy, would be reinstalled as the powerful ruler over Judah. In keeping with the cultural belief in miracles, Jesus considered himself an apocalyptic messiah. He would miraculously bring back the Kingdom of God to oppose the brutal Roman occupation. In the Sermon on the Mount he repeated the Ten Commandments, which involved the covenant with God to protect the Jews. He also went to Jerusalem at Passover, despite its being an especially dangerous time. During this holiday, the desire of Jews for liberation from slavery and freedom was intensified. As a result, the Romans posted greater guards in Jerusalem to prevent any uprising. Jesus had his Last Supper, which celebrated the Passover Seder. Jesus hoped to be like Moses and miraculously have the power to liberate his Jewish people from Roman oppression.

Alienation between Jews and Jewish Christians occurred with the revolt against the Romans from 66 to 70 CE by the Jewish Zealots. Jewish Christians were not part of the revolt, and indeed many observant Jews themselves opposed the revolt of the Zealots. Christians were not protected by Roman law, as were the Jews who had been allies of Rome during the Punic wars. Christianity was considered a separate religion, and thus Christians were being burned or slaughtered in the Roman arena since the time of Emperor Nero. Thus, Jewish Christians and many observant Jews were opposed to a military revolt against the powerful Roman army, which would only lead to devastation. The division increased between Jewish Christians and observant Jews with the second revolt against the Romans by Simon bar-Kochba from 132 to 135 CE. Rabbi Akiba had declared bar-Kochba as the Messiah, who would bring on the end of days. The Jewish Christians did not accept bar-Kochba as the Messiah, since they already believed Jesus was the Messiah. The revolt was crushed, and vast numbers o f Jews were killed including Rabbi Akiba, who was flayed alive.

The greatest split between Jews and Gentile Christians occurred when Constantine (288?-337 CE) prevented Jews and Christians from worshiping together. He changed elements in the Christian religious service and moved the Sabbath from Saturday to Sunday. This change was to honor the sun god Apollo, whom Constantine still worshiped. He focused on the crucifixion of Jesus, and cast the Jews as Christ killers to displace the Romans as killers of Christians. This did not acknowledge that Jesus and all his early followers were Jews, nor that it was the Romans who killed Christians for

centuries. Constantine profited politically by setting up this division, to divide and conquer. He also opposed other Christian sects, such as the Gnostics. Constantine institutionalized the Christian religion into an orthodox body that empowered the noble and religious leaders. This will be elaborated on in chapter 7.

John Chrysostom of Antioch, around 390 CE, criticized Judaizing Christians and Jewish Christians who still worshiped together for observing both Sunday and Saturday and celebrating Jewish holidays. He blamed the Jews collectively for killing Jesus, which was later used to justify genocide against the Jewish population. In the third century, Hippolytus, a Greek pagan who converted to Christianity, rose to authority in the Catholic church. He wrote a treatise on heresies, calling nonbelievers the anti-Christ. By naming all nonbelievers the anti-Christ, it further polarized, demonized, and dehumanized people as a group. Jews were not seen as individuals but by this group stereotype, and it further enabled Christians to commit violence against Jews and Muslims during the Crusades. Later, calling a person the anti-Christ justified burning large number of so-called heretics in the auto-de-fe by the Catholic church d u ring the Inquisition. This was justified they believed, since being burned at the stake saved their souls from burning in hell for eternity.

With the passage of time, the attitudes toward God and miracles changed in the culture. Belief in miracles was considered an illusion by Spinoza (1632-1677). This position was also held by the philosophers o f the Enlightenment, such as Descartes, Locke, and Hume. In the Enlightenment, reason and scientific method, instead of the Bible, were used to discover how the world and the universe operated. Religion no longer was the dominant power, as it was divested from its alliance with the political rulers, who had been divinely endowed to rule. Governments were organized to be representative of the will of the people and not to be controlled by the nobility allied with religious leaders. The rule of law was applicable to everyone, and no one was above the law. Despite the Enlightenment goals that glorified reason, emotional prejudices continued to exist. Religious tolerance did not evolve despite the grand ideals of liberty, equality, and fraternity, which intellectually were declared for all the people. These lofty ideals o f the Rights of Man did not affect emotional bigotry. Jews were supposedly accepted as an individual citizen but not as a group. Ethnocentric tribal values and emotional stereotypes continued to dominate in Europe.

Freud was born after the Enlightenment, and as a young man he was strongly influenced by the work o f Charles Darwin. After graduating from medical school at the University o f Vienna, he worked in Brucke's labora tory and made im p o rtan t discoveries concerning neurons. However, Freud's academic career was brought to a halt due to anti-Semitic laws passed in turn-of-the-c entury Vienna (Schorske 1981). He left the university to enter private practice but used the same scientific method of observation to understand mental functioning and neurotic illness. Freud developed a theoretical basis for his work by postulating the libido theory, which was based on the second law of thermodynamics in physics. However, Freud's greatest contribution was to recognize the very limitations o f reason. He discovered the influences o f repressed unconscious emotions.

What can be said about Freud and his lifelong struggle with the oppression of Jews? In the nineteenth and twentieth century Freud had to confront anti-Semitism from his early infancy to the last days of his life.

Freud had problems with the passivity of his father, who submitted passively to anti-Semitism. His father was a defeated man and not a model of masculine strength. Freud could not accept the passive and emasculated identity of his father. Freud saw himself as a conquistador, who would fight back and would not be a passive victim.

Freud, like Einstein, valued his Jewish heritage. Freud saw himself as a secular Jew who rejected the religious belief o f his father. Freud dismissed the belief in God as a projection of the father from childhood. He called the cultural belief in religion to be an illusion. However, Einstein did not reject his belief in God. He believed in Spinoza's concept o f God, which is not anthropomorphic, but is revealed in the lawful harmony of the universe. Spinoza's Deist God did not perform miracles and was not involved with the day to day doings of humankind. This contributed to Einstein being more independent in his personal life, as he was embraced by his religious belief. Not having this comfort of group support, Freud sought it by establishing a circle of professionals who were mostly Jewish. Freud's ambition was to challenge the culture and to bring about a universal psychology to understand all human behavior. Since his work had universal applicability, as a secondary effect, he hoped Jews would no longer be victimized. Jews would not be the outsiders but would be part of all of humanity.

Psychoanalytic theory produced a different understanding of human behavior. It was based on clinical observation and inductive understanding o f individuals and not on the deductive response to group stereotypes, as espoused by religious ideology.

Even though the Enlightenment tried to eliminate religion from politics, the existing political leadership in Vienna had been elected on an anti-Semitic platform. Like the Enlightenment, Freud also attempted to remove religion from politics, but he also failed. Later, the Nazis evolved a political structure that included a secular/pagan religion. Nazism was considered a holy order with sacred blood, the SS troops were its warrior priests, and Hitler was its messiah.

Freud had established a worldwide reputation as a researcher in neurobiology and was the founder of psychoanalysis. Yet he and his immediate family were threatened to be murdered by the Nazis. His daughter Anna had been called in by the Gestapo, and the entire Freud family was in danger of being sent to a concentration camp because they were Jewish.

Through the outside help of Christian colleagues, he and his family were ransomed out of Austria in 1938, and they settled in London, England. Freud's immediate family was saved but four of his five sisters who could not escape were sent to concentration camps and murdered by the Nazis.

3 Maintaining the Illusion of Power by Using Anti-Semitism

To maintain the illusion of power when religion and politics are joined in a theocracy, an outside group needs to be scapegoated. In this way the blame for disasters and defeats can be displaced, and the divine and absolute authority of the leader can be maintained. Even though Jesus and his followers were Jews, the traditional scapegoated group in Europe became the Jews. Instead of Jesus saving the Jews, his crucifixion was used to persecute the Jews. Scapegoating Jews as a group was not rampant for the first few centuries after the death of Jesus. Although there was some friction between Christians and Jews, they generally worshiped together. This occurred because Christianity was not tied to politics. The Romans persecuted and slaughtered the Christians who did not accept polytheism and the divinity of the emperor. Christianity derived from Judaism, and they often joined in prayer. This was in keeping with the emphasis of Jesus on inclusiveness despite gender, class, ethnicity, or social standing. Jesus was a healer and not a destroyer. He believed in the equality of people, rich or poor, male or female, and preached the Torah, the essence of Judaism, and the golden rule as described by Hillel.

What were the factors that created this complete turnabout in the very core of the teachings of Jesus? How did the humanistic teachings of Jesus become overshadowed by emphasis on the passion of his crucifixion? How did the messenger become more important than his message, and how was his death used to inflame hatred against the Jews? Why do some right wing fundamentalist Christians still believe that Jews need to be converted to be saved from being burned in the lake o f fire when Jesus returns? Historically, this is the opposite to what Jesus preached to his Jewish sect. James, the older half brother of Jesus and the council of the Apostles, felt to be a follower o f Jesus one needed first to become Jewish. Being punished and killed for not accepting one's religion was a Roman tradition and not that of Jesus.

Despite the brutal persecution of Christians by the previous Roman emperor Diocletian (284-305 CE), the religion had grown extensively throughout the Roman Empire. Christianity had become widespread and established its own religious hierarchy. Christianity offered the pagans social services, increased self-esteem by being told they were made in the image of God, and promised an afterlife after death. When Constantine became emperor (306-337 CE), he legitimized Christianity and used it to consolidate his political power (Carroll 2001). Constantine allied the religious and Roman hierarchies and introduced Roman values into the religion. The Roman fascination with death and dying was now focused on the crucifixion of Jesus. Previously, the slaughter of Christians and gladiators in the Roman Coliseum was used to mollify the plebians.

By creating divisiveness between Christians and Jews, he displaced the frustration and anger that had been expressed in the Coliseum onto a new target for persecution, the Jews. By eliminating crucifixion as a capital punishment,

and by accusing Jews of killing Jesus, it covered up the brutal slaughter of Christians by Romans for hundreds of years. Also, by scapegoating Jews, he could sustain his illusion of divine power by blaming Jews for natural disasters and defeats. Jews were a small vulnerable group, which made it easier to use them as the target for persecution. Jesus was not seen as a Jew, and blaming Jews collectively for the death of Jesus was increased by John Chrysostom, Hippolytus, and other Christian leaders.

The gentle, loving, and compassionate teachings of Jesus became subverted into an angry religion, that like the Romans persecuted nonbelievers (Chilton 2000). As mentioned, Jesus and all of his apostles and followers were observant Jews who worshiped a monotheistic, universal Jewish God. The preaching of Jesus and the apostles reflected the Jewish commandments about moral and ethical relations between people. As mentioned, these humanistic values had also been propounded by the famous academies of the sages Hillel and Shammai, who lived at the same time as Jesus. In all likelihood, Jesus was influenced by their teachings. Jesus and his disciples respected and perpetuated the Jewish laws. He cleansed the Temple of money lenders and animals to uphold the integrity o f the Jewish religion. He did not believe in excluding people but embraced all as equals. He cared for the poor and the sick, and he freely associated with the o utcasts of society, such as lepers, prostitutes, and even with Jewish collaborators who collected taxes for Rome. He considered women on an equal basis

36 *The Quest for Power*

with men, including Mary Magdalene who was possibly favored among his disciples.

Jesus did challenge an area of the traditional Jewish culture that may have caused some opposition. He was against divorce, *a Get*, which at first glance would be surprising in view of his respect for women's rights. However, according to the existing Jewish tradition, only men could divorce their wives. At that time, after the divorce the men did not have the responsibility to help support their ex-wives and children financially. By discouraging divorce, he was protecting women and their children who would be helplessly destitute. Thus, Jesus had a widespread concern for women and children. Jesus upheld the law and was protective of all his fellow human beings. He did not believe in persecuting or killing others but advocated freedom and integrity.

Jesus, out of deep human compassion and respect, hoped to liberate his fellow Jews from the brutal domination of the Romans. It was precisely at Passover when Jesus decided to come to Jerusalem. Passover is the holiday that celebrates the liberation of Jews from Egyptian slavery by Moses. The belief in miracles was reinforced, since Jews historically had fought for their freedom and often been victorious against overwhelming odds. Their religious belief, in following the covenant with God about individual and social behavior, bolstered their courage.

Just before coming to Jerusalem in 30 CE, Jesus gave his Sermon on the Mount in the Galilee. Like Moses, Jesus preached the Ten Commandments to his Jewish followers from the mount, which was a high place similar to Mount Sinai. The sermon also included the beatitudes, and the golden rule. His sermon relied on the Jewish emphasis of performing good deeds in accordance with the Covenant with God. These could be found in the Jewish Bible, such as Psalm 37 and Isaiah 61:1-2, and elsewhere. The eight

beatitudes mentioned by Jesus are quoted by Luke and Matthew. The beatitudes included blessed are the poor (Matthew changed this to poor in spirit), mourners, the hungry (Matthew changed this to hunger for righteousness), those persecuted for righteousness, the meek, the merciful, the pure of heart, and the peacemakers. Essentially the beatitudes he felt were a reflection of God's view and not those of the power-obsessed Romans. This would offer hope and courage for the Jews who attended his sermon. He preached that the powerless (the Jews and all others) would replace the powerful (Romans) when the Kingdom of God would be established in the near future.

Jesus believed in the biblical passages that the Messiah's coming would miraculously bring on the Kingdom of God, the apocalypse, and the end

of days. Jesus hoped to defeat the theocratic Roman subjugation of Judea through the power of religion to achieve freedom for everyone. As the Messiah, the son of God, he would bring on the day of judgment. When the end of days came into being, the Roman domination of Judea would cease, and the universal Jewish God would be the sole ruler of all the earth. Although Jesus knew he would suffer crucifixion, he bravely accepted this in the belief he would bodily return in the resurrection. At the end of days the dead were believed to be bodily resurrected, which was the firm belief of the Pharisee sect of Jews.

There is circumstantial evidence that Paul was not correct in his interpretation of the crucifixion, by saying that Jesus died for man's sins. The Romans had tried to impose their belief in the divinity of their emperor and polytheism on others, which the Jews strongly refused to accept. Jesus, like any person who created unrest or a hint of rebellion, threatened Roman power and was accused of a capital offense punishable by crucifixion. Even members of the crowd listening to a charismatic leader were also punished. Those leaders who were not Roman citizens were crucified as the prescribed form of capital punishment, while Roman citizens were beheaded. Crucifixion was a slow and tortuous death, resulting from slow asphyxiation and loss of blood. All those crucified were left on the cross for days, so others could see the victim slowly die in agony. Crucifixion inspired fear, which intimidated others against revolt against Roman power.

How is it that the Romans were so militaristic and brutal? The myth concerning the origin of Rome is that in 753 BCE the twin brothers Romulus and Remus were suckled by a she wolf. This experience supposedly instilled fierce animalistic power in them that was passed on to their descendants. This mythological fable of the origins of Rome probably gave rise to the saying that man is wolf to man. The story continued that Romulus and Remus invited the neighboring Sabines to a meal. Then they surprised and defeated the men and kidnaped the Sabine girls, who were raped and made their wives. The Romans developed as a violent, militaristic nation, with a lust for conquest and power. They were constantly at war with surrounding tribes and nations or fighting internal rebellions within the empire. Many of their emperors were assassinated and some committed suicide. They had little respect for the people that they captured, and imposed the Roman culture and religion on them. If the conquered peoples submitted to domination, they could eventually become Roman citizens

and their god would be included in the Pantheon in Rome. But, conquered peoples who did not submit were killed or enslaved in great numbers. Some male slaves were used to row Roman galleys or worked in the mines. Slaves were worked so hard that they usually perished after a short while. Female slaves were often used as prostitutes or to do menial labor. Conquest and death permeated the Roman culture. Christians who did not convert to Roman paganism were thrown as meat to the lions in the arena to entertain the public.

The Romans had a morbid fascination with death and dying, which is called necrophilia. Rome instituted mortal battles between gladiators and enjoyed watching them kill one another as well as seeing helpless people being brutally devoured by wild animals in the arena. As a form of dining entertainment, Romans sometimes enjoyed having slaves fight one another to the death. Large Roman crowds gathered in the Coliseum, which held perhaps 70,000 spectators to view the macabre spectacles. Plebeians sat in the upper tiers, while wealthy Romans and senators sat closer to the arena. In this way the social hierarchy was reinforced. The emperors used this brutal entertainment to pacify the plebeians and to support their position of power. The crowd could emotionally displace and ventilate their frustration and anger as they screamed for blood. They also could feel superior to their victims in the arena and enjoyed participating in determining the life or death of the defeated gladiators. This gave the plebeians an illusion of supremacy and control over death. But, the emperor made the final decision of life or death of the defeated gladiator, which also emphasized his ultimate power. He was the decider.

The gladiators who fought to the death were slaves or convicted criminals who were physically fit and trained to fight in the arena. One gladiator used a net and a trident and the other had a sword and a shield, the instruments with which to attack each other. The gladiators knew they were about to die and proclaimed it as they entered the arena. However, they hoped their brave performance might save them, since the crowd and then the emperor decided their fate. Romans enjoyed watching wild animals attack defenseless people who screamed with terror and pain as they were torn to bits and devoured. That was the fate of a large number of Christians who did not renounce their religion and pray to the pagan gods of Rome. In summary, this fascination of Romans with death and dying served as a form of entertainment, reinforced the social hierarchy and the emperor's divine authority, and supported the brutal militaristic values of Rome.

Pagels (1989) notes that not only were a vast numbers of ordinary Christians murdered but also a great many of its leaders as well. Saint Peter was crucified upside down, Saint Paul was beheaded, Polycarp, Bishop of Smyrna, was burned alive, Ignatius, Bishop of Antioch, was torn to pieces and devoured by wild animals, Bishop Pothinus of Gaul was brutally tortured to death. Thousands upon thousands of Christians died horribly painful deaths in the arena, which Roman emperors organized as entertainment for Roman citizens. The crowd was infused with the illusion of power over the defeated gladiators, signalling with their thumbs for life or death. In all other respects the plebeians had little power over their own constricted lives and death. As mentioned, ultimately, the games reinforced the emperor's power, since he alone had the final power of life or death over the defeated gladiator. In one such prolonged arena event in Rome organized by Emperor Trajan, 9,000 gladiators died.

When the Roman general Pompey conquered Judea in 63 BCE, he slaughtered the priests in the Jerusalem Temple and butchered 12,000 Jews.

This is according to Flavius Josephus (37-95 CE), a Jewish historian who wrote what many believe are accurate accounts of the Jewish wars. Previously, Josephus had been the general of the Jewish army in the Galilee, which had been defeated by Roman forces. He endeared himself to Vespasian, the general of the Roman army in Judea, by predicting he would become emperor of Rome. When Nero committed suicide in 68 CE, it ended the dynasty that had existed from Augustus through Claudius. What followed was a bloody combat for leadership between four commanders of the army, Galba, Otho, Vitellius, and Vespasian. Vespasian, who was the commander of the Roman army in Judea, emerged victorious to become emperor of Rome, and he started the Flavian hereditary dynasty. Vespasian's assuming power in Rome was facilitated by the conquest o f Judea by his son Titus. Vespasian built the Colosseum using 40,000 Jewish slaves and plunder from the Holy Temple in Jerusalem. Titus, his son, built a triumphal arch near the Colosseum, which exists today. It shows Roman soldiers carrying the holy candelabra and trumpets that they looted from the destruction of the Holy Temple in Jerusalem.

The Jewish former army general and historian, Josephus, went to Rome and became a Roman citizen. He noted that the resulting brutal yoke of Roman oppression by Vespasian and his son Titus created a turbulent political atmosphere. There were many charismatic leaders in Judea, magicians, prophets, and would-be messiahs that drew dangerous crowds and fostered an atmosphere of rebellion (Rivkin 1918). Many apocalyptic preachers who considered themselves the Messiah gathered crowds around them, which the Romans experienced as a threat to their political power. These previous Jewish messiahs were quickly arrested by the Romans and summarily crucified for fear of insurrection. Jesus was not alone in the hope that a messiah would restore the sovereignty of Judea, nor was he the only one crucified by the Romans. This explanation of the purpose of the crucifixion of Jesus is consistent with the belief in a messiah saving Judea. It does not seem at all reasonable that the powerful and bloodthirsty Romans suddenly became passive and complied to the bidding of Jews to kill Jesus.

Why did so many messiahs arise at that time? Jesus was not alone in believing that a messiah could arise to save the Jews from persecution, since it was a widespread belief in the culture. The wishful thinking for salvation arose out of the profound emotional despair and helplessness that the Jews felt. They did not have the military might to oppose the Roman army and put an end to their subjugation and suffering. They understood their predicament by believing that God was not in ascendance. They had followed the covenant yet God had not protected them. They believed that evil forces must now be dominant, and many hoped that with the occurrence of an apocalypse, God would regain supremacy. The Jews hoped that through a religious miracle, their universal God would be restored to his throne and his protective mantle could cover them again. The Pharisee sect in Judea believed this, that the Kingdom of God would return in the apocalypse. Then the Roman theocracy would be miraculously defeated and God alone would reign over the world. Jesus, like the Pharisees, believed

that the dead would be resurrected physically and goodness would prevail for everyone in the world.

The Dead Sea scrolls were discovered on 1947 in Qumran, being written

between the third century BCE and the first century CE. It informed us
o f the religious beliefs also of the Essene sect. They believed that a religious
Teacher of Righteousness would bring about the Kingdom of God. It is
questionable whether this Teacher of Righteousness referred to Jesus. The
scrolls described a battle between the forces of darkness, the Romans, and
the forces of light, the Jews. Also, a three-foot stone tablet called Gabriel's
Revelation by two Israelis, Yardeni and Elizur, was discovered near the
Dead Sea recently. This provides some evidence that the teachings of Paul,
which initiated a split between Jews and Christians, may not be accurate. It
was dated in the first century, before the birth of Jesus. Professor Israel
Knohl of the Hebrew University noted it that told of a messiah who would
die, be resurrected in three days, and bring on an apocalypse. Some have
questioned the validity of this stone tablet, while others consider that Jesus
followed this tradition concerning a messiah who would be resurrected in
three days to redeem Judea. It is believed to have been written by a slain
man named Simon, who is described by the historian Josephus. This
archaeological find is considered important evidence and confirms the
Dead Sea Scrolls, about a messiah bringing on an apocalypse to remove the
yoke of Roman oppression. All these findings seem to confirms that Jesus
followed this messianic tradition to liberate his fellow Jews from the
Romans and not to heal the sins of people, as St. Paul stated.
A psychological explanation for the rise of these messiahs can be found
in the work of British psychoanalyst Wilfred Bion (1959), who discovered
basic assumption groups. When groups feel helpless and cannot find a
rational solution to save themselves, they may resort to a form of basic
assumption group. Since their survival is threatened, they may join together,
regress from logical thinking, and share a collective wish fulfilling fantasy.
One basic assumption group that Bion called pairing involves the
shared fantasy that a messiah will arise to rescue the group.
On a neurological basis, this basic assumption response appears to
come from the limbic system, especially the amygdala, where emotions and
survival instincts are processed. Briefly, the limbic system is the primitive
midbrain, similar to reptiles and lower animals, and automatically comes
on line to protect survival. A fearful sensation that signals danger immediately
is sent directly to this fear center in the limbic system. The impulse
bypasses conscious perception, located in the more advanced portions of
the brain. This circuit serves as a rough and ready emergency survival
response to rapidly and automatically deal with danger. This primitive
emotional region of the brain functions when one cannot reasonably cope
with danger, when survival is threatened. The right cerebral cortex, which
is involved in attachment, is responsible for the group's shared emotional
fantasy. The chapter on biological survival and adaptation goes into greater
detail about the neurological basis, when the fear center of the brain predominates
under conditions of helplessness.
Jesus, a charismatic teacher, believed he was the true Messiah, and
hoped that he would fulfill this biblical prediction to insure survival of the
Jews. It is likely that this was the secret information he conveyed to Judas

Iscariot and Mary Magdalene, although other Gospels state he revealed it
to all his disciples. As mentioned earlier, during the Sermon on the Mount,
three of his disciples saw Jesus talk to Elijah and Moses. Also Matthew (2)

states that bystanders heard Jesus on the cross call to Elijah to save him as he was dying, but then he cried out feeling abandoned. According to the Jewish Bible, Elijah was the prophet who appoints the Messiah. The crucifixion of Jesus was his heroic attempt to save his fellow Jews, apparently not to forgive people's sins. A more detailed account will be covered in the chapter on Jesus as an apocalyptic Jewish martyr.

Despite all the evidence that Jesus bravely tried to save the Jewish people by hoping to be an apocalyptic messiah, his crucifixion was totally turned around. Instead of his death saving the Jews from the brutal oppression by the Romans, his crucifixion was used to justify the persecution and murder of his own beloved people by the Romans and later by others in Europe.

A myth developed that Jesus was a Christian and not a Jew, and his followers were not Jews either. But, Christianity did not exist then and was created by Paul years after the death of Jesus. Another myth developed that all Jews collectively were responsible for his death. This myth is contradicted by the parallel belief that God killed Jesus, his only son. The myth about the Jews portrays the Roman Pontius Pilate passive and simply giving into the wishes of the Jews. The Jews are portrayed as powerful and the Romans simply complying to their wishes. This contradicts the reality of who had the power and who used crucifixion as the form of capital punishment. It was not the Jewish people but the Romans. This version not only exonerates the Romans for killing Jesus as a troublemaker but also the killing of many other Jewish messiahs and the slaughter of a multitude of Christians over hundreds of years. One explanation for why the Romans were not blamed and held accountable for murdering other Jewish messiahs and so many Christians is that history is written by the victors, the Romans.

In summary, despite the persecution of Christians by the Romans, Christianity spread rapidly throughout the Roman Empire. Slaves and plebians were exploited and offered little respect by the Romans. Christianity enhanced their self-esteem, since they were told they were made in the image o f God. In addition they were cared for by Christian social agencies, and they were promised a life after death. Christians became a potent force despite efforts to destroy them. Constantine stopped killing Christians and legitimized Christianity. But he himself did not convert to Christianity until his deathbed. By combining Christianity with his political position as emperor, Constantine was able to consolidate his absolute political power. The Orthodox church had grown and had become institutionalized, establishing its own hierarchy. Allying the two hierarchies reinforced the political power o f Constantine and the church. This occurred despite the fact that Jesus was not political and against the abuse of power. Instead of Jesus's teachings concerning the poor, the meek, and embracing the outsiders of society, Constantine allied the church with the rich and powerful and created social division. Constantine instilled Roman class values into Christianity. The divine right of Christian kings to rule was established, being a modification of the divinity of the Roman emperors. This joining of politics and religion created a powerful theocracy, which continued

from the Middle Ages until the Enlightenment and resulted in violence and holy wars against nonbelievers.

Constantine also subverted the very moral teachings of Jesus by focusing on the brutal crucifixion of Jesus. The gentle teachings by Jesus of forgiveness, love, and acceptance were lost. Even on the cross, Jesus said, "forgive them; they do not know what they do." Essentially the Romans killed the humanistic message of Jesus and preserved the image of his crucifixion. By creating a myth that portrayed the death of Jesus as a victim of the Jews, he instilled a lust for vengeance. He did not acknowledge that Jesus and all his apostles and followers were thoroughly Jewish.

As mentioned, there were a number of motives why Constantine changed the emphasis of Christianity to the crucifixion and blamed the Jews. Constantine was able to consolidate the populace to his side by establishing a common enemy, the Jews. This polarization consolidated his autocratic power. It also erased the guilt of centuries of Roman brutal genocide against the Christians, by displacing the target of blame from the Romans onto the Jews. Also, the crucifixion reflected the Roman fascination with death and dying as exemplified by gladiators fighting to the death and people being devoured by animals in the arena. Finally, most people in the Roman Empire were illiterate and had worshiped statues of pagan idols. Thus, visually seeing a statue of Jesus on the cross made the transition to Christianity easier for pagans. We now know that illiterate individuals use their right brain and see their world in graphic functional images, which are accompanied by fables. Illiterate people think in terms of stereotypes and uncritically accept fables as reality, even when they are not true.

Constantine's legacy of anti-Semitism continued into the Middle Ages of Europe. Since the Christians were not allowed to be money lenders, this task fell to the Jews in Europe. The Jews were exempt from the Christian prohibition of usury. Being people of the book, Jewish men were also literate, unlike the general populace. This ability to read the Torah occurred after the Temple was destroyed, since animal sacrifices were no longer possible. The Sanhedrin was abolished, and the Sadducee high priests no longer were the most powerful. The Jewish religion changed following this tragedy, from sacrificing animals in the Temple to one of studying the Bible. Not having a Temple destroyed the hierarchical hereditary power of the Sadducees, who were priests and rich land owners. As a result, the Pharisees were elevated to power, and they emphasized reading the Torah. Thus, knowledge was of prime importance and a meritorious and more egalitarian society evolved.

The Jewish religion would have ended after the Temple's destruction in 70 CE had it not been for Rabbi Yochanan ben Zakkai. He appealed to the Roman Emperor Vespasian, who agreed to allow Jews to set up religious academies at Yavneh in Judea. Learning the Torah replaced sacrifices in the Temple. Jewish men were taught to read the Bible in synagogues by rabbis. The Jews became more autonomous and less conforming by discussing the Torah from different perspectives.

Because Jewish men could read, the nobility used them to serve as tax collectors. This assignment placed the Jews in a difficult position. The anger at the nobility for imposing taxes could be safely displaced against the diaspora Jews, who did not have the power to retaliate. As for the nobility, at times they borrowed money from the Jews who, unlike the Christians, were allowed to engage in banking. But, instead of paying

back their debt, the Jews were sometimes killed, exiled, or fined. This unethical behavior by Christians was rationalized as acceptable, since Jews did not accept Jesus as the son of God and were implicated in his death. All Jews were stereotyped as a group and called the anti-Christ. This served to dehumanize the Jews and to enable and rationalize Christian abuse as just punishment.

Shakespeare (1654-1616) is considered the greatest playwright of all times. His genius in the use of language enabled him to describe the psychology and actions of individuals and groups that took place during the time he lived. Shakespeare was born in the small provincial town of Stratford, England, where his father was the mayor. His father owned a glove factory that became bankrupt when Shakespeare was thirteen. This had a traumatic effect on him, according to his biographer Greenblatt in *Will in the World* (2004). Both his parents were secretly Catholic in a country that had become Protestant.

England had changed from being a Catholic country to becoming Protestant one. King Henry VIII (1491-1547) wanted to annul his marriage to Catherine of Aragon, who could not provide him with a male heir. His appeal to the Pope was refused, so he abolished papal authority and made himself the head of the Church of England. The Inquisition was actively in force at the time, and people were being burned at the stake as heretics in Europe. After establishing the Protestant religion, Henry oppressed the Catholics and plundered their abbeys. When his son, Edward, became king he tried to eliminate all the remaining Catholics. He died after five years and his sister Mary assumed the throne. In retaliation, she persecuted the Protestants, and after burning 300 Protestants, became known as "Bloody Mary." After two years she died of ill health, and Elizabeth I (1533-1603) became queen in 1558. Elizabeth returned England to Protestantism, but retained the hierarchical titles of bishops and archbishops. There remained religious conflict however, and the constant threat of Catholic insurrection to regain political power. Thus, Elizabeth put to death Mary Queen of Scots, who was Catholic. In 1588, Spain sent a naval fleet of 130 ships, the Armada, to conquer England and return the government to Catholicism. But the Armada was defeated by efforts of the English fleet and storms. Despite continued intrigues and the threat of the Inquisition, Elizabeth firmly established the Protestant religion in England.

Shakespeare had two great fears. One was becoming poor again, after experiencing his father's bankruptcy. The second was being found out and persecuted as a secret Catholic, in view of the continued religious conflict in Elizabethan England. He hid his Catholicism but secretly remained loyal to the Roman Catholic church in which he had been brought up. When he gained wealth from his plays, Shakespeare applied for a crest, so he could be called a gentleman. Then he could, for all appearances, be considered an insider. Because of his social climbing aspirations, other writers referred to Shakespeare as "an upstart crow."

One can assume that because he was a hidden Catholic in Protestant England, he himself was concerned about being a member of an unacceptable religion. This may have contributed to his writing a play that reflecting the attitudes of his time in England toward Jews. The ultimate outsiders in England were Jews. Because of his financial insecurity and his hidden Catholicism, he played to the crowd as if one of them and expressed their

religious prejudices.

The prime example of the pervasive anti-Semitism existing in England is reflected in Shakespeare's play *The Merchant of Venice.* Shylock is a Jewish

money lender living in Venice. His daughter, Jessica, steals some of her
father's money and elopes to marry Lorenzo, a Christian. But she is not
condemned for this theft, nor for the betrayal of her family and her religion.
In fact, she is later rewarded for these actions.

Shylock, like other Jews in Venice, lived as a virtual prisoner. Jews
were locked up in the Ghetto at night and restricted to money lending
and trade. As mentioned, these occupations were assigned to them
because money lending was not allowed for Christians. And since Jews
were more literate than others, they also engaged in trade. Because of
anger over the constricted life and humiliation he constantly suffered as
a Jew, Shylock made an agreement with the Christian merchant Antonio.
Shylock would loan Antonio money w ithout any interest. However, if the
loan was not paid, Antonio must forfeit an equal pound of flesh. Then
the news came that Antonio's ships were presumed lost, and he was
unable to repay the loan.

At the ensuing trial, Shylock demands his pound of flesh. He is told by
the judge that if he sheds any Christian blood, his lands and goods,
according to Venetian law, will be confiscated. This Venetian law is supposedly
based on the myth of Jews being responsible for the blood of
Jesus. Because Shylock has plotted against the life of a Christian, the judge
deeds half of his fortune to Antonio and the other half to the state.
Antonio refuses the money and then tells Shylock that he must give the
money to his son and daughter. Another of A ntonio's requirements is to
force Shylock to convert and become a Christian. All this is pleasing to the
audience of the Globe theater.

Throughout the play Shakespeare appeals to the crowd's prejudice and
uses stereotypes of all Jews. Shylock is not addressed by his name as a person
throughout the play but is only called Jew. However, possibly out of
Shakespeare's own concerns about being a secret Catholic and also an o u tsider,
Shakespeare might have expressed sympathy for Shylock in one
speech. Shakespeare could avoid taking responsibility for discussing his
own reactions to religious bigotry by having Shylock speak for him. In this
way Shakespeare could secretly empathize with Shylock and express his
own feelings as an outsider, a hidden Catholic, and also as an object of persecution.
In Act III, Shylock comments how he is mocked and his nation
scorned. He proudly states,

I am a Jew! Hath not a Jew eyes? Hath not a Jew hands, organs,
dimensions, senses, affections, passions? Fed with the same
food, hurt with the same weapons, subject to the same diseases,
healed by the same means, warmed and cooled by the same
winter and summer as a Christian is? If you prick us, do we not
bleed? If you tickle us, do we not laugh? If you poison us, do we
not die? And if you wrong us, shall we not seek revenge? If we
are like you in the rest, we will resemble you in that.

Here Shakespeare reveals the humanity of Shylock as a person.
However, in the Act V, the whole trial is revealed to be a sham. The judge
and clerk at the trial were not real but played by the Christian lady, Portia,
and her maid servant, Nerissa. While Shylock's estate is confiscated and his
spirit broken, the others enjoy the farce played on the Jew. Shylock's daughter,

Jessica, who had stolen from and betrayed her father, the Jew, gets her
"special deed of gift" from him that leaves him penniless. Then
Shakespeare wrote a surprised happy ending, possibly to avoid suspicion of

his sympathies for Shylock and to please the crowd. Three of Antonio's ships arrive in the harbor richly laden. Thus, instead of a tragedy all turns out to be a time of merriment for the Venetians but not for Shylock. Shylock's estate is stolen, he is forced to convert, and he is betrayed by his daughter who has assimilated with the Christian majority.

This play demonstrates the angry vindictive attitude toward Jews as a group in England. They are seen only in group stereotypes, which denied their individuality and diminished them as human beings. As an outsider, Shylock is not treated according to the prevailing ethics and morality of the Christian world. Morality only applies to the Christians and not to inferior outsiders. The play's message is that it is enjoyable to steal from Jews, to humiliate them, to trick them, and to coerce them to convert. This is one step away from throwing Christians to the lions by the Romans, but here Shylock is only murdered emotionally. The golden rule preached by Jesus, of not treating others as one would not like to be treated by them, is broken and not applicable to outsiders. Where is the encompassing humanity, compassion, and moral integrity that Jesus, a Jew, preached, and for which he sacrificed his life? Jesus was a social reformer for justice and against fraud, and a moral teacher of ethics. These so-called "Christian" Venetians sadistically make merry at the expense of another human being's suffering whom they have cheated and humiliated. The play is a perversion of the religious theology as espoused by Jesus. Instead, it reflects the rigid English society, where others are seen by social or religious class.

Shylock made his pact with Antonio probably to seek vengeance for the past injustices and humiliations he had experienced by the Christians. He offered the loan without interest but would extract a pound of flesh for nonpayment. Antonio out of self-interest agreed to this bargain, since he assumed he would have money when his ships would arrive. The one person to deliver a speech that is truly Christian regarding compassion for all human beings is Shylock. Shylock speaks the words of Jesus and not those of the so-called "Christian" Venetians. He declares he is a human being who suffers pain like all other people, and he asks others to empathize with him. From this perspective, Shylock reflected the true values of Jesus, the golden rule. His forced conversion was a violation of his identity and totally un-Christian. The Venetian "Christians" are the ones who should have converted to true Christianity.

The Venetians sadistically emotionally destroy Shylock, because he is an outsider. Jesus had great compassion for all human beings, including outcasts such as lepers and prostitutes. In fact, one of the reasons for his compassion was that Jesus himself was considered an outsider. Jesus came from the Galilee and not from urban Jerusalem. People from the Galilee were seen as provincial troublemakers. Shakespeare also considered himself an outsider, coming from Stratford and not London. His position as an outsider was increased, since he also hid his Catholicism in a Protestant England. In conclusion, there was no Christian justice or moral integrity in *The Merchant of Venice,* only sadistic pleasure in robbing and humiliating another human being. The Venetians betrayed Jesus and Christianity by being deceitful and punitive.

The Merchant of Venice reflects the state of anti-Semitism throughout Europe. The Inquisition was in force in the Western world and Jews were given the choice of converting to Christianity or exile. Those Jews who converted, *conversos,* were partially accepted in the culture, but if the conversion was only a cover-up and this was discovered, they were burned at the stake.

What inflamed anti-Semitism were the canonical Gospel stories of Judas, which stated he betrayed Jesus for money. These characteristics of greed and betrayal were projected onto all Jews, even though Jesus himself was a Jew. The very name Judas sounded like Jews, and illiterate Christians in Europe made this association. These stereotyped prejudices were projected onto all Jews as a group, who were dehumanized and violated.

Shylock, whom the Venetians addressed only as Jew, represented the group stereotype of all Jews.

England promulgated the blood libel, where Jews were accused of using the blood of Christian children for Passover matzos in Norwich in 1144. Shylock became the example of the stereotype for all Jews, who were depicted as bloodthirsty, deceitful, and vengeful. Jews were persecuted, forced to convert, and expelled, and their property was stolen. The play is similar to the Edict of Expulsion decreed in 1290 by King Edward I of England. The king needed money after coming home from the Eighth Crusade. By making trumped up charges about the ritual murders of Christians by Jews, he defaulted on his loans from the Jews and expelled them from England. About sixteen years later, King Philip IV of France also expelled the Jews and killed the Knights Templar to gain their money, also after false accusations. In 1492, King Ferdinand and Queen Isabella expelled the Jews or burned at the stake those Jews who remained and converted but secretly observed Judaism.

Benjamin Disraeli (1804-1881) was born Jewish but baptized a Christian. He served as leader o f the House of Commons, chancellor o f the exchequer, and prime minister of England. Despite his dedicated service to England, he was depicted in cartoons as a Jew with a big nose and curly hair. He was called "our modern Shylock" and "the devil" and portrayed as ritually murdering the infant Britannia (Kirsch 2008). Evidence of persistent anti-Semitism in England is reflected currently in the trade union and academic boycotts of Israel.

How does one explain the pervasive English anti-Semitism as expressed in *The Merchant o f Venice*? A possible explanation comes from the history of England. England was subject to repeated Norse invasions and then conquered by the Romans and Normans. The vanquished Celts and Anglo-Saxons were demeaned socially and subjugated to the will of the conquerors, particularly the Normans. A rigid hierarchical class structure was established that offered little possibility of upward social mobility. Political power rested on being born into the right family, as well as going to the right prep schools and colleges. However, there were exceptions for unusually gifted individuals. If one did not belong to the top privileged class, one could feel superior and look down upon a group lower in the hierarchy, which included Jews and women.

It is interesting that a number of female novelists in the nineteenth century wrote about gender and social inequalities that existed during their lifetime. Charlotte Bronte wrote *Jayne Eyre* and her sister Anne wrote *Wuthering Heights.* Jane Austen's *Pride and Prejudice* dealt with its characters

struggling with gender and social stereotypes, while one person, Darcy, responded to people as individuals. One of the most brilliant novels was *Daniel Deronda,* written by George Elliot, who was a woman.

Deronda is the one person who sees people as individuals and not in terms of social stereotypes. The novel exposes the bigotry stemming from these group stereotypes, which included not only gender and social class but also religion. Deronda's mother, who is Jewish, turned him over as a young child to her Christian lover so he could be raised as an English gentleman. Thus, he would not suffer the humiliation of social discrimination as a Jew. Before she dies, the mother reveals he is Jewish. Deronda then marries a Jewish woman, a singer like his mother, and sets out for Palestine as a pre-Zionist settler.

After studying social behavior in monkeys and apes for many years at Emory University, Frans de Waal published a book on *Primates and Philosophers.* He focused on humans banding together, who only adhered to moral restraints and shared values within their own tribal group. Outsiders were seen as a threat and the group's moral values did not apply to them. These moral restraints were learned in the group, despite genetic loading. In threatening times, tribalism helped survival within the group, but at the expense of humanism. For survival in tribal societies, reasoning came after the quick decisions were made based on the emotion of fear. Thus, the automatic acceptance of stealing, betrayal, and fraudulent behavior against outsiders, as described in *The Merchant of Venice,* can be understood also as derived from its primitive tribal origins. There was no guilt in cheating and humiliating outsiders of the tribe to satisfy one's own greed. In addition, cruel behavior toward another human is made easier by using stereotyped thinking that is demeaning and dehumanizing. This is not Christian behavior but is similar to the behavior of primitive tribes that evolved out of the need for survival. The greatest miracle is that Jews have survived at all, despite the centuries of persecution based on inaccurate emotional myths and beliefs that were held to be absolute truths.

Mark Twain wrote an article titled "Concerning the Jews" in *Harper's Magazine* of September 1898:

The Egyptians, Babylonians, and Persians filled the planet with sound and splendor, then faded and passed away. The Greeks and the Romans followed and made a vast noise, and they are gone. Other peoples sprung up and held their torch high for a time, but then it burned out. They sit in twilight now or have vanished. The Jews saw them all, and beat them all. While other forces passed, he remains. What is the secret of his immortality? The Jews became a nation when they left Egypt and were given the Torah on Mount Sinai. They have preserved this holy code meticulously, observing its precepts, studying it, and passing it down from generation to generation.

Historically, during the time of the Enlightenment, which advocated humane values for individuals, there was a simultaneous rise in nationalism. Thus, the emphasis on rationality and science was limited, since emotions and group prejudices emerged strongly. Outsiders were excluded as xenophobia increased resulting in anti-Semitism. One prime example was the Captain Alfred Dreyfus case in France. Dreyfus was falsely accused of revealing French army secrets to the Germans and imprisoned on Devils Island. Despite evidence exonerating him, he was convicted because he

was a Jew. Dreyfus after a number of years was eventually exonerated and set free.

There were repeated episodes of massacres of Jews during the Middle Ages, and they continued into modern times. There were slaughters o f Jews at Chmielnitski and pogroms in Russia/Poland. But the greatest genocide occurred from 1933 to 1945, before and during World War II, in Nazi Germany. First books were burned by the Nazis, and then the people of the book were killed and burned. This was the first time that a modern enlightened European country had a national policy to exterminate all the Jews in Europe. The Nazis used modern technology, establishing killing factories in concentration camps that murdered six million human beings because they were Jews.

The history of the Jews mirrors the biblical story of Joseph, who was favored by his father Jacob. Joseph was given a multicolored coat by his father, which was visual evidence of his preference. This evoked jealousy in his brothers who threw him into a pit and sold him into slavery. Because of his psychological ability, Joseph interpreted the Pharaoh's dream and rose to prominence in Egypt. How much of the persecution of Jews is a result o f jealousy, because the Bible states they were God's chosen people and given the Bible?

How could the Jews flourish despite being conquered, persecuted, and killed over the centuries? Darlington in his book *Evolution o f Man and Society* (1969) offers a possible historical theory. The Bible stated that when Judah was defeated by Nebuchadnezzar in 586 BCE, the Jewish leaders, soldiers, and artisans were taken to Babylonia. Left behind were the less intelligent, poor, and unskilled Jews, who may have been absorbed into other cultures. Assimilation and loss of the ten tribes had been the case when the northern part, Israel, was conquered earlier by the Assyrians. When many o f these elite Jews returned from Babylonia, they had learned a good deal and may have elevated the genetic pool for intelligence. Another explanation is that in 64 CE, the sage Joshua ben Gamla mandated universal education for all Jewish males starting from the age of six. As mentioned, learning was accentuated after the Romans destroyed the Temple in 70 CE. The Jewish religion changed from sacrificial rites in the Temple to reading the Bible and praying in the synagogues. Jewish men became literate and exercised their reasoning powers by commenting on the Torah. Reading and commentaries involve activity in the left brain.

With their gradual emancipation, Jews have made important contributions to civilization. According to an article by Murray in *Commentary* 2007, he noted that from the time of H omer to the first millennium, Jews did not make significant contributions, although Jewish physicians did practice in the Middle Ages. An outstanding one was Moses Maimonides (1135-1204), who was also a world famous philosopher and theologian. From 1200 to 1800, only two Jews are well-known, Spinoza and Montaigne. But after being freed from social restrictions, Jewish contributors from 1870 to 1950 in literature was four times the number of their proportion of the population. In music and the visual arts it was five times, in biology eight times, in chemistry six times, in physics nine times, in mathematics twelve times, and in philosophy fourteen times. In the first half of the twentieth century, Jews won 14 percent of the Nobel Prizes for

literature, chemistry, physics, and medicine. In the second half of the twentieth century, Jews won 29 percent. In the twenty-first century this figure increased to 32 percent. This is all despite the fact that Jews represent only two tenths of one percent of the world's population. Envy undoubtedly may have therefore increased.

In modern times, with the globalization of the world, there seems again to be both progress and regression in human relations. There is a recognition of the universal humanity of all people but also a simultaneous increase in tribalism and conflict. The sociologist Emil Durkheim noted that, during times of change, there is an increase in violent behavior and suicide. But at the same time this has been accompanied by a potential for a greater universal cooperation.

In the Christian religions an atmosphere of mutual respect and dialogue is occurring with Judaism, and includes other religions. Pope John Paul II agreed that the Jews were not responsible for the death of Jesus. The Pope acknowledged that this collective emotional myth spread by the church had created anti-Semitism and resulted in devastating genocides. He apologized and asked Jews for forgiveness. He also released documents concerning the horrors of the Inquisition. Pope John Paul II also established bridges with other religions and preached the universal brotherhood of humankind. Since then, the Roman Catholic church has been involved in ecumenical meetings with other religious groups for some time to find common ground. There has been a groundswell to reconcile the relations among Jews, Protestants, and Roman Catholics.

The healing of Christian-Jewish relations were an important part of Vatican II, written by Popes John XXIII, Paul VI, John Paul I, and John Paul II. Pope Benedict XVI has attempted to overcome the breach in the Roman Catholic church that occurred in 1054 CE. Pope Benedict XVI met with the Ecumenical Patriarch Bartholomew I, leader of the Orthodox Christians, to resolve long-standing theological differences. Both leaders made the statement that they are committed to safeguarding human rights and religious freedom, to preserving our environment, and to advocating for justice and peace for all. They both hope to alleviate poverty, disease, and the threats of terrorism for all humankind. People can maintain their individual and separate identity as well as be members of the brotherhood of humanity. As mentioned, there have also been other efforts to create dialogues between people to foster religious understanding and build inter*Samuel Slipp* 53

faith relationships. One is the Interfaith Youth Corps that operates in colleges to foster religious tolerance and understanding. The exchange of students between different countries having diverse religions also contributes to the breaking down of stereotypes and mutual understanding. Now many countries cooperate to provide disaster relief when one country suffers a natural calamity. The global economy, electronic technology, and threats to the earth hopefully will result in greater international understanding and cooperation.

4 Jesus Seeking Freedom by the Power of Religion

Jesus was against the brutal Roman political authority and the religious leaders who collaborated with them. Jesus and his sect believed he was the apocalyptic Jewish Messiah, who would bring on the Kingdom of God. He hoped that an apocalypse would miraculously occur and remove the theocratic Roman domination of Judea. Jesus believed that his death as the Messiah would bring on the apocalypse and establish the Kingdom of God over the world. This would restore God to power, eliminate the brutal Roman oppression, and bring freedom to Judea.

Jews in the time of Jesus were persecuted by the Romans because they would not accept the divinity of the emperor and had historically fought to maintain their national freedom. Jesus observed the Jewish commandment that there was only one God, and no Roman emperor was divinely chosen to rule over Judea. Rome was a theocratic nation whose welltrained army conquered vast territories around the Mediterranean, Europe, and England. Rome demanded that conquered individuals submit to their pagan religion and accept the divinity of the emperor.

From what we know historically, Jesus was a charismatic teacher who preached for a kinder, honest, and just society for his Jewish brethren. He was able to gather a sect of Jewish followers that strengthened his opposition to the Romans and the quisling Jewish leaders who complied to their wishes. The most holy place, the Temple, was befouled by animals brought into the Temple as well as by the presence of corrupt money lenders. Roman coins needed to be changed to Jewish currency, since the Roman coins contained the head of the divine Roman emperor. He cleansed the Temple of the animals and money changers to preserve the sanctity of the Temple. This was a direct affront to the Romans and their collaborators, and a brave statement for Jewish integrity. This act went along with the Jewish tradition of a messiah, who would miraculously restore the sovereignty of Judea. Some Jews desperately hoped Jesus was the Messiah who would have the power to eliminate the theocratic rule of the Romans. However, other Jews did not believe him to be the Messiah, since he had been a lowly carpenter and an outsider from the Galilee. Also, previous messiahs had been arrested and crucified since they were seen as fomenting rebellion. Other Jews reasoned that religious faith alone could not defeat at this time the most powerful military machine of the Romans.

At the time Jesus lived, there were four major Jewish sects existing in Judea. There were the Sadducees who were the aristocrats of Jewish society with the most power. They constituted the high priests of the Temple and their council, the Sanhedrin, as well as wealthy landowners. They were

a hereditary group descending from Aaron, the brother of Moses. According to Ehrman (2005), the Sadducees retained their political power in Judea by collaborating with the Romans. They had previously had a

Hellenistic Party under the Greeks, and out of expediency, they worked with the Romans to preserve their power. The second group, the Pharisees, represented a larger number of the Jews, who had less status. They relied on meritocracy by studying the Torah and believed in the coming apocalypse when the dead would be physically resurrected. The third group was the Essenes, who were a monastic class that left the city to live near the Dead Sea and were devoted to manual labor, study, prayer, and acts of kindness. They also believed in the apocalypse. The fourth group, the Zealots, sought to fight the Roman oppression directly. The Zealots, under the leadership of Eleazar, were a group derived from the Pharisees, and they advocated military revolt. Many Zealots were poor landless Jews who lived in the Galilee, where Jesus also had resided. They were violently against collaborating with the Romans and intent on restoring justice and freedom to Judea. During the revolt against the Romans, when Jerusalem was under siege in 70 CE, the Zealots also fought other Jews. These included the Sadducees, who considered the revolt against the might of the Roman army to be suicidal. The Zealots were especially enraged at the Sadducees, who had collaborated with the Romans, and killed some of them during the revolt.

Jesus did not seek to establish a separate religion; what he did was to create another sect within Judaism. He preached the Hebrew Bible, was a disciple of John the Baptist, and became a preacher. As mentioned, Jesus was probably influenced by the great Jewish scholars Hillel and Shammai, who lived at the same time and taught the golden rule of mutual respect between people.

What was the probable origin of the frightening concept of the cataclysmic end of days, which the Pharisees, Essenes, and Jesus believed?

Where did this apocalyptic thinking come from? Many believe the Jews learned about an apocalypse during their exile as captives in Babylonia during the sixth century BCE. When Cyrus of Persia conquered Babylonia in 539 BCE, he introduced the Zoroastrian belief that was then the religion in Persia. The religion had been founded by the prophet Zoroaster, also called Zarathustra. The exact date of its origin is unknown, but it was before the sixth century BCE. The religion was written down in the book called Avesta and was dualistic in its prophecies. There was a conflict between the forces of good and the forces of evil, as well as between light and darkness. Sharamazda, or Ormuzd, was the good and wise god, while Ahrimon was the evil god. There were bands of angels around the good god and demons around the evil god. Mithra was the divinity for light and truth. After the final battle, in which the evil Ahrimon is defeated, the good kingdom is set up by a messiah. In this good kingdom the dead will be resurrected, there will be everlasting life, and the world will be judged.

Ahrimon was probably the prototype for Satan and the anti-Christ. Cyrus was unique among conquerors in tolerating defeated peoples to practice their own religion. Most other conquerors imposed their god on the defeated nation. Romans, however, put the defeated god into the Pantheon in Rome. Yet, it is most likely that the Jews in captivity derived their idea of

an apocalypse from the benign Zoroastrian religion and introduced it into the belief systems of the Pharisees and Essenes.

The book of Daniel was written during this time of exile to Babylonia in the sixth century BCE and contains his prophetic visions of four apocalypses. This prophecy is claimed to have been fulfilled in the history of Persia. The narratives first take place in the court of Nebuchadnezzar, then of his successor Belshazzar, and later of King Darius. King Darius, the Mede, is considered to be the son of the Persian King Cyrus, who was part Mede. The son of Darius, Xerxes sought revenge against Athens for its previous defeat of the Persian army at Marathon. Xerxes assembled a huge army and attacked Athens by land and by sea. Athens enlisted the support of Sparta, since they considered that Persia sought to conquer all of Greece. The historian Herodatus related how the 300 Hoplite Spartan warriors under their king Leonidas, as well as 700 Thesbian and 400 Theban Greeks, opposed the massive Persian army at the pass of Thermopylae in 480 BCE. The Spartans and Thesbians sacrificed their lives as martyrs, which gave the combined Greek army time to assemble. The combined Greek military force and the Greek naval victories, under the leadership of Themistocles, enabled the Greeks to win the war. In 360 BCE, Philip II became king of Macedonia. Using catapults and siege machines that he invented, he won military victories and unified Greece as a nation in 338 BCE. Philip was assassinated in 336 BCE, and his son Alexander became king. Alexander the Great (356-323 BCE) sought revenge by conquering Persia, and all the lands East from the Mediterranean Sea to the Indus River, which included Judah and Egypt. However, he did not consider himself divine, was a student of Aristotle, and also tolerated religious diversity. This enabled him to spread Greek culture and language widely.

There are three apocalyptic visions in Daniel, and one prophecy supposedly affected the destiny of Israel. Daniel describes the wars between the Kingdom of the North and the Kingdom of the South. Many biblical scholars interpret this final part of Daniel probably was written in the second century CE because it described the Jews under the Babylonians, the Medo-Persian empire, the Hellenistic empire o f Alexander, and the Roman Empire. The wars described in Daniel between the Kingdom of the North and the Kingdom of the South are thought to represent the split in the Greek army of Alexander the Great after his death. The North Kingdom was the Seleucid king of Syria, Antiochus IV Epiphanes, and the South Kingdom were the Ptolemaic rulers o f Egypt, who fought each other. They were not tolerant of religious diversity and sought conquest and power.

There is mention of a messiah in Daniel, and a first reference to the Kingdom of God and the resurrection of the dead. The apocalypse described by the book of Daniel, as well as the apocalypse described in Ezekiel and Isaiah, were considered to be the source o f the apocalyptic thinking by the Pharisees and Essenes. Jesus is considered to have been influenced by this impending end of the world thinking, probably by the Pharisees and especially the Essenes. The apocalypse is vividly described in the Essene Dead Sea Scrolls found in the caves of Q umran.

How did the death of Jesus, who hoped to save the Jews as a messiah from Roman oppression, become perverted to justify persecution of the Jews? Biblical scholars recognize Jesus was an apocalyptic messiah, who hoped that through a religious miracle he would eliminate the theocratic

Roman rule. He hoped that by his crucifixion he would bring on the Kingdom of God and he would be bodily resurrected, a belief held by the

Pharisees and Essenes. Instead, his martyrdom was totally turned around and was used to blame the Jews for his death. Instead o f Jesus saving his fellow Jews, his crucifixion was used to instill hatred and to persecute the Jews for many years as Christ killers. This was directly opposite to the intent of Jesus, who remained a Jew, who martyred himself for his fellow Jews, and whose followers were all Jews. Scapegoating the Jews for the death of Jesus was used to divert anger and attention away from the abuses of a powerful hierarchical society that existed when politics and religion were combined by Constantine.

It does not seem to be generally recognized that all of those who believed in Jesus as the Messiah were also Jews. Many Christians when asked about the religion of Jesus do not see him or his disciples as Jews. Instead they consider all of them to be Christians. They only see Jews as responsible for the death of Jesus. But the Christian religion did not exist when Jesus was alive, and it was only developed by Paul many years after the death of Jesus. It was not called the Christian religion originally, but was so named in the Greek city of Antioch in 45 CE. What is not openly acknowledged is that Jesus himself remained an observant Jew. This was also true of his apostles who were all observant Jews. All those who originally believed Jesus to be the Messiah were also Jews. There is an impression among many that the Romans were loath to crucify people and only crucified Jesus under Jewish pressure. This is not the case. Jesus was not the only person crucified by the Romans. There were many others crucified before and after him. Crucifixion was the official Roman form of capital punishment inflicted on millions of people. Crucifixion was deliberately used by the Roman to terrify people into submission and to discourage rebellion.

Ausubel (1961) notes that the Jews suffered under the Roman yoke, feeling exploited, insecure, and helpless. Many Jews resorted to wishful thinking and hoped for a messiah who would miraculously rescue them. This was supposed to occur when their suffering became unendurable as prophesied by Ezekiel and Enoch. Then the day of last judgement would come and the Kingdom of God would bring everlasting peace and happiness to everyone in the world. Jesus was not the only one that the Romans crucified as a messiah. Josephus, the Jewish historian, mentions only three of the other messiahs who preached against the Romans. They were Judah of Galilee, Theudas, and Benjamin the Egyptian. All these messiahs were arrested by the Romans and suffered the same capital punishment of crucifixion as Jesus. During one early rebellion, the Romans crucified two thousand Jewish rebels and sold many thousands more into slavery. Thus, many Jews who faced the reality of their helplessness did not believe that any messiah would miraculously save them, and they were also pessimistic against armed revolt as well. The Roman army was the most powerful military force in the world at the time.

How did it come to pass that Jews were blamed only for the death of Jesus and not the other Jews who were crucified similarly as messiahs? It is difficult to answer, since that time is shrouded in the mists o f ancient history, and there are many different versions concerning their deaths. It is virtually impossible to come to a definitive conclusion. Various versions of

what might have happened exist. But first of all, there is a logical inconsistency in the case of Jesus for blaming the Jews when the Gospels indicate the death of Jesus was the wish of God. Thus, it makes no rational sense to blame the Jews for the death of Jesus when God wished it.

In the Gospel according to Mark, Jesus is said to have cleansed the Holy Temple of money changers and animal sellers. Money had to be changed from Roman coins to Jewish shekels to buy a sacrificial animal for the Temple ritual. This was because Roman coins contained a picture o f the Roman emperor, who declared himself as god's son, divi filius, DE Specifically, Roman coins pictured the divine Tiberius Caesar Augustus, son of the divine Augustus. Using the Roman coins were against the first two commandments, not to worship another god or its image. Jews would not break these commandments and not worship Emperor Tiberius as a divinity. The Romans got a percentage of profit from the money changers. By the order of the high priest, Caiaphas, the animals that were to be used for ritual sacrifices were now actually brought into the Great Court of the Holy Temple. The result was that the Holy Temple became befouled with ill-smelling dung. Caiaphas was subservient, a puppet, to the Roman prefect Pontius Pilate. Thus, one can make the assumption that Caiaphas was a vehicle through which the Romans wished to demean the Holy Temple and the Jewish people for not worshiping the emperor.

Mark states that Jesus was arrested after cleansing the Temple and brought before the Sanhedrin, the Jewish privy council of the high priest, Caiaphus. However, in the Gospel according to John, it states Jesus cleansed the Temple three years earlier. Thus, the timing sequence is contradictory, and it is unclear which is correct. If it was three years earlier, the Sanhedrin had no role in arresting Jesus and turning him over to Pontius Pilate for execution. We encounter a number of different accounts of events leading up to the arrest of Jesus. This and other contradictions occurred in the Gospels, so it is difficult to reconcile the differences.

Mark is considered by scholars to have w ritten the original manuscript of his Gospel, which was generally drawn upon by Matthew and Luke. But the question is when and where did Mark write his Gospel and for whom was it directed? What were the circumstances and the context that influenced his writing? Mark had moved to Rome, and scholars suggest that he wrote his Gospel there from the late 60s to 70 CE. Mark aimed his Gospel at Gentile readers, and he was critical of the Jews and the Jewish apostles of Jesus. He repeatedly mentions how the behavior o f the apostles of Jesus was inadequate. He wrote his Gospels at the time the Roman emperor Nero (54-68 CE) blamed the Christians for setting fire to Rome and ordered many o f them slaughtered. Some Christians were wrapped in pitch and set on fire, while others were torn to pieces by wild animals in the arena. The persecution of Christians continued after the suicide of Nero. This was also the time when the Jewish revolt in Judea occurred, which was defeated by Titus. Thus, for Mark to blame the Romans would have only inflamed the existing fury against the Christians and he himself might have been accused of rebellion and crucified or killed by wild animals in the Coliseum. One can speculate that by blaming the observant Jews in Judea for the revolt, he may have hoped to deflect the target of vengeance away from the Christians, who were already being persecuted and killed by the Romans. By vindicating and not blaming the Romans, perhaps they might

lessen their persecution of Christians. The Jews were already guilty of rebellion against Rome.

Other historical accounts say nothing about the Jews having had anything

to do with the crucifixion of Jesus. This is in the writings of two
famous historians living in Rome at the time. One was Josephus, the
famous Jewish historian, who provides one of the most accurate histories
available of the time. He does not mention that Jesus was ever tried by the
Sanhedrin, only by Pontius Pilate. In addition, the famous Roman historian
Tacitus, in his Annals (15:44), also only mentions that Jesus was executed
by Pontius Pilate in the reign of emperor Tiberius. But nothing at all is
said about the Sanhedrin being involved in any way at all.
What other evidence is there that it was only the Romans who arrested
and executed Jesus and that the Jews were not involved? When Jesus
claimed to be the son of God, he directly challenged the basis for the power
of the Roman emperors, who considered themselves divine. Roman
emperors identified themselves as the son of god by using the initials DF.
Only the Roman emperor could be the son of god and anyone claiming
this position was questioning the emperor's authority to rule. This alone
was a capital offense to the Romans and punishable by crucifixion.
How and when did the divinity of the emperor come into being?
Octavian, after avenging the assassination of Julius Caesar by defeating
Mark Antony, declared himself Caesar Augustus, Rome's first emperor. The
emperor's divinity began when Caesar Augustus saw Hailey's comet in the
sky, and Augustus believed that this was the soul of the divine Julius Caesar
ascending into heaven. By his identifying the emperor as divine, religion
and politics were combined to enhance the absolute power of Augustus.
Augustus was then able to replace the Roman republic in 27 BCE and
establish his imperial hereditary dynasty.
What if the earlier Gospel of Mark was accurate, not politically motivated,
or a distortion by a later scribe. What if Caiaphas was indeed
involved in the crucifixion? First of all, Caiaphas was not a legitimate high
priest. He was not a descendant of Aaron, the brother of Moses, which was
a strict hereditary requirement. His appointment by the Romans as high
priest was a clear violation of Jewish law. Caiaphas was therefore not a
legitimate person to fill the position of high priest of the Temple (Rivkin
1997). However, this assured the Romans that the loyalty of Caiaphas
would not be to the Jews but to the Roman prefect, Pontius Pilate. To maintain
his position of authority, Caiaphas continued to comply to the bidding
of Pilate. When John the Baptist was critical of Caiaphas, he had him executed.
Since Jesus was the pupil of John the Baptist and considered himself
a prophet, Jesus was also a threat to the authority of Caiaphas.
Chilton (2000) offers another version of when the Holy Temple was
cleaned by Jesus and includes the possible role o f Caiaphas in the execution
o f Jesus. Caiaphas ordered animal sellers to trade in the Great Hall of the
Temple, since it was more profitable to the Romans. This action was against
the Pharisee's rules, which resulted in conflict among many Jews about
dung fouling the Temple. Jesus was influenced by the Targum formula
established by the prophecy of Zechariah, which would bring on the
Kingdom of God over the entire earth. Sacrifices in the Temple were to be
offered by pilgrims themselves in the Galilean fashion, to occur on the festivals
of Sukkoth, Passover, and Shavuot, and traders were to be eliminated

from the sanctuary (Zeckariah 14:9-21). Jesus came to Jerusalem on
Sukkoth accompanied by between 150 and 200 of his Jewish disciples. Jesus

came to act against the rule of Caiaphas and uphold Zeckariah's prophecy. Jesus felt empowered to do this, since he considered he had fulfilled Isaiah's prophecy. He was born in Israel, felt anointed by the Lord's Spirit, and therefore felt able to speak on God's behalf as the Messiah. Chilton states it was during the festival of Sukkoth that Jesus cleansed the Temple, thereby directly opposing the authority of Caiaphas. As a result, Jesus had to go into hiding to avoid being arrested by Caiaphas. Jesus was arrested in Jerusalem during the Passover, which was much later. This version provides a different time table, which provides evidence and may be more accurate. What do we know about Caiaphas as an individual? In 1970, archeologists unearthed the house of Caiaphas, and they found frescos with graven images forbidden in Jewish law. This is against the second commandment, not to have graven images. His house was similar to a sumptu62 ous Roman mansion, similar to those discovered in Pompeii. This would have been totally inappropriate for a Jewish high priest, but more in common with the Roman nobility. This finding can be read as indicating that Caiaphas disregarded upholding the Jewish law. He identified with the Roman culture and assimilated the Jewish religion with Roman values. In 1990, the ossuary (bone box) of Caiaphas was accidently discovered, which indicated he had a wife and four children.

Caiaphas and also the Sadducees, who were the power elite in Judea, maintained whatever political authority they enjoyed by having to collaborate with the Romans. Essentially, Romans had the power and not Caiaphas nor the Sadduccees, who constituted the priests of the Sanhedrin court. Chilton makes a point that the prefect Pontius Pilate was threatened by the execution by the Emperor Tiberius of his mentor Sejanus, his family, and his followers in Rome. Chilton considers that the execution of Sejanus may have weakened Pilate and enhanced the power o f Caiaphas, or at least increased their working relationship. However, the opposite might also have been true as well. Feeling threatened with the lose of his powerful position, Pilate could have become more autocratic and controlling, demanding greater submission from Caiaphas to prove himself to Rome. Ehrman also points out the close allied working relationship between Caiaphas and Pontius Pilate. When Pilate was deposed by the Roman legate in Syria, Vitellius, in 37 CE for being incompetent in the management of Judea, Caiaphas at the same time was also dismissed.

According to the Gospels, Jesus had revealed a secret to Judas Iscariot, while in the Galilee, that he was the Messiah who would bring on the end of the world. The brutal Romans would then be replaced and Israel would regain its sovereignty. One Gospel states that Judas then conveyed this information to Caiaphas (Mark 8:27-31). The Gospels state that Judas betrayed Jesus, but some feel the Greek word for being handed over was mistranslated as betrayed. In addition, the Gnostic Gospel of Judas informs us that Jesus instructed Judas to turn him over to the Romans. Judas reluctantly complied to this order from Jesus. If Caiaphas believed that Jesus might bring on an apocalypse, it would have been a disaster for him. The Gospel of Mark indicates that this information from Judas Iscariot was

what further motivated Caiaphas to arrest Jesus. However, Caiaphas already had a warrant out for the arrest of Jesus for being a pupil of John the Baptist and for challenging his authority by cleansing the Temple of animal dung.

Prior to the trial by Pontius Pilate, Caiaphas and the Sanhedrin supposedly tried Jesus first. But Ehrman (1999) points out there is a question about that trial o f Jesus by Caiaphas and the Sanhedrin. The trial occurred at night and during the Passover holiday. According to the Mishnah, (Sanhedrin 1:4-5) trials were prohibited at night and also during Jewish holidays. In addition for a capital offense for which Jesus was on trial, there was a requirement to have two separate hearings before twenty-three members of the Sanhedrin prior to a conviction. Clearly none of these requirements were met. Either the trial never occurred, or else if it did take place, it was not a legitimate trial.

The eminent scholar and medical missionary, Albert Schweitzer (1948), noted that according to Jewish law, two witnesses were required for a conviction by the Sanhedrin. One witness was Judas, but there was no other witness. This would have made it impossible to convict Jesus. If Jesus had only kept quiet, he would not have been convicted at all. Jesus apparently did not want to save himself and did not keep quiet. When Caiaphas asked Jesus if he was the Messiah, Jesus replied, "I am, and you will see the son of man sitting on the right hand of God and coming upon the clouds of heaven" (Mark 14:62). In the apocalypse of Enoch, the son o f man is merged with the Messiah. W hen Jesus spoke, he became the second witness, and it was enough to convict him according to Schweitzer. The conclusion drawn by Schweitzer is that Jesus did not want to keep silent and save his life; instead he apparently wanted to bring on the apocalypse by his death.

In the Gospel version of the trial, Jesus predicted that the Temple would be destroyed by God because of the priests' corrupt complicity with the Romans (Mark 14:58). The priests had compromised themselves to sustain their political power. The earlier cleansing of the Temple by Jesus was only a sample of what would happen when the apocalypse occurred. Because of their sinfulness, the priests themselves would also be cleansed away. Erhman writes that Jesus quoted the prophet Jeremiah that the Temple cult had become corrupt, "a den of thieves" (Mark 11:17). Caiaphas may or may not have believed Jesus proclaim that God would destroy the Holy Temple when the Kingdom of God arrived, but Jesus was seen as a troublemaker who challenged his authority. Thus to preserve the Temple, which was the center of power for Caiaphas and the Sadduccees, and to prevent revolt, Caiaphas supposedly turned him over to Pilate (Mark 15:2) Jews had no authority to order crucifixion, only the Romans did. Crucifixion was the official Roman form of capital punishment, and only Pilate was the one with the power to order it.

The story of Pontius Pilate washing his hands of the death of Jesus in front of a Jewish crowd seems to be a malicious myth. If this event actual64

The Quest for Power

ly ever did occur, it appears to be a blatant piece of political showmanship. If this myth had any veracity, it may have been done to make it appear the Romans were only doing Jewish bidding. Blame could then be externalized

to avoid Roman responsibility. Pilate is portrayed in this myth as powerless, and the emotional pawn of the Jews. However from a real historical perspective, this event most likely never occurred. The historian Josephus clearly stated that Pontius Pilate was a brutal and powerful governor, who was unconcerned about public opinion. Ehrman makes an important point that Pilate had no reason to have the trial of Jesus out in the open, nor would he have asked for the crowd's opinion. This would only have made him appear weak, and in no way did he want any perception of him that devalued his power. Thus, the myth about the Jews screaming for the blood of Jesus to Pilate after he asks for their opinion is not at all historically accurate. It is a false myth, since the Jews were powerless. This myth caused terrible anti-Semitism and repeated episodes of genocide, and ultimately the Holocaust.

In addition, the Gospel of Matthew (27:24-25) claims the Jews cursed themselves, "His blood is upon us and on our children." This does not make any sense at all, especially when there is evidence that Jesus himself wanted to die as the Messiah and it was also God's will. That people would curse themselves and their children is so improbable and irrational as to be absolutely absurd. This sentence was in all likelihood inserted into the Gospel by one of its later translators and was not in the original texts. It contradicts the sections of the New Testament that indicate Jesus was responsible for his own death. Similarly, Chilton (p. 265) states, "Pilate's own temperament, make the theory of general Jewish guilt for the death of Jesus completely implausible in historical terms." Chilton also states that the version of Jewish guilt was put in later by scribes in the Greek world, because they wished to ingratiate themselves with their Roman rulers. They were probably unaware of the massive destructive consequences it would have later.

In the Gospel according to Matthew 2, the last words of Jesus on the cross before he died were "Eli, Eli, *lema sabachthanP.*" In Aramaic this means, "My God, my God, why hast thou forsaken me!" But this Gospel also states that other bystanders said, "He is calling Elijah," and others said, "Let us see if Elijah will come to save him." How can these last words of Jesus be explained, since it does not correspond to his belief of being the Messiah? If this Gospel is correct, could it be that Jesus himself feared he would not become the Messiah, and cried out feeling abandoned by God. He then called on the prophet Elijah to come in the desperate hope to be proclaimed as the Messiah and save him from death. The Messiah was supposed to bring on the day o f judgement. Then Jesus would not die, despite being crucified, since the dead would be bodily resurrected. Tragically, Jesus died, the apocalypse did not occur, but his apostles strongly continued to believe he would return in their lifetime.

In 1961 an Italian archeologist found an inscription at the Roman military headquarters in Jerusalem that indicated Pontius Pilate had more power than a procurator. Pilate was a prefect. A procurator was an administrator who collected taxes, while a prefect was powerful and controlled the military. Thus, Pilate was not the helpless passive tool doing the bidding of the Jews. Pilate had come from Cesarea, headquarters of the Roman occupation, to Jerusalem with a military force, since Passover was a potential time for insurrection. Pilate held all the power in the grip of his hands and militarily controlled the governing of Judea. He was not helpless, his hands were not clean. His hands, through surrogates, were responsible

for driving nails into the arms and feet of Jesus. According to the historian Josephus, Pilate confiscated the grand palace that King Herod had built in Jerusalem and used it for himself. It was the highest point in the city, near the Jaffa gate. This was physical confirmation that he was the highest and most powerful Roman in Judea.

The apostles of Jesus were simple hard-working Jewish peasants from Galilee, uneducated fishermen who could not write or read (Acts 4:13). What was passed down and written into the Gospels came from oral traditions and not in writing. What we now have is not the original writings of the Gospels by Greek scribes but handwritten copies of copies of copies, etc., etc. Even the original Greek scribes were not professionals but amateurs who were simply literate members of the different Christian sects.

Ehrman (2005) comments that the subsequent scribes of the Gospels inadvertently or intentionally changed or inserted their own items into the Gospels. This resulted in a very large number of discrepancies, so it is impossible to be sure of the accuracy of the Gospels that were handed down. John Mill, a fellow at Queens College, Oxford, spent thirty years reading a hundred Greek manuscripts of the Christian Bible and found 30,000 variations. Others have found an even greater number of differences in the various Gospels.

There were anti-Jewish scribes in the second and third century who copied the Gospels. For example, Erhrman notes that Jesus asked, "Father forgive them, for they do not know what they are doing" (Luke 23:32-34). But this saying was not found in all the manuscripts. It was either eliminated or added to, so it is not clear whether Jesus is referring to forgiving the Romans or the Jews. If the forgiveness was for his fellow Jews, was Jesus praying to forgive them. Or was he praying for forgiveness of the Romans or both the Jews and Romans? The church father Origen claimed that God had not forgiven the Jews for not accepting the divinity of Jesus, and therefore Jerusalem was destroyed as punishment (Against Celsus 4, 22).

Ehrman also notes that in the Gospel of John, Jesus says that "salvation comes from the Jews," which is changed in some Syriac and Latin texts to "salvation comes from Judea." It is not the Jews but Jesus's death in Judea that brings salvation. Anti-Judaism prejudice developed in the church and influenced the writing of the Gospels.

Ehrman cites two major examples in which insertions were made into Gospels that were not in the most original manuscripts. One is the story of the woman who was caught in the act of adultery as described in John (7:53). According to the law of Moses, she was condemned to death by stoning. Jesus was placed into a no-win dilemma when he was asked what should be done to her. If he followed his humane teaching of mercy and compassion, he was breaking the law of Moses. If he told them to stone her, he was going against his own empathic and forgiving teachings. He said, "Let the one who is without sin among you be the first to cast a stone at her." Everyone left, and he told the woman to go and sin no more. However, this story is not found in the oldest manuscripts of John. In addition, the style of writing is different than his, and words that are alien to the Gospel are used.

The other major insertion mentioned by Ehrman is most significant to the Christian story of the resurrection of Jesus. In the Gospel according to Mark, Jesus was buried by Joseph of Arimathea the day before the Sabbath

(15:42). The day after the Sabbath, Mary Magdalene and two other women visit the tomb to wash and anoint the body of Jesus. When they arrive, they find the stone at the entrance to the tomb rolled away. They enter the tomb and find a young man in a white robe, who informs them, "Do not be startled! You are seeking Jesus the Nazarene, who has been crucified. He has been raised and is not here, see the place where they laid him." He then instructs the women to tell the disciples they should go to Galilee and will meet Jesus there. But the women run from the tomb and remain silent, telling no one "for they were afraid" (Mark 16:4). This is the end of the most original manuscript. They told no one, and in addition the disciples had ran off when Jesus was arrested and crucified, for fear that they would also meet the same fate as Jesus.

But twelve more verses were added later by a scribe, in which Jesus himself actually appears to Mary Magdalene. She tells the disciples of this appearance, but they do not believe her. Then Jesus appears to two others and to the disciples. Jesus is said to commission them to go forth and spread the Gospel "to the whole creation." Those who believe and are baptized "will be saved," and those others "will be condemned." The signs of the believers will be speaking in tongues, take snakes in their hands, and if they drink poison, it will not harm them. They can heal the sick by placing on their hands. Then these verses tell o f Jesus being taken up to heaven and seated at the right of God. Erhman states there is "indisputable evidence" that these last twelve verses in Mark were added later by a scribe. They are not in the earliest manuscripts, the writing style is different, and there is no mention of the earlier story in Mark o f what Mary Magdalene saw and that she remained silent.

It is therefore most likely that the story of the Jews cursing th em selves and their children was also not in the original manuscripts at all, but was added later by a scribe. The Gospels were translated from the oral words and written down by hand. The original Gospel o f Mark was composed between 60 and 70 CE when he lived in Rome. As mentioned, this was the time that the Roman emperor Nero started killing Christians who were accused of setting fire to Rome. It also was during the Jewish rebellion in Judea, which was defeated in 70 CE by the Roman army under Titus. Out o f self-preservation, Mark could n ot blame the Romans, which would only bring down further punishment for the Christians. The traditional Jews were a defeated group, and about a million Jews died in the revolt. The Roman general Titus appointed Haterius Pronto to kill the elderly and infirm and to spare only "m en in their prime." The able bodied men were made slaves or became gladiators to be killed in the arena for entertainment. About 40,000 Jewish slaves were used to built the Colosseum. According to Josephus 11,000 of the Jewish prisoners died o f starvation even before they became slaves in Rome (Hertzberg 1999).

One reason for cursing the Jews came from the anger at traditional Jews for not accepting Jesus as the divine Messiah. Also many Christian Jews, as well as traditional Jews, were against the rebellion by the Zealots. They would curse these militant Jews for bringing on the defeat and resulting debacle. Neither faith nor military rebellion would have been successful, in restoring sovereignty to Judea. Rome had the mightiest military machine in the Greco-Roman world and defeated adversaries of much

larger countries. By the time Emperor Trajan reigned, the Roman army had conquered forty nations, including more than half of present day England, Germany, Romania, Armenia, and all those countries bordering on the

Mediterranean. To commemorate his achievements, Trajan built a tall column depicting his many victories.

Another possible explanation for anti-Jewish sentiment came from the Gospel letters of Paul. But Paul's incendiary language and antagonistic behavior against his fellow Jews provoked them to oppose him. He seemed unaware of the effect of his behavior on others. Originally when Paul was traveling on the road to Damascus, he was intolerant of the Jewish followers o f Jesus, whom he planned to persecute. How could this man, who was so anti-Jesus, turn around so completely and then express anti-Jewish sentiments in his epistles? How can this be understood psychologically? Paul was basically an intolerant and angry individual. Paul even heard Jesus criticize him on the road to Damascus asking why he wanted to persecute him.

After his conversion to be a follower o f the Jesus sect, he remained the same intolerant person that he always had been. This time the target of his aggression turned from the Jews in the Jesus sect to traditional Jews. Paul employed binary thinking, which polarized groups into us against them, thus making this switch easy.

Paul also used the psychological defense of splitting, seeing things as all good or all bad, with no shades of grey. He sought absolute answers and was intolerant of religious diversity. He angrily confronted resistence to his teachings by traditional Jews, whom he demeaned. He made disparaging comments about traditional Jews, and called them names that instilled hate in his Gentile followers. He called the traditional Jews "circumcisers," "the devil's son," and "enemy of all righteousness" (Acts 13:10). Paul even demeaned the original Twelve Apostles of Jesus, calling them "idolaters and hypocrites" for their keeping the Sabbath and for observing kosher rules. Most of the Gentile Christian converts were poor and uneducated, and he was able to influence them and instill prejudice. Paul brought uncircumcised Gentile converts into the Holy Temple in Jerusalem, which was a flagrant offense against Mosaic law. This provocative act, probably out of hubris, was a direct attack on the Achilles heel of the Jews. Past conquerors of Judea had tried to impose their religion on the Jews and brought pagan idols into the Temple. Jesus himself would not have allowed uncircumcised Gentile converts into the Temple. Jesus even cleansed the Temple of money changers and animal sellers to purify it as a holy place to worship the Jewish God. Paul's rebellious act against the Jewish Law resulted in a riot, and so incensed the crowd they wanted to kill him. The Roman guards rescued him, and he was arrested as an agitator. Paul claimed his right as a Roman citizen, and he was not immediately tried and crucified. Paul was imprisoned in Caesaria for two years. The new Roman governor Porcius Festus then sent him to Rome, where he was placed under house arrest. After another two years of imprisonment, he was beheaded during the reign of Nero (Acts 21-31).

Despite the arrest of Paul by the Romans, religious tolerance between the Jews and Christians generally continued. Many traditional Jews, Jewish Christians, and Gentile Christians worshiped and ate together for centuries. There was never a "parting of the way" until the Roman emperor Constantine de-Judaized the service in the Christian church that had been

modeled after the Jewish synagogue worship (Khnghoffer 2006). He separated the traditional Jews from the Christians.

The martyrdom of Jesus was in keeping with the history of Jewish resistance to being dominated by the conquerors of Judea. In the past, when the Jews would not submit or could not revolt against their powerful oppressors, such as the Assyrians or Babylonians, one form of defiance was martyrdom, called in Hebrew *kiddush Hashem,* to die in God's name (Hertzberg 1999). There are many examples of this self-sacrifice for national freedom. One incident occurred when Pontius Pilate tried to force Roman battle standards, carved with graven images of the divine emperor, to be placed in Jerusalem. In response there were many Jews who calmly offered to die to prevent this. Another incident occurred when the psychotic Roman emperor Caligula (37-41 CE) ordered a statue of himself as a divinity to be placed in the Holy Temple. According to the ancient historian Philo, Jews came to the Roman legate, Petronius, and offered to martyr themselves to prevent this (Hertzberg 1999). Fortunately Caligula was assassinated by the Romans themselves before this provocative action occurred. However, the most remembered example of martyrdom occurred at the end of the revolt o f the Zealots against the Romans. Josephus and other Jews warned the Zealots that the rebellion against the Roman Army in 66 CE was suicidal. Nero was the emperor at that time, and he was a cruel and venal tyrant. The Jewish Zealots did not listen to reason, but were driven by emotion. They wanted to stand tall, preserve their cultural identity and reestablish their national freedom. As a consequence, most Zealots were killed during the Jewish war in Jerusalem. The remaining 1,000 Zealots retreated to the mountain fortress of Masada near the Dead Sea and defended it for three years. Anticipating imminent defeat as Masada's defenses were being breached by the Romans, their leader Eleazer ben Jair made a decision. He was aware of the massacre of Jews that had occurred in Caesarea, Damascus, and Egypt. He also knew that if they surrendered, and they were not killed, they would become slaves of the Romans. The decision arrived by all was to take their own lives, to die bravely in freedom, which was probably the most famous example of martyrdom, of *kiddush Hashem.*

Hermann Samuel Reimarus (1694-1768), a noted Bible scholar and professor in Hamberg, Germany, tried to understand the life and motivation of Jesus. He admired the moral teaching of Jesus, but denied the story of the resurrection. Reimarus considered Jesus was another of the many apocalyptic spiritualists who were crucified by the Romans. Schweitzer also considered that Jesus was an apocalyptic believer, who thought the end of the world was about to happen. Klinghoffer (2006) also noted that more recent scholars agree that Jesus preached a coming apocalypse, the Kingdom of God, in his lifetime. He hoped that the Roman theocratic political authority could be defeated by supernatural means, by a miracle, and not by active rebellion. Jesus was a martyr for Jewish freedom.

Is there further evidence that Jesus sought his own martyrdom as the Messiah? Jesus stated to his disciples that he anticipated that he would die when he went to Jerusalem. During the Passover holiday, many thousands of Jews came to Jerusalem to celebrate their liberation from Egyptian slavery. There was a pervasive hope among many people that a miracle by God would again occur on this date to liberate them. As mentioned, Passover was

a potentially turbulent time for a potential rebellion. The Romans anticipated such problems and posted more guards, who were placed on high alert to prevent any disturbances. Jesus undoubtedly knew this was a dangerous time and also that previous Jews claiming to be the Messiah had been crucified to prevent any hint of revolt. Jesus was consciously aware that he was susceptible to arrest and execution and accepted this eventuality.

Jesus may have believed that the sacrifice of his flesh and shedding of his blood would miraculously bring about salvation of the Jewish people. He started the Eucharist, a meal in which he said the wine is my blood and the bread is my flesh. This indicated that he would be the sacrifice instead of the blood and animals used for sacrifice in the Temple. This represented a challenge to the sacrificial practice in the Temple, which he wished to be replaced symbolically. However, this created a problem for traditional Jews, since drinking of blood was forbidden. In the Last Supper with his disciples, one of the oldest Greek manuscripts quotes him as taking a cup, giving thanks, and saying, "Take this and divide it among yourselves, for I say to you that I will not drink from the fruit of the wine from now on, until the Kingdom of God comes" (Luke 22:17-19).

Ehrman notes that most scholars are convinced that Jesus predicted the coming of the Kingdom of God, in which there would no longer be injustice, sickness, and suffering. Then the rich and poor, slave and free men, and women and men would all be equal. This message was appealing to the poor, sick, outsiders, and women. To buttress this belief in miracles, Jesus is described as a miraculous healer, having brought the dead Lazarus back to life and having cured sick people.

Jesus was compassionate to all regardless of class, gender, sickness, including sinners, outcasts of society, and even tax collectors for the Romans. The New Testament depicts him as having empathy for all suffering humanity. As mentioned, Chilton (2000) notes Jesus himself felt like an outsider. He not only came from provincial Galilee but was also considered illegitimate, a *mamzer*. Chilton also comments that the Greek word *parthenos* means maiden, but it was mistranslated into Latin as virgin in the second century. This created the story o f the miraculous virgin birth of Mary. The birth of Jesus in a stable, the wise men, and the rest o f the story is considered a myth by Chilton.

Chilton notes Jesus was named Yeshua, after Joshua the successor of Moses. Jesus was considered a *mamzer* in the community, because Mary was pregnant prior to marrying Joseph. Joseph came from Bethlehem in the Galilee, and Mary lived in Nazareth. Being impregnated prior to marriage by a man outside the community made the child a *mamzer*. Jesus was circumcised, which assured him that he was part of the covenant of Israel. Growing up in Nazareth, Jesus was isolated as an outsider in the community. Joseph died when Jesus was about twelve years old. Chilton notes that Jesus was excluded from his father's funeral, because he was a *mamzer*. His own life experiences of being excluded must have contributed to his deep compassion for all others considered as outsiders. The poor, the hungry, and the alienated Jews were the people that Jesus wished to embrace, to feel included, and to help psychologically.

5 The Gnostic Gospels:
Power through Knowledge

The Gnostic Christians did not legitimize the linkage between religion and politics established by Constantine, and thereby challenged the hierarchical power of the emperor and the Orthodox Christian church. The term Gnostic denotes knowledge, which was paramount in this sect, and the sect members stood against submission to authority. As a result, Constantine condemned the Gnostic Christians as heretics and ordered their writings destroyed. However, some of the Gnostic Gospels were buried to avoid being destroyed. The Gnostic Gospel according to Judas was discovered in 1970 on the east bank of the Nile at El Minya, Egypt, as a leather bound manuscript of papyrus. It was translated by R. Kasser of Germany and later authenticated by carbon dating. It was found to be written around the third century. Clearly this Gospel could not have been written by Judas Iscariot, one of the twelve disciples of Jesus, who would have been dead by then. According to Matthew, Judas killed himself in remorse after the crucifixion of Jesus. This copy of the Gospel o f Judas is probably from an original Greek manuscript that was written by the Gnostic followers of Jesus, likely between 130 and 180 CE. The Gnostic Gospels are mentioned by Irenaeus, Bishop of Lyons France, in his work *Against Heresies* written in 180 CE, which provides added evidence that this Gospel existed prior to 180. Bishop Irenaeus rejected all the Gnostic Gospels as heretical, since they claimed the resurrection of Jesus was spiritual and not bodily (Pagels 1989). In Judea, the concept of the spirit surviving after death had been believed by the Jewish Sadducees, while the Jewish Pharisees believed in the bodily resurrection.

The Gospel of Judas indicated that Jesus specifically instructed Judas to betray him to the Romans in order to be executed. Thus, the action of Judas depicted in this Gospel was not a betrayal of Jesus for money but rather a reluctant submission to the wish of Jesus. The Gnostic group felt that the body was a prison for the spirit, and thus Jesus wished to release and free his spirit. This Gospel adds evidence to the hypothesis that Jesus sought to be crucified as a martyr, to release his spirit, and to bring on the Kingdom of God. Jesus hoped to fulfill his messianic mission to bring on the day of judgement, an apocalypse, and to save his fellow Jews from the domination and abuse of the theocratic Roman empire.

These Gnostic Gospels also indicate that Judas was actually one of the favorites of Jesus. Jesus even confided secret mysteries to him that were not revealed to his other disciples. The Judas Gospel states that Jesus said to Judas, "Step away from the others and I shall tell you the mysteries of the Kingdom. It is possible for you to reach it, but you will grieve a great deal. For someone else will replace you, in order that the twelve disciples may again come to completion with their God." This Gospel also notes that Jesus criticizes the other disciples for being ignorant. For several days

before the Passover Seder, Jesus supposedly revealed the Gnostic mysteries to Judas. The spirit had to be released from the prison o f the body of flesh according to this Gospel.

This Gnostic Gospel considers that Judas acted according to the instructions of Jesus to help bring on the Kingdom of God, which was supposed to occur on the death and spiritual resurrection of Jesus as the Messiah. The Gospel of Judas therefore respects and praises Judas for his brave action, which Jesus clearly considered as God's plan. As further evidence that Judas was obeying the wish of Jesus in the Gospel of John, Jesus says to Judas at the Seder, "Do quickly what you have to do" (John 13:27). This appears to be a command by Jesus to Judas to follow the instructions Jesus gave to him. How else would Jesus have been aware that Judas was going to turn him over to the Romans, unless he knew ahead o f time that Judas was supposed to follow his instructions. Also, if the death of Jesus was God's plan, how could Judas be blamed for carrying out this divine plan? One explanation for this contradiction can be offered. If the death of Jesus had nothing to do with human beings, and was God's plan, it was out of the control of the church authorities. By blaming Judas and scapegoating the Jews, the illusion of absolute divine power by the church and political authorities could be sustained.

The Gospel of Judas also states that Jesus told Judas, "You shall be cursed for generations . . . and you shall come to rule over them. You will exceed all of them. For you will sacrifice the man that clothes me." This Gospel does not state that Judas hanged himself, instead it claims that the

other disciples stoned him to death, not knowing that he was complying to the wish of Jesus. Another version of the death of Judas in Acts is that Judas died as a result of an accidental fall. However, what if the version of Matthew (27:3-10) was correct and Judas did hang himself. If Judas was such a despicable character, a betrayer of Jesus for money as described in the synoptic Gospels, Judas would not have killed himself. He might simply have enjoyed using the money for his own pleasure. But Judas is described as being despairing, since the apocalypse did not occur. He may have thought that the painful death of Jesus was therefore useless.

One can examine this historical event from a modern psychological perspective. Supposedly Judas had reluctantly obeyed the instruction of Jesus and unwillingly contributed to his death. But it was all in vain, since the apocalypse did not occur and all the dead, including Jesus, were not resurrected. The Kingdom of God did not come into being, and the Romans' political power over Judea remained as strong as ever. Judea was still under the heel of Roman domination and Jesus had suffered terribly and seemed to have been killed needlessly. The efforts o f Judas were in vain, and following the instructions of Jesus had only brought Judas grief and condemnation. This would explain why Judas suffered remorse and guilt for his submission to the wish of Jesus. Judas found himself in an impossible situation. If we recreate the situation hypothetically it may have been as follows. The other disciples did not know that Jesus had secretly instructed Judas, and thus they hated and rejected him for betraying Jesus. Jesus had predicted Judas would suffer grief and be cursed. The guilt he felt for this useless, destructive act of his beloved Jesus, and the condemnation of the other disciples, trapped him. There was no way out

of his impossible dilemma. It is usually when a person feels trapped with no exit that they are motivated to commit suicide. This may well have been the dilemma faced by Judas. He felt trapped by these circumstances and killed himself.

There were other hidden Gnostic Gospel manuscripts discovered besides the Gospel of Judas that also tell a different story than the canonical Gospels. In 1954, an Arab peasant, Muhammad Ali al-Samman, discovered a large red earthenware jar near the town of Nag Hammadi in Upper Egypt. Pagels (1979) comments that the peasant who found them was fearful of opening the jar. He feared that a destructive jinn, or spirit, might be released. But he reconsidered his decision, since it might contain gold. He opened it to find thirteen papyrus books bound in leather. But an ironic twist occurred. When he brought them home, his mother burned some of them in the oven for heat. They were eventually sold on the black market to antiquities dealers in Cairo, but the government found out and confiscated them. Ten and a half of these codices were placed in the Coptic Museum in Cairo. But most of the codices were later smuggled out of Egypt and offered for sale.

At the urging of Professor Gilles Quispel, the codex was bought in 1952 by the Jung Foundation in Zurich. Jung was a student of ancient religions and wished to study them. But because the codex was illegally removed, Dr. Pahor Labib, the director of the Coptic Museum, recovered them and kept control over their publication. However, UNESCO intervened so that scholars could have free access to the manuscripts. Between 1972 and 1977, all the codices were published. Dr. James Robinson of the UNESCO committee created an international team to copy and translate the manuscripts, which are now available to all scholars.

Gnostic Christianity arose after the Romans destroyed Jerusalem in 70 CE, and in all probability this sect resulted from the despair and selfreflection suffered by the traumatized Christians. People felt even more abandoned and not protected by God th an they had previously.

Apocalyptic messiahs had not brought on the Kingdom of God for the Jewish followers of Jesus, and the covenant with God did not protect the traditional Jews. Many of these Christians searched for a new meaning to their lives. Some proposed that there was an evil and a good God to explain the events that occurred. Others felt that the world that God created was now seen as evil, and the body was a prison for the spirit. This latter thought may have been related to the Jewish Sadducee belief in the spirit being released from the body after death. The crucial issue for the Gnostics was that they questioned Christ's actual bodily resurrection on the third day after his death. They believed the resurrection could not have taken place literally, but could only be understood symbolically. The actual body of Jesus was not resurrected, and they believed it was only his spirit that was liberated from the prison of his body. The Gnostics considered that those who believed that the dead could come back to life in bodily form were frauds.

But why were these Gospels hidden, and is there any evidence that they may have been correct? Pagels comments that in the Gospel of the Hebrews, John (2:12) noted that Jesus anticipated his arrest and joined his disciples in Gethsemane where he sang and danced with them. How could this be, when he knew that he would probably be brutally crucified? It was

as if he was celebrating a happy occasion. One can speculate that he rejoiced in the thought that his crucifixion would bring on the Kingdom of God and eliminate Roman control of Judea. His loyalty to his fellow Jews would be rewarded and he would be their heroic messiah. That might have been a probable cause for celebration. However, the disciples were frightened when Jesus was arrested, and they fled to the Mount of Olives. Pagels also notes in the Nag Hammadi manuscript, the Apocalypse of Peter (Hippolytus 6:17), Peter observes Jesus on the cross as glad and laughing. Peter states that Jesus said, "He whom you saw being glad and laughing above the cross is the living Jesus. But he into whose hands and feet they are driving the nails is his fleshly part, which is the substitute." The Gnostic Gospel states that Jesus experienced the crucifixion as the time when he would discover and set free his divine spirit (Dialogue of the Savior 139:12-13). With his spirit set free, the Kingdom o f God did not materialize externally, but was seen by the Gnostics and others to be spiritual. For example, Luke (17:21) stated that Jesus implied that the Kingdom of God is within you, while others anticipated an actual external apocalypse would occur. The mortal death of Jesus did not stop the persecution of Jewish and Gentile Christians as well as the Gnostics Christians by the Romans.

The long Roman persecution of Christians who remained faithful to their religion, instead of converting to the Roman pagan religion and worshiping the emperor as divine, created a dilemma. The Orthodox sect of Christianity was in conflict with the Gnostic Christian sect, since the Gnostics did not relate the martyrdom of Jesus to the external political domination by Rome. The Gnostics turned to inner reality while the Orthodox Christians were externally oriented. Pagels states the Orthodox Christians also saw self-sacrifice and self-mortification of the body as imitating the sacrifice of Jesus. The Gnostic Christians disagreed that selfmutilation made people more like Jesus or more Christian. They emphasized that individuals needed to search for the truth internally, and that by doing so the divine God within each person could be discovered. Pagels noted the Gnostic Christians condemned the cult of martyrdom, as advocated by Tertullian, as a "hideous folly." It was not God's will and his p u rpose for humanity to commit violence against themselves.

The Gnostic form of Christianity was felt by some scholars to be influenced by Hellenistic and Oriental beliefs as well. This included the Hindu and Buddhist religions that stressed turning inward for enlightenment. The Gnostics did not consider that God wanted Christians to martyr themselves to insure being rewarded in heaven. However, Bishop Irenaeus, who was a pupil of Polycarp and Papias, opposed the Gnostics, especially the Valentinean subgroup. He emphasized that the willingness of Christians to be martyred was proof of their Christian faith. Later, Irenaeus provided personal proof of his own faithfulness, since he himself was martyred by the Roman emperor Septimius Severus.

In some respects, Pagels notes that the Gnostics concepts had some similarity to modern psychotherapy. Gnostics felt that individuals needed guidance to discover their inner true selves, but once they were mature, an apprenticeship was no longer necessary. Also Valentinus (Irenaeus 1:11) is quoted as considering the importance of nonliteral emotional elements of language as well as inner emotional experiences originated from the depth, the abyss. This has some similarity to Freud's recognizing the

importance of the emotional unconscious. Ehrman (1999) notes that in the Gospel of Didymus, the entire issue of the crucifixion, resurrection, and miracles of Jesus is not mentioned. This goes along with the ideology

of the Gnostics that only the sayings of Jesus are important since they p ro vide
knowledge. There are 114 sayings of Jesus, many of which are also in
the Synoptic Gospels. It was knowledge by individuals and not conformity
to organizations that offered power.

The bodily resurrection of Jesus remained the pivotal conflict
between the Orthodox and Gnostic Christian groups. Pagels noted that
the bodily resurrection of Jesus legitimized the authority and the hierarchy
of the Orthodox Christian church, which still relies on this to today.
The Orthodox Christians believed that when Jesus bodily arose after
death, he appointed Peter to be the "rock" upon which to establish the
hierarchy of the church. Jesus then ascended bodily to heaven. The
appointment of Peter by Jesus provided legitimacy to the leaders of the
church, who were successors of the Apostle Peter.

In summary, the Gnostics emphasized that Jesus was not resurrected
bodily, but that only his divine spirit was released. For the Gnostics the
process of inner learning was necessary to reach the truth and reach the
divinity residing within each individual. They believed the individual's
understanding the self and the relationship to others was significant, not
the submission to an external authority. The Orthodox Christians considered
that the church and its clergy represented the revealed truth of God
that needed to be accepted. The Gnostic teachings were therefore a threat
to the power and authority of the hierarchical Orthodox Christian church
that developed. The Gnostic Christians claimed direct access to God could
occur w ithout the necessary intercession of church authorities. As a result,
the Orthodox Christians declared that anyone who denied that Christ was
resurrected in the flesh was a heretic.

What evidence do we have about whether Jesus was resurrected bodily.
As previously mentioned, there is conflict about whether Mary
Magdalene ever witnessed the resurrection of Jesus. One early version
states she simply saw Jesus was missing from his tomb and she remained
silent. However, in the Gospels according to Mark and John, Mary
Magdalene was said to have been the first to see the resurrection of Jesus
and not Peter. However, Pagels notes that the Roman Catholic and some
Protestant churches name Peter as the first one to witness the bodily resurrection.

In the Gnostic Gospel of Mary (10:15), a conflict existed
between Mary Magdalene and Peter. This Gospel also states that Mary
Magdalene was the first to enter the tomb and only later Peter entered.
Mary Magdalene was a very important leader in the sect of Jesus, being
present at the crucifixion and also the first to enter the tomb to wash and
anoint the body o f Jesus. Peter also challenged Mary Magdalene about the
special secrets that Jesus had confided in her, which apparently may have
been the mystical Gnostic teachings. This conflict between Mary
Magdalene and Peter over leadership was mediated by Levi who defended
Mary Magdalene. To discredit Mary Magdalene she was not identified as
one of the favorite disciples of Jesus, but as a prostitute. This accusation
was later withdrawn by the church.

Pagels also notes that while the Orthodox Christian hierarchy became
patriarchal, some Gnostic Christian groups, such as the Valentinians, considered

women as equal to men. Women were respected as prophets,
teachers, healers, priests, and even bishops. This would be closer to the
egalitarian relationship that Jesus seemed to have had with women, who

were his companions. Women continued to hold positions of leadership after the death of Jesus. In the early days Christians met in private homes and public buildings, including synagogues, where they shared communal meals together. As mentioned, this practice of sharing a communal meal was instituted by Jesus to replace baptismal immersion, which he had learned from his teacher, John the Baptist (Chilton 2000). In the Gospel of Philip (63:32), Mary Magdalene is said to have been loved by Jesus above all the other disciples, who were jealous of her. In the Dialogue of the Savior (139:12-13), Mary Magdalene was noted to be a special disciples of Jesus. The Orthodox Christians did not consider Mary Magdalene to be one of his disciples. However, Chilton {NY Sun, April 2, 2008) reviewing Pagel's first book, contradicts her statement that the Gnostics were feminists. Chilton noted the Gnostics also denigrated women as corrupt.

Women were represented by Sophia, the feminine counterpart of the masculine God, and were considered hysterical, jealous, and vindictive.

The Gnostic Gospels were condemned and ordered to be destroyed by the Roman emperor Constantine and Athanasius, the Archbishop of Alexandria in the fourth century. These gospels represented a challenge to the absolute power that Constantine claimed for himself when he combined the church with his political position as emperor. By joining politics and religion, he justified the continuation of endowing the emperor with divinity, which had been established since the time of Caesar Augustus. Accepting the Gnostic Gospels, which were against a hierarchical church, would have denied that he had divine authority derived from God. To save the texts from being destroyed, the Gnostic Gospels were hidden in jars and buried, some in northern Egypt, and only found in the twentieth century. Another piece of possible evidence has added to this ancient controversy about the bodily resurrection of Jesus. The evidence is not absolute but circumstantial, and comes from the field of archeology. In 1980, several boys entered a crypt and found ten limestone ossuaries, burial bone boxes, in the East Talpiot section of Jerusalem. The boxes were from the first century and were examined by archaeologists of the Israel Antiquities Authority. The contents were buried according to Jewish law. Once the dead body had deteriorated, the bones were collected and put into ossuaries. These ossuaries were catalogued and stored in a warehouse. However, in 1996, an archaeologist, Amos Kloner, examined the inscriptions of these bone boxes. This created new interest and a film was made by Emmy-winning filmmaker Simcha Jacobovici and produced by Oscarwinning James Cameron, who made the film *Titanic.* They titled the film *The Lost Tomb of Jesus,* and it was shown on television. They claimed that they were not out to disprove Christianity but only to present the findings of archaeologists and researchers.

The inscriptions on the ossuary boxes were in Aramaic, the language used in the time of Jesus, and were translated. The film essentially raises the question whether Jesus was bodily resurrected, since they feel they found his bones in one of the ossuaries. This box was inscribed with "Yeshua bar Yosef," which translates to Jesus son of Joseph. Another box was inscribed with "Mariamene e Mara" which they feel refers to Mary

Magdalene. According to Professor Bavon of Harvard, this is the way the name of Mary of Magdalene was spelled by the second-century theologian Origen. This spelling was also used in the fourth-century text, the

Acts of Phillip, which was recovered from a monastery at Mount Athos in Greece. The other boxes were labeled "Maria," for Mary the mother of Jesus, as well as "Matia" for Matthew. There were many Matthews in Mary's family as referred to in the Gospels. One box was labeled "Judah," son of Jesus. By again referring to the Gospels, the older half brothers of Jesus were called James and Yoses, while his full brothers were Judah and Simon. The name on one box was inscribed as "Yoses," which was not a popular name in Judea at the time. Yoses is mentioned in the Gospel of Mark. The filmmakers feel this unpopular name adds further evidence for this being the family tomb o f Jesus. Andrew Feuerverger, a mathematics professor at the University of Toronto, figured that the odds of these six names all appearing together were at least 1 in 600, and perhaps the odds were even greater.

The DNA of what was thought to be Jesus and Mary Magdalene were also able to be examined and compared. The DNA was discovered to be different, so they were not genetically related. However, the filmmaker jumped to the unwarranted conclusion that they may have been man and wife and were buried together. Some early Christian Gospels seem to imply that Jesus and Mary Magdalene were physically affectionate. Unfortunately, the remains of the other boxes were not available for DNA testing. A team of scholars were brought in, and they confirmed the names as possibly being that of Jesus, his mother Mary, Mary Magdalene, the son of Jesus, a relative of Mary, and the brothers of Jesus.

However, other archaeologists and Bible scholars strongly disagree with the conclusions that were drawn from these ossuaries. They feel that the interest in whether Jesus was married to Mary Magdalene was created by the fictional novel, *The Da Vinci Code,* by Dan Brown. They consider the documentary film contained inaccuracies. There are also a great many myths about where Mary Magdalene is buried. There are five churches in France that claim to have boxes with the bones of Mary Magdalene. Having her bones attracted pilgrims to the church. The relics thus had economic value to the church and attracted the illiterate masses of people to view them. A relic is like a fetish, where a part of the person represents the entire person.

The existence and death of Mary Magdalene in France is based on a legend about her coming to southern France with others in a rudderless boat. She is said to have lived in a cave and to have evangelized the pagans. Another m yth has it that she and the Virgin Mary went to Ephesus in present-day Turkey where they were invited by the Apostle John. Mary and Mary Magdalene were supposed to have resided in a house, died there, and are buried in Ephesus. The house still exists and is visited by tourists. Thus, there is considerable controversy about where the mysterious figure of Mary Magdalene spent the last days of her life. What is important is that Jesus respected Mary Magdalene. She had a leading role in the Jewish sect that Jesus established and was not a prostitute. Not her bones in a church or the house that she lived in are what is significant. It is the message of equality, respect, and empathy for all that Jesus preached that is important. Mary Magdalene was described in the Gnostic Gospels as a

leader who carried the compassionate message o f Jesus to others. But physical images, like the crucifixion, and relics became privileged and tended to overshadow the message that Jesus preached. The invisible God of the Jews was replaced by relics and pictorial male images of God and Jesus. These external images and relics seemed to have helped the transition of Gentiles to Christianity from pagan religions, where gods were represented by external statues. Picturing God and Jesus in human forms focused on concrete external images, which were similar to the gods that pagans had worshiped. Since most Gentile converts who accepted Christianity were illiterate, a concrete visual image of God and Jesus was more easily comprehended than the invisible God of the Jews. Also, the Gnostic Christian movement considered the spirit as most important and was more intellectual and individualistic. Additionally, the visual images of God and Jesus had greater emotional impact and facilitated the spread of Christianity.

The movie *The Passion of Christ* by Mel Gibson focused on the crucifixion of Jesus and seemed to blame the Jews and not the Romans. The movie is in direct opposition to the official position that the Catholic church has recently taken. The Catholic church has sought forgiveness for provoking anti-Semitism and genocide by preaching that the Jews were responsible for the crucifixion of Jesus Christ. The Vatican Council II and the pronouncements of Pope John Paul II have apologized for the false persecution of Jews, and emphasized the compassionate teachings of Jesus.

Pope John Paul II clearly stated that the Jews were not responsible for the crucifixion of Jesus then or now. Jesus himself and his followers were all Jews. Christianity arose from Judaism, which Pope John Paul II called the elder brothers of Christianity. The humanistic and inclusive teachings of Jesus are now emphasized in the Catholic church and demonstrated by ecumenical meetings of religious leaders from different faiths.

6 Paul's Creation of Christianity: A Religion about Jesus

Although Paul never met Jesus, he established Christianity, a religion about Jesus. Due to the conscientious efforts of Paul, he spread the Christian religion widely in the Greco-Roman world by converting many Gentiles. If not for Paul's energetic missionary work to spread his Gospel, the small Jewish sect of Jesus probably would have faded into the mist of history. Although Paul was a Jew himself, he facilitated the spread of Christianity by dismissing as unnecessary the 613 rules Jews lived by. Paul felt that most Jews did not strictly follow these rules of behavior, thus it was only necessary for converts to believe in Jesus to be relieved of their sins. In his zeal to convert people, he condemned traditional Jews for following these rules and was intolerant of diversity.

Paul was successful in creating Christian communities in the Gentile world since he spoke Greek as well as Aramaic. In his letters to these communities he was able to answer many questions they asked and thus sustained their continuing belief in Christianity. As a result of his efforts, Christianity gradually became a powerful force and was institutionalized with a hierarchy of priests and bishops. The Roman emperors could not stamp out the spread of Christianity despite centuries of their being brutally slaughtered in the arena. Unable to stop the spread of Christianity through persecution, Constantine legitimized Christianity. By bringing them in the fold, he enhanced his political power. Constantine then used Paul's negative remarks about traditional Jews to justify changing the target o f Roman persecution from Christians to Jews. This had not been the original intent o f Paul, who only sought to convert Jews. By Constantine stopping crucifixion as the Roman form of capital punishment and emphasizing the crucifixion of Jesus, he was able to displace guilt for the Roman killing of Christians onto Jews, who were accused of killing Jesus.

Paul (10:67) was originally named Saul. He came from the town of Tarsus in Asia Minor, which is Turkey today (Acts 9:30). He was brought up as a traditional Jew, descending from the tribe of Benjamin. He also spoke Greek, was a tentmaker, and became a Roman citizen (Acts 18:3). He was not one of the original twelve Jewish disciples and never actually saw the living Jesus. Nevertheless, his contributions to Christian theology are considered by many to be greater than any other author in the New Testament. In addition, he was the second largest contributor to the New Testament after the Gospel of Luke. Paul contributed thirteen letters, epistles,

which were directed at the Gentile churches he founded throughout the eastern Mediterranean.

Saul's conversion started when he was traveling on the road to Damascus, when he was about twenty-seven years of age. His purpose was to persecute those Jews who believed in Jesus as the Messiah. On the way, he saw a bolt of light, fell to the ground, and heard the voice of the dead Jesus. He heard Jesus say in Aramaic, "Saul, Saul why do you persecute me?" After this experience, Saul suffered blindness. He continued to Damascus, where one of the followers of Jesus, Ananias, laid hands on him, curing his blindness. Then he was baptized into the Jewish sect of Jesus. This experience is considered as a divine revelation by religious individuals and accepted as a literal truth. It is difficult to provide an accurate diagnosis for Paul's vision and his subsequent blindness, since we only have written accounts of what happened. But, according to current neurological knowledge, the episode he experienced closely resembled an epileptic seizure. In ancient times epilepsy was considered to be a connection with the divine. Later in the Middle Ages, epilepsy was seen as a form of demonic possession. As a result, women with epilepsy were burned at the stake as witches. The phenomenon Saul experienced corresponds to the series of events that occur in an epileptic seizure. The bolt of light was the aura that occurs just before a seizure. Falling to the ground is typical, even without convulsions, and hallucinations can occur. Martha Morrell, clinical professor of neurology at Stanford University School of Medicine {NY Sun, August 3, 2007), supports this tentative diagnosis that Saul suffered an epileptic seizure. She also mentions that Julius Caesar, Alexander the Great, and many other historic figures suffered from epilepsy.

We now understand the neurological changes in the brain to explain Paul's experience. Brain scan studies of patients with hallucinations have shown activation in Broca's area (for speech processing and perception) in the frontal lobe, the hippocampus (for memory), the auditory cortex (recognizes sounds and speech), and Wernicke's area (understands language) in the temporal lobe. Researchers noted that due to pathologies and under some conditions, the hippocampus or the auditory cortex is unable to distinguish inner from outer voices. Another possibility is that Wernicke's area is flooded with signals from Broca's area to produce auditory hallucinations. Most of these studies were done on schizophrenic patients, but there is a history of others, with or without pathological conditions, that have experienced visual and auditory hallucinations. The person actually has a perceptual experience of hearing speech. There are a number of recorded instances in religion where individuals have heard voices talking to them that have been considered due to divine revelation. In summary, what Saul experienced is characteristic of an epileptic seizure.

Saul's subsequent blindness could have been the result of the debilitation that follows a seizure. When his blindness was cured by laying on of hands, it could not have been o f organic origin. It probably was a conversion symptom, hysterical blindness, resulting from the strong emotional response to his experience on the road. After this, Saul not only changed his name to Paul, but also his religion from traditional Judaism to belonging to the sect of Jesus. His actual identity changed as a result of

hearing Jesus speak to him. He now believed that Jesus was the Messiah, and instead of persecuting his followers, he became their advocate (Galatians 1:11-24).

After arriving in Damascus, Paul preached in the synagogue, Bab Kisan, attempting to convert the traditional Jews into believing that Jesus was the Messiah. He seemed to be unaware of the impact his preaching would have on his fellow Jews. Instead of converting the traditional Jews, he created a riot, and he had to escape by being lowered down a wall in a basket (Acts 9:23). Three years later Paul was able to join the Jewish Apostles of Jesus in Jerusalem. This was accomplished through the good efforts of a friend of Jesus, Barnabas. Here again Paul provoked conflict with the Greek-speaking Jewish Apostles. He was rejected by them and returned to Damascus. The Apostles also distrusted him, in view of his having formerly persecuted the Jewish followers of Jesus. For the next fourteen years, Paul preached to Gentiles and Jews and set up Christian communities throughout many parts of the Greco-Roman world.

Paul then again attended the Apostolic Council in Jerusalem in 48 CE (Acts 11:27). While meeting with the Apostles, Paul provoked a conflict with Simon Peter and James, the older half-brother of Jesus. Both Peter and James felt that to become a Christian one first had to be circumcised and become a Jew. Paul accused Peter of not totally following the Mosaic law, essentially calling him a hypocrite. He accused Peter by saying, "You are a Jew, yet you live like a Gentile and not like a Jew. How is it then, that you force Gentiles to follow Jewish customs?" (Gal 2:11-14) Paul claimed that everyone broke the Mosaic law and sinned, and therefore he rationalized why observe it, since it was irrelevant.

In Galatians and Philippian epistles, Paul concluded that the Mosaic law only made people feel sinful and need not be followed. However, this was in direct conflict with what Jesus said, "whoever goes against the smallest of the laws of Moses, teaching men to do the same, will be named least in the Kingdom of Heaven, but he who keeps the Law of Moses, teaching others to keep them, will be named great in the Kingdom of Heaven" (Matthew 5:19).

James, the leader of the Jewish followers of Jesus, was finally persuaded by Paul to compromise. The religion needed to be made easier for it to be spread universally among the Gentiles. They submitted to Paul's demands that Gentiles did not need to keep the covenant with God and did not need to be circumcised. Gentiles did not have to keep kosher, but restrictions were placed on not eating food offered to idols or meat of strangled animals (Acts 15:29). In addition, Paul reestablished immersion, as had been advocated by John the Baptist. As mentioned, Jesus had eliminated baptismal immersion and substituted the communal meal. But, Paul countermanded the decisions of Jesus on these issues, which then became institutionalized in the Christian religion.

How was Paul so successful in converting so many Gentiles to Christianity? First of all Paul could speak Greek beside Aramaic, so he could speak the language of the Gentiles as well as the Jews. Greek was a universal language throughout the Middle East following the conquest o f Alexander the Great. Paul told the Gentiles that the pagan idols they worshiped were dead, and there was only one tru e universal God, the Jewish God. He said people were made in the image o f God, which

instilled a sense o f dignity among Gentiles, since most o f them were poor or slaves. He stated that Jesus Christ was God's son and died for man's sins, so their sins would be forgiven if they believed in Jesus.

What was most appealing in what Paul preached was that having faith
in Jesus would also grant them eternal life after death. They would be
rewarded in heaven to make up for the impoverished life they lead on
earth under Roman rule. Paul must have been a charismatic leader, with
very strong dedication, since he was successful as a missionary among
the Gentiles.

What also facilitated the conversion of the Gentiles was that many
people in the Roman Empire admired the Jews who stood up to and
fought the overwhelming military might of Rome. As mentioned, by Paul
criticizing and eliminating the 613 behavioral requirements for traditional
Jews, he made it easier to spread Christianity. He preached a simple and
absolute doctrine, that is, that faith alone was necessary, not behavior. For
traditional Jews it was much more complicated, since they had to follow
and behave according to the 613 laws of Moses. Jews were individually
responsible for their behavior according to the covenant established by
Moses with God. If a Jew sinned against another, only the offended person
could forgive them. In Christianity faith alone in Jesus Christ would
absolve a person o f sin; acceptance was thus unconditional. Belief in
Christ would also be rewarded by salvation after death.

Paul preached two origins for Jesus, which may have helped convert
two different groups. In one, Jesus was a descendent of King David, and in
the other Jesus was a result of a virgin birth. Even though they contradicted
one another, the first was more suitable for converts who were traditional
Jews and the second for Greeks who were Gentiles. However, it is
possible that this contradiction was a result of later scribes who interpreted
the word for maiden as virgin, since maidens were assumed to be virgins.
On the other hand, the Gospels may have been changed by later
scribes to suit the needs of the Jewish and Greek communities.

The Gospel according to Matthew infers that traditional Jews might
be converted more easily to Christianity by stating that Jesus was a descendent
from David and Abraham through his father. This heritage was a
requirement in the Jewish Bible for a messiah. But for Greeks, Mary is
described as a virgin who is impregnated by God. This was similar to
Greek pagan legends of demigods, such as Achilles, who had both human
and divine parents. This was also true of the Egyptian goddess Isis who
was divinely inseminated to give birth to Horus. However, the Gospels
were copied so many times and changed so often, it is uncertain what any
of the Gospels originally stated. However, Ehrman notes that in the earliest
manuscripts of the Gospels, Jesus is said to be the son of Joseph, the
husband of Mary (Matt 1:16). This was changed by later scribes to read
that Joseph was not married to Mary, only betrothed, and states that she
was a virgin.

Paul (Corinthians 1) preached that Jesus would return as the Messiah
during Paul's own lifetime. Since the apocalypse had not occurred when
Jesus died, Paul anticipated Jesus would soon return from the dead. Paul
stated that Jesus having arisen from the dead was "the first fruit" of the
time of judgment, and the apocalypse would occur shortly, with good
defeating evil. Paul declared he was a Pharisee, and stated that at the time

o f judgment all who believed in Jesus, including the dead, would be bo d ily
resurrected and enter Christ's eternal kingdom up in heaven. However,
unbelievers would be punished eternally below. This polarized and established

a punitive attitude that was not characteristic of Jesus. Jesus was
accepting and forgiving of all. It seemed more characteristic of the personality
of Paul, who saw events in black and white terms.

Paul wrote epistles around the year 50 CE to the congregants he had
converted in order to resolve their questions and to prevent splintering of
the Christian movement. These included Paul's epistles Romans 1 and 2,
Corinthians, Galatians, Ephesians, Philippians, Colossians 1 and 2,
Thessalonians 1 and 2, Timothy, Titus, and Philemon. Questions were
brought up and answered in the epistles concerning abuses of the communal
meal, chaotic services, visiting prostitutes, eating meat sacrificed to
pagan idols, and ethical issues. In the Thessalonica epistle, he addresses a
Christian community that was severely persecuted by the Romans. He also
may have written the epistle, Hebrews, to the Jewish Christians who were
considering abandoning Christianity and returning to traditional Judaism.
Because Paul claimed the end of days was very near, he advocated that
people should not be attached to things in this life. As a consequence, he
discouraged marriage and advocated celibacy. He preached against masturbation,
since he considered it would pollute the flesh. Essentially Paul
felt it was important for Christians to maintain their physical body, since
when Jesus returned and the day of judgment arrived, God would raise
the actual bodies of the dead.

As mentioned, Paul seems to have been a strongly opinionated individual,
which helped motivate him to accomplish the difficult task of
being a missionary to the Gentiles. However, he left a long trail of conflict
behind him, because of his provocation and insensitivity to his effect on
others. In summary, his conflict with others began in the Jewish temple,
Bab Kisan, in Damascus, where he provoked a riot and had to be rescued.
He also created conflict with the Greek-speaking Jewish Apostles of Jesus
at the Jerusalem Council. He had a dispute with Simon Peter over circumcision,
accusing him of Judaizing the conversions of Gentiles. He had conflict
with James over whether Gentile converts could ignore the 613 laws
of Moses. He also demeaned the Apostles of Jesus for their orthodox
Jewish beliefs, and finally he fought with Barnabas, who had helped him
to meet the Apostles of Jesus in Jerusalem. His actions seemed to have selfrighteous
beliefs, which resulted in his attacking others for their divergent
religious beliefs, instead of being like Jesus who was tolerant and accepting
of diversity.

In summary, Paul wanted to persecute the Jewish Christians, and then
he turned against the traditional Jews. He called people who did not agree
with him derogatory names as he tried to intimidate them and impose his
views. His anger and conflict with traditional Jewish belief created problems
between Gentiles and traditional Jews. Instead of following the tolerant
and egalitarian views of Jesus, Paul created a number of conflicts
that as Volkan stated became part of the collective emotional memory of
Christians. Had he not held his views to be absolutely true, been more tolerant
of diversity of religious beliefs, and not demeaned traditional Jews,
European history might have taken a different course.

Intellectually Paul espoused the ideas of compassion, patience, forgiveness,

love, and gratitude, all the traits advocated by Jesus (Galatians
5:16-26). Yet in his condemnations, intolerance, and self-righteous behavior

throughout his life, his actions spoke louder than his words. Jesus
deeply respected the Temple in Jerusalem, cleansing it to keep it a holy
place for Jewish worship. Paul, unlike Jesus, brought in uncircumcized
Greek Christian converts into the Holy Temple. This was contrary to the
beliefs of Jesus, who considered the rules concerning the Holy Temple
should not be violated. As mentioned, Paul's actions created a riot in the
Temple, and Paul was arrested by the Romans. Since he was a Roman citizen
he was not crucified but was incarcerated in Caesaria and then sent
to Rome, where he was eventually beheaded by the Romans.
Paul held other values that today are questionable. Paul did not condemn
slavery (Philemon 16), but he advocated treating slaves like b rothers.
He also stated women were created for men and were forbidden to
teach or have authority over men. Women were thus prevented from
being ordained in the church, which was unlike Jesus who respected
women disciples. Women according to Paul were delegated to a secondclass
position socially. He also condemned homosexuals, adulterers, masturbators,
thieves, and drunkards who he claimed would not inherit the
Kingdom of God. He needed to impose his absolute beliefs, but this drive
helped achieve his missionary goals.
What about Paul's belief that the apocalypse would occur in his lifetime?
It did not occur when Jesus died, nor did it occur in Paul's lifetime
The apocalypse is also mentioned by St. John in Revelation in the Bible.
However, this ancient belief of a second coming of Jesus and an apocalypse
has persisted to this day. Despite being unscientific, the tripartite
collective thinking of heaven, earth, and hell still persists in some fundamentalist
evangelical Christian religions. They believe the Rapture will
occur, where believers in Jesus Christ will be elevated to heaven and n o n believers
will burn eternally in the lake of fire below.
Scientifically this tripartite thinking based on Paul's beliefs in the
Bible does not fit with our current knowledge of the universe. We have
sent space craft to explore the moon and the planets, and the depths of the
earth have been explored and hell was not discovered. Thus, there is objective
scientific evidence contradicting the religious belief that heaven is
above the earth, where people will ascend up into the clouds, or that people
will descend into hell below the earth. Yet, this collective emotional
memory that is not based on rational facts persists despite the findings of
science as Volkan noted.
The belief in the Rapture persists, since it psychologically serves to
help some people in the fundamentalist evangelical movement. Collective
emotional memory can be greater than conscious rational knowledge.
Despite objective evidence to the contrary, believers in the Rapture adhere
to it fervently. We now live in anxious times, and people feel helpless. It is
not the Romans that oppress us now but the fear of terrorism and natural
disasters. The neurological basis for this emotional memory will be discussed
in a separate chapter on brain functioning.
Insecurity has arisen due to terrorist attacks and the fear of a nuclear
holocaust. In addition, there have been natural disasters related to the

danger of global warming. Global warming could result in raising the level
o f the oceans to flood our coastal cities, as the polar ice caps melt. Global
warming can also cause drought near the equator and famine, and bring

death to many animals. There are more frequent natural disasters, as occurred in Indonesia and New Orleans. Also there are diseases such as the Ebola virus, HIV, West Nile Virus, Lyme disease, a deadly form of tuberculosis, and Avian flu, which are difficult or immune to treatment. Additionally, there are other bacterial infections, such as Staphylococcus aureus and other diseases, which have mutated and become resistant to antibiotics. These factors have created the fear that life has become precarious and even though faith in science had been like God our protector, it has its limitations.

As in all religions, people are comforted by the collective believe in a higher authority who has the power to protect, love, and comfort them. This can serve as a backup when science is not effective in many instances and even destructive. Some religions provide an absolute truth, which creates a sense of security to mitigate the chronic stress, helplessness, and anxiety people experience. It also is appealing to people who may have felt unfulfilled, empty, and isolated in their lives. They feel loved by the divinity, which bolsters their self-esteem. People gain a sense of social support by emotionally joining with other believers. As mentioned, this may be more an issue in the United States, which is made up of many nationalities, so that religion can serve as a substitute community and provide a sense of belonging. Religion also promised a happy life after death, eternal peace, and being reunited with lost loved ones.

People believing in the Rapture use as evidence the Revelations of St. John in the New Testament. They hold that believers in Jesus would be lifted to heaven and nonbelievers would roast forever in hell. Ehrman notes that the apocalypse, the day of judgment, as described by St. John's Revelations, does not apply today, and was only relevant to the time St. John lived. St. John was like Paul; both felt that the end of the earth was at hand. The apocalypse would occur immediately to end Roman theocratic rule and human life would become immortal.

Revelations included evidence concerning the oppression of Judea by the Romans during the first century. In Revelations (John 17), the whore o f Babylon is dressed in purple, which was the imperial color of the divine Roman emperors. Rome was like Babylon, both o f whom conquered Judea. The whore is seated on a beast with seven horns and seven heads (John 13). The number seven refers to Rome, which was built on seven hills. Some fundamentalist Evangelicals consider that the number 666 refers to Satan. But, the anti-Christ beast's number 666 comes from adding up the Greek letters that spell out Caesar Nero. Nero was the ruthless and venal tyrant who started the slaughter of Christians. Nero also killed his own relatives, his brother, his pregnant wife, and his mother, Agrippina, who may have poisoned her husband, the previous emperor Claudius.

In 64 CE, the Roman emperor Nero blamed the Christians for setting fire to Rome. Christians were also accused of killing and using the blood of children in their rituals, which was later attributed to Jews. It was Nero who started the brutal slaughter of Christians, which continued for centuries thereafter. Nero saw the Christians as troublemakers and wished to

eliminate them. Christianity was considered a separate religion from Judaism and not protected by Roman law. As mentioned, since the Jews had sided with Rome in the Punic wars, they were rewarded with religious tolerance. This tolerance ended with the Jewish revolt against Rome d u ring

Nero's reign.

The Roman emperor Nero not only slaughtered ordinary Christians
but their leaders as well. St. Paul was beheaded and St. Peter was crucified
upside down. Revelations by St. John cryptically hoped that the brutal
Samuel Slipp 91
Roman tyranny would be destroyed in the apocalypse, but this wished for
event did not occur. Rome continued its slaughter of innocent Christians
for hundreds of years.

If the Rapture did not originate with St. John, and only referred to the
Roman emperor Nero and his slaughter of Christians, how did the idea of
the Rapture start? It began in 1830 when a fifteen-year-old Scottish-Irish
girl, Margaret MacDonald, had a vision of Jesus rescuing people and saying
he would return. This story was published in 1861 and widely d stributed.
At the end of the nineteenth century, John Nelson Darby spread this
story throughout England. He stated that when Jesus returned, he would
only rescue believers, who would enjoy immortality. C. J. Scofield stated
that nonbelievers would suffer eternal hell in the lake of fire. Some of the
others who wrote about the Rapture included William Eugene Blackstone
in *Jesus is Coming*, Dr. John Wolvoord in *The Rapture Question*, Hal Linsey
in *The Late Great Planet Earth*, and Tim LaHaye in *Left Behind*.

The Roman Catholic Church, the Greek Orthodox Church, and moderate
Protestant Churches do not adhere to the idea of the Rapture. The
Vatican rejected this scenario, since Jesus was compassionate, not punitive,
and forgave sinners. Thus, other Christian religious denominations
do not hold that nonbelievers would go to hell as prescribed by some fundamentalist
Evangelical believers in the Rapture. Jews do not believe in
salvation as a reward for believing; ethical behavior is its own reward. The
foundation for the Rapture belief started with Paul, who taught that those
who believed in Jesus would have their sins forgiven and that they would
enjoy eternal life in heaven.

The Gospel according to Mark was written during and after the time
that Nero was emperor of Rome. The Gospel according to Mark came
first, and served as a source for the Gospels of Matthew and Luke, hence
they are referred to as synoptic Gospels, from the Greek meaning seen side
by side. As stated previously, these Gospels were written during and after
the rebellion by the Jewish Zealots against the Romans. It is estimated that
up to a million Jews were killed during this revolt. The Holy Temple in
Jerusalem was burned down and sacked in 70 CE by T itus's Roman army.
The Gospel scribes undoubtedly had to be influenced by the Roman backlash
against Jews. These writers probably feared for their own lives if they
blamed the Romans for the crucifixion of Jesus. As mentioned earlier, the
Jewish Christians defensively sought to differentiate themselves from
rebellious traditional Jews by noting that Jesus preached faith not military
rebellion. We do not have the original writings of the scribes, but only
copies of copies of copies, so it is unclear what was in the original writings.
According to Ehrman (2005), the original scribes who wrote the
Gospels were amateurs and inadvertently or intentionally changed them
in places according to their beliefs.

The split between Jewish Christians and traditional Jews was amplified
when Rabbi Akiba declared Simon Bar-Kochba the Messiah, and

anticipated the end of days. In 132 bar-Kochba's army defeated the Roman legions in Judea. Even though bar-Kochba was declared a messiah and led a successful military revolt initially, the Jewish army was defeated three years later, in 135 CE. This occurred after Emperor Hadrian dispatched a large Roman army under Julius Severus. First of all the Jewish Christians already had a messiah in Jesus and rejected bar-Kochba as the messiah. They and many traditional Jews recognized the futility of combating the powerful military force of Rome.

The Roman army was the existing superpower at the time. The Roman army was a well-disciplined fighting machine, which accounted for their victory. The Roman soldiers were well armored and had spikes under their sandals to secure their grip to the ground. They could defend themselves with their large curved rectangular shields, which they could bring together to form a "turtle" to fend off arrows. They had ballistic machines (like artillery that threw stones), arrows, javelins, knives, and short swords that they used very effectively. They also had cavalry, which was employed against an enemy's lightly armed infantry. Nevertheless, the Jews emotionally hoped for national freedom and to maintain their cultural integrity. This hope was strong enough among the Jewish rebels to attempt to fight against such an overwhelming force. The defeat of the rebellion by the Romans was devastating, with a great many Jews killed and Rabbi Akiba being flayed alive.

The Romans then changed the name of the land from Judea to Palestine.

7 Emperor Constantine: Christianity Used for Power

Christians initially were slaughtered by Nero (54-68 CE), who accused them of setting fire to Rome. Christians in large numbers were brutally murdered by the Romans. They were either burned alive, crucified, beheaded, forced to fight to the death as gladiators, or simply thrown into the arena where they were torn apart and devoured by wild animals. Christians continued to be executed in Rome for centuries when they failed to worship the pagan gods and the emperor as divine. Rome was a theocratic political nation in which the gods from conquered nations were placed in the Pantheon. Feeding Christians to the lions in the Coliseum placated the crowds, giving them an illusion of power over the victims, and served as an entertaining sport.

An attempt to destroy all of Christianity occurred in the reign of the Roman emperor Diocletian (284-305 CE). Despite the persecution, there were over three million Christians in the Roman Empire at the time, and the faith was rapidly growing. Christianity had become institutionalized with its own hierarchical structure, making it difficult in governing the Roman Empire. Diocletian thus began the "great persecution" that lasted about ten years and killed a great many Christians. In addition, to better govern the vast Roman Empire, Diocletian divided the empire into the East and the West and appointed two rulers for each empire, the Tetrarchy. All this drastically changed after Emperor Constantine Chlorus, who ruled the Western empire, died in 306 CE (Carroll 2001). The army p ro claimed his son Constantine (288-337) emperor of the West, b ut he first needed to depose his rival ruler in the West, Maxentius. Constantine fought his opponent across northern Italy. But in 312 CE, as the story states, Constantine saw a shining cross in the sky at the Milvian Bridge over the Tiber river. Above the cross were the words, "In this sign you will conquer." He placed a cross on the shield of each of his soldiers, and his army defeated the Roman army of Maxentius to become the sole ruler of the Western Roman Empire. Constantine then proceeded in 323 CE to conquer the Eastern Roman army of Licinius as well. Constantine was then able to declare himself the sole emperor of the entire Roman Empire. To further his grab for political power, Constantine stopped the killing of Christians, making Christianity the legal religion of Rome. Thus, he combined politics and religion to enhance his power as a divine emperor.

However, in the process he hijacked Christianity's essence. According to Will's *What Jesus Meant* (2006), the main teachings of

Jesus were that he was against violence even toward the Romans, who exploited and tyrannized the Jewish population. Jesus preached a religion of tolerance, nonviolence, love, and forgiveness but hoped to eliminate the abusive political power of Rome through religious faith. As mentioned, Jesus was egalitarian concerning the poor and wealthy, and male and female, and he was against political hierarchies. Constantine did not adhere to the teaching o f Jesus, which were responsive to the needs of the people. Like previous Roman emperors, who were considered the son of God, Constantine initiated what became the divine right of Christian kings to rule. Constantine established a different theocracy than had existed previously, by combining the Christian religion with politics. This was the exact opposite of the teachings of Jesus, who was against the abuse of political power.

Constantine infused the Christian religion with Roman class hierarchy and militarism, not the egalitarian and compassionate teachings of Jesus. Christianity was no longer associated with the poor, the sick, and the outcasts of society whom Jesus defended but became allied with the rulers and powerful elite. It was no longer the meek that would inherit the earth, as Jesus had hoped, but the militarily powerful rulers. Conformity to the Roman emperor's edicts was continued; people obeyed the divine emperor and the church elders. Originally, the emperor Augustus had called himself princeps, the first citizen of Rome, but Constantine saw himself as the domini, the lord over slaves. Power now came from the top down and not from the bottom up as Jesus had preached. Constantine crowned himself with divine power that was absolute.

Constantine was an astute and clever politician. He was aware of the spreading of Christianity throughout the empire. Unlike Diocletian who fought to stop the spread of Christianity, Constantine recognized it was too late to defeat the Christians, who had become too numerous. He viewed them as representing a potentially unifying force for his ambition. By enlisting Christians to his side, he consolidated his grasp of power. Belief in the Christian religion was not o f prime importance to Constantine, since he himself did not convert and continued to worship Apollo, the sun god. As a result, he changed the day of the Sabbath from Saturday to Sunday. He used religious belief to reinforce his political power. By allying himself with the religious hierarchy, Christians were no longer trouble makers for Rome. His divinity had more universal support, and his authority became more widespread. All his decisions now had divine sanction by not only Romans but by Christians as well, and his edicts could not be questioned. Although he used Christianity to consolidate his power, he only converted to Christianity shortly before dying.

According to James Carroll's superb book *Constantine's Sword* (2001), the crucifixion had no previous symbolic significance in Christianity before Constantine. But Constantine emphasized the crucifixion of Jesus and stopped crucifixion as the official form of Roman capital punishment. In this way he was able to submerge the compassionate and egalitarian teachings of Jesus by focusing on the external visual image of the crucifixion. As mentioned, the messenger and not the message became the

focus of attention.

There were a number of reasons for Constantine's focus on the crucifixion of Jesus. First of all, most of the Roman populace were poor and illiterate. Thus, being unable to read, having a concrete symbol of the religion made it easier for illiterate people to become Christian. This fit in with their previous pagan worship, since they were accustomed to worshiping idols. Also, visual imagery of the crucifixion and relics related to people more emotionally, creating a sense of connection. Finally, observing death and dying in the arena had been of central importance in the Roman culture, and seeing the death of Jesus probably continued this fascination of the Romans.

The externalized image of God was against the Jewish second commandment of not worshiping a graven image. In addition, after the destruction of the Temple, Jewish men became literate as they studied and commented on the Bible. This ability to symbolize helped them to accept an invisible God. Jews also focused on internal values that d e te rm in ed b ehavior th a t was in the rig h t side o f the Ten Commandments. It was less im p o rtan t to Constantine how a person lived ethically in a morally just society, since for him Christianity appeared to be a means to an end. He was a great sinner, since a good deal of his behavior was immoral and driven by a lust for power. He killed many o f his relatives and his immediate family, just like many previous Roman emperors.

In 325 CE, Constantine sent his mother, Helena, to Jerusalem to find the sight of the crucifixion and the grave of Jesus. As mentioned, it served his political purpose to have external religious evidence about Jesus. That would make the Christian religion more acceptable to people who were poor, illiterate, and formerly pagan. Helena needed to find concrete visual evidence about Jesus. This would make it easier for the vast number of illiterate and poor Romans to convert to Christianity.

Finding the place of crucifixion and burial of Jesus was an almost impossible task that Constantine assigned to his mother Helena. It was almost 300 years since Jesus had been crucified and buried. Legend had it that his burial was not far from the site of his crucifixion, but the exact site was shrouded in mystery. Helena questioned many people in Jerusalem and was told that the Roman emperor Hadrian (117-138) had built a pagan temple to the gods Jupiter, Juno, and Minerva over the tomb of Jesus. On the basis of this tale, she had Hadrian's temple torn down. But there needed to be more evidence that this was indeed the correct place. However, Hadrian's temple was situated inside the city walls of Jerusalem, but according to Jewish tradition, graves had to be outside the city walls. Another alternative site needed to be explored by Helena.

Other people claimed that the tomb of Jesus was in the garden outside the city wall which was supposed to have been that of Joseph of Aramathia. Joseph of Aramethia was a wealthy Jew who supposedly allowed Jesus to be buried in his tomb. Also, there apparently was a stone over the entrance to this burial site. This garden site might have seemed more possible. But the garden site of Aramethia was not characteristic of the tombs during the time Jesus lived. On further inquiry, Helena discovered that Hadrian's temple had originally been outside the city wall so this resolved that problem. In 41 CE the city had expanded its wall to include

Hadrian's temple, so now it was inside the city. It was a possible site again, since it conformed to Jewish law. Hadrian's temple was built over a quarry that did contain rock cut tombs like those that were used during the first century.

After Hadrian's temple was torn down, Helena was able to examine the quarry that was revealed. What was needed was a place where people could come and worship at a shrine. What may have convinced her was that Christian pilgrims had left graffiti marks with the name of Jesus on a rock cut tomb located on the western wall of the quarry. This was enough evidence to convince Helena. Helena had the Church of the Holy Sepulcher built over the quarry, which she considered to be on the sight where the crucifixion and burial of Jesus had occurred. She also claimed to have found the true cross upon which Jesus was crucified and brought home a wooden relic. It is very unlikely that this relic was from the original cross upon which Jesus was crucified three hundred years earlier. However, the relic of the cross satisfied the Roman desire for an external symbol of the death of Jesus. Bringing home a visible relic was a victory for Helena, having fulfilled her mission for Constantine.

However, there still remain considerable debates about where Jesus was actually buried, and other sites have been suggested. As mentioned previously, a tomb was discovered in the Talpiyot neighborhood of Jerusalem that contained bone boxes with the names of Jesus, the son of Joseph, Mary, Mary Magdalene, Yose (brother of Jesus), Matthew (relative of Mary), and Judah son of Jesus. As an added complication to finding the burial site of Jesus was the usual procedure that the Romans followed after crucifixion. This was to let the body rot on the cross, allow it to be devoured by animals, or be thrown into a common grave. The Romans wanted crucifixion to be symbolic of a brutal and humiliating death to instill fear and terrify the populace against rebellion. Vast numbers of people were crucified as the official form of capital punishment by the Romans. This was not only in Judea but throughout their empire. For believers, the Shrine of the Holy Sepulcre, which has been rebuilt, is considered to be the actual site of crucifixion and burial of Jesus. However, historically it is difficult to pinpoint the exact burial site given the lapse of three hundred years and the scant evidence that Helena was able to assemble.

Constantine ruled to separate the Jewish and Christian religions. Jesus was no longer depicted as a Jew, which made it easier to blame Jews for his crucifixion. By eliminating crucifixion as the official form o f capital p u n ishment practiced by the Romans, it furthered this perception. It was as if the crucifixion of Jesus was a single special occurrence. The prolonged Roman systematic and cruel persecution of great numbers of Christians was covered over and now the target changed from Christians to Jews. Constantine wanted to further differentiate Christians from Jews by not allowing them to pray together in synagogues. He also changed the character of the Christian religious service to make it different from that practiced by the traditional Jews. Even though Constantine had issued his "Edict of Tolerance" in 313 CE, several years later he issued repressive laws. These divisive laws were instituted to make Christianity the one true religion, just as he was the one true emperor o f the Roman Empire. The laws excluded not only Jews from civil rights but also pagans. Jews could

not marry Christians, and he denounced Jews as "a nefarious and perverse sect" (Ausubel 1961).

By this maneuver, Constantine and the Romans were relieved of responsibility for brutally killing Jesus, as well as for killing Saint Peter (crucified upside down) and Saint Paul (beheaded), and countless n um bers of Christians who were eaten by lions and martyred over the centuries in the Roman arena. Blame for this savage killing and lack of morality was displaced from the Romans onto the Jews. This divisiveness was to make the Jews the scapegoat and served to divert anger away from Constantine. He created the prototype for political anti-Semitism used by demagogues for centuries. Scapegoating an outside group also brought people together against a common enemy.

By combining religion and politics, Constantine's power was perceived as divine and absolute. Most people complied to this autocracy, since they felt protected by a powerful ruler. When disasters or defeats occurred, the illusion of the rulers absolute power could be preserved by blaming nonbelievers. As mentioned, John Chrysostom of Antioch around 390 CE further tried to divide Jews and Christians. He condemned Judaizing Christians and Jewish Christians for celebrating both Sunday and Saturday, as well as the Jewish holidays. He reinforced this divisiveness by condemning all the Jews collectively for the death of Jesus. Two centuries later Emperor Justinian (527-565) created an anti-Semitic code, which became the official Christian state policy up until recently.

In 325 CE Constantine convened the Council of Nicaea , which confirmed the divinity o f Jesus. As Christ, Jesus was declared to be of the same single essence as God the father. The Council rejected the Gnostics who disagreed. In the novel *The DaVinci Code,* Dan Brown claimed that Constantine created the new Bible canon. However, this is not accurate, since the Gospels according to Mark, Matthew, Luke, and John had been accepted as authentic around 202 CE by Irenaeus the bishop of Lyons, France. Irenaeus was opposed to the Gnostics and rejected them because the Gnostics focused on Jesus's teachings and knowledge. As mentioned, the Gnostics emphasized that the spirit within individuals was important and not the body. They considered the spirit to be trapped in the body and the awakening of God inside people as essential. This was an individualistic religious approach that taught that each individual needed to seek the truth. They opposed the belief in the bodily resurrection of Jesus and submission to the hierarchy of the Orthodox Christian church.

As mentioned, Bishop Irenaeus focused on the crucifixion and the actual bodily resurrection of Jesus. Some versions o f the Gospels state that after his bodily resurrection, Jesus is said to have told Peter to be the rock upon which the church would be built. The bodily resurrection of Jesus was the basis for the legitimate authority of the church, which he named Orthodox Christianity. Irenaeus was himself martyred along with many other Christians during the persecution ordered by the Roman emperor Septimius Severus (193-211 CE).

Out o f self-interest, Constantine destroyed all the Gospels he could find that contradicted his power base. This included the Gospels of Andrew, Bartholomew, Magdalene, Philip, Thomas, and Judas. As previously noted, hidden Gnostic Gospels were discovered in Egypt, authentica ted by carbon dating, and recently translated. As

also mentioned, the Judas Gospel states th a t Jesus actually instructed Judas to give him up to the Romans, so his spirit could be liberated from being trap p ed in the flesh. This was according to the views o f the

Gnostic Christians.

The Judas Gospel states that Judas did not betray Jesus but reluctantly followed the wish of Jesus. As mentioned previously, in the New Testament, Jesus told Judas, "Do what you have to do" at the Passover dinner (John 13;27). This can be interpreted to be a request that Judas follow the orders given to him by Jesus. In addition, Jesus told his disciples that after his death, they would receive his holy spirit. During the Pentecost, all the disciples felt his spirit and spoke in tongues.

In summary, Constantine emphasized there was one emperor, one Roman Empire, one holy essence of Christ and God, one religion, and one Bible. He had defeated the armies of his wife's father and then his b rother-in-law, Maxentius, whom he drowned. In 324 CE, he also killed his other brother-in-law, Licinius, to become the sole ruler of all the Roman Empire. In 326, he ordered the murder of his wife, Fausta, and his son, Crispus. He was a militaristic power-hungry leader like so many previous Roman emperors, and he used Christianity to rationalize his un-Christian actions. Constantine justified his executing his son Crispus by stating that if God can kill his Son, so can God's co-regent do likewise.

Constantine's behavior was not that of a respectful, charitable, and compassionate Christian as preached by Jesus. Instead, he was like so many brutal and militaristic Roman emperors. His aim was self-aggrandizement and maximizing his power. Making Christianity legal was clearly not out o f a genuine religious belief but was more likely a political strategy to consolidate his power. As mentioned, he remained a pagan all his life, and he was only baptized shortly before dying. Constantine built a great palace with extensive grounds as well as a hippodrome that rivaled the circus maximus arena in Rome. These were external manifestations of his self-aggrandizement and political power.

As a consequence of the civil wars that Constantine fought, he probably weakened the entire Roman Empire. He assured his own survival and power, but not that of the Roman empire. In 378 CE, near Adrianople (present-day Turkey), Germanic warriors annihilated the field army of the Eastern Roman Empire and killed its emperor Valens. There followed a series of events that lead to Rome being sacked by barbarians in 410 CE and the eventual collapse of the Roman empire.

8 Maintaining the Illusion of Divine Power

The illusion of absolute power by the ruling class in Europe contributed to the compliance of the general population. The populace felt protected by the power of a divinely appointed monarch and church. This illusion of divine power in the theocracy could be maintained by shifting blame for disasters and defeats onto the Jews. There were additional factors contributing to the rise of anti-Semitism. First, since Jews were literate they were often assigned by the Christian nobility to be their tax collectors. This set up Jews to be the target of anger, since the peasants could not express their feeling exploited to the powerful nobility for fear o f retaliation. Second, Christians were forbidden to be money lenders, so Jews became involved here as well as in commence. Third, when Jews accumulated money through these pursuits, anti-Semitism was fomented by the nobility to justify robbing Jews whom they owed money. Finally, by establishing a common enemy, "the other," whom the peasants could differentiate themselves, group cohesiveness of the community was enhanced.

Just as nonbelievers o f the pagan gods were persecuted and killed by the Romans, nonbelievers were persecuted and killed by the Christians. Jews were a vulnerable target, since they were a powerless minority that had been disbursed th ro u g h o u t Europe by the Romans as punishment for rebelling. The church demonized the Jews, calling them Christ killers and in league with the devil. Jews were n o t seen as individuals b u t only by their religious group identity. Stereotyped a ttitudes were projected onto Jews as a group, which demeaned and d eh u manized them. Jews were seen as being greedy and unethical, since they were associated with Judas, who supposedly had betrayed Jesus for money. Not only were Jews restricted occupationally b u t they were also restricted physically to ghettos, which were locked up as a prison each night.

St. Augustine considered that the Jews killed Christ out of ignorance but should be kept alive as failed and suffering witnesses of their misdeed. St. Thomas Aquinas, on the other hand, considered that the Jews killed Christ out of maliciousness. The Passion plays in Germany perpetuated the hatred of Jews by casting them as the betrayers and killers of Christ. In 1095, Pope Urban II launched the crusades, and whole Jewish communities in Europe and in Jerusalem were massacred. In 1219 Jews were forced to wear yellow badges and were seen as the anti-Christ and associated with the Devil. Jews were blamed for poisoning wells that caused the Black Plague and were murdered en mass. The blood libel of killing children for their blood, which was first attributed to Christians by the Romans, was

displaced onto the Jews.

Jews were expelled from England in 1290, so the king could avoid

repaying loans that he had borrowed from them. Jews were only allowed
to return from Holland by Oliver Cromwell in the sixteenth century, but
even then it was to help pay for his civil war. In 1492, more than 100,000
Jews were expelled from Spain during the Inquisition, and many were
burned at the stake by the church. The justification for burning people
was to save their souls, so that they would not burn eternally in hell.
In 1519 Martin Luther persecuted Jews for refusing to be converted
and advocated labor camps, where he could continue his missionary
efforts to force their conversion. The Nazi's adopted the past anti-Semitic
practice of forcing Jews to wear a yellow star of David. They also established
so called labor camps but not to force conversion. Despite having
the words "work will make you free" in German over the entrance of
Auschwitz, these concentration camps were killing factories. In Russia, a
fake document, *The Protocols of the Elders of Zion,* was published falsely
accusing Jews of attempting world domination. Jews were massacred during
pogroms and young Jewish boys were conscripted into the Russian
army to serve for many years and pressured to convert.
Through the Middle Ages until the eighteenth century, the alliance of
the Christian religion and the nobility reinforced each other's power. If
Jews were not murdered there was pressure on them to convert to support
Christian belief. The Enlightenment changed the way events in the world
were experienced. It changed from reliance on absolute faith and theological
explanations to understand the world to rational and scientific
inquiry. A popular book written by Voltaire (1694-1778), *Candide,* was a
satire on the theological justification for human suffering. It ironically

Samuel Slipp 103

criticized the German philosopher von Leibnitz, whose work was based
on a belief of absolute faith in religion. No matter how horrible an event
happened to the hero, Candide, Dr. Pangloss stated it was all God's will "in
this best of all possible worlds." These disasters included an earthquake,
war, shipwreck, rape, disease, and injustice, as well as the Inquisition. This
book however includes several anti-Semitic events, one in which Candide,
the hero, kills a "choleric Hebrew."
The philosophical and scientific writings of Bacon, Descartes,
Hobbes, Locke, Newton, Spinoza, and others resulted in the political revolutions
that undermined the divine right of Christian kings to rule.
Autocratic rule by the alliance of the nobility and the church was challenged
in order to empower the people. The American and French revolutions
resulted from Enlightenment thinking and enabled the creation of
secular governments responsive to the needs of its citizens. Power would
now come from the below up and not from the top down, which previously
had existed in despotic European hierarchies..
The Enlightenment had an influence on the Jewish religion itself as
well. Benedict (Baruch) Spinoza (1632-1677), one of the most famous
philosophers in history, wrote about reconciling secular and religious
views. Spinoza was a Dutch Jew whose ancestors were Marranos, who left
Portugal during the Inquisition. Marranos were Jews who were forced to
convert to avoid being burned at the stake. Yet a great many Marranos

secretly maintained their Jewish traditions at the risk of their lives. In his
Treatise on Religion and the State, Spinoza wrote that the Bible was written

in a metaphorical or allegorical way so as to appeal to the popular
mind. God was not anthropomorphic but was inseparable from the
processes of nature. He denied God's direct intervention with people,
that miracles ever occurred, and he denied the existence of an afterlife
after death. Spinoza considered Jesus to be a noble prophet but not
divine. He also wrote that all people were created equal and could see no
importance in Jewish ceremonial law. He was a strong advocate for the
separation of state and religion, and he also prophesied the rebirth of the
land of Israel in the future.

In terms of philosophy, Spinoza criticized the mind-body dualism of
Descartes (1596-1650), who was famous for saying, "I think therefore I
am." For Spinoza, the mind and emotions were not separate; they interacted
and worked together. Spinoza stated, "Passion without reason is
blind, and reason without passion is dead." He felt that instincts exist for
self-preservation as well as for seeking pleasure over pain. Many of these
same themes were reflected by later philosophers such as Fichte's ich,
Schopenhauer's will to live, Nietzsche's will to power, Bergson's elan vital,
and Freud's eros.

Freud built his foundation for psychoanalysis on an awareness that
reason was influenced by unconscious emotions. The result of Spinoza
openly expressing the denial of the immortality of a soul and criticizing the
literal interpretation of the Bible was that he was excommunicated in 1656
by the Jewish religious leaders in the Netherlands. The Jewish community
felt that they had been welcomed and adopted by the liberal Dutch and did
not want to make any waves that might cause antagonism or expulsion.
The Inquisition was a threatening event elsewhere in Europe.

Moses Mendelssohn (1720-1786) also explained the belief of Judaism
in rational terms but retained its traditional laws and ceremonies. He
authorized the translation of the Bible so that it was written in both
Hebrew and German. The Jewish Enlightenment movement that was created
in Germany was called the Haskalah. Abraham Geiger (1810-1874),
a member of this scientific school of Judaism, saw rituals as derived from
human construction, which could be reformed to fit the current assimilated
generation. He created the Reform Jewish Religion to save Judaism
from being totally lost to assimilation, since many Jews had converted to
Christianity. They had converted because of the restrictions and pressure
that was exerted by the Christian community. Unless Jews converted, they
could not gain a higher education, were limited in business, and were
unable to participate in society on an equal footing. Jewish converts
hoped they would no longer be outsiders and would gain the advantages
of being part of the wider society. Some examples of prominent Jewish
converts were Heinrich Heine, Felix Mendelsohn, and Karl Marx. Later,
some Jews who despite being educated could not find employment, so
they joined revolutionary movements to change society hoping to eliminate
these restrictions.

How did the Enlightenment affect the relationship between
Christians and Jews? Grand ideals were proposed in the Enlightenment.
Power would not be the exclusive domain of the king and the church, but

power would be granted to all the people. In America, Jefferson wrote the
Bill of Rights and the American Congress signed it in 1776. These founding
fathers were an unusually gifted group of men, which included John

Adams, Franklin, Hamilton, Jefferson, Washington, and others. However, compromises were made concerning slaves and women to preserve the union of the thirteen states from fragmenting. But the founders successfully dealt with many issues facing a democracy, including the role of religion, states rights, religious freedom, and the equality of all men.

In the French Revolution of 1789, the Declaration of Rights o f Man and Citizen declared that all citizens were also endowed with equal rights, that religious tolerance was advocated, and that the rule of law was to be applied equally to all. The French motto was "Liberty, Equality, and Fraternity," but these rational ideals were not enough, since virulent anti-Semitism persisted just as before. Supposedly there was no prejudice against a Jewish individual citizen, but it existed against Jews as a group. However, this was not proven to be the case, as demonstrated by the case of Captain Alfred Dreyfus in France. As Volkan noted, the persistent collective emotional memory was stronger than the new rational declarations of liberty.

In 1894, Captain Alfred Dreyfus, of the French army general staff, was falsely accused of selling military information to the Germans. He was blamed for the military defeat of France and courtmarshaled. This resulted in his being convicted, stripped of his rank in a humiliating ceremony, and sentenced to Devil's Island for the rest of his life. Colonel Picquart, chief of the Army Intelligence Bureau, examined the document that had been used to incriminate Dreyfus, and he found it to be a forgery. On investigation, he concluded it was Major Esterhazy who was really the guilty person. However, this information was squelched, and Picquart was removed from his office and sent to a dangerous assignment in Tunisia, where there was an Arab revolt. Probably it was with the hope he would be killed there and silenced. However, due to the accusation of Colonel Picquart about the innocense of Dreyfus, Major Esterhazy was tried but was acquitted. The stereotype of Jews as betrayers of Jesus undoubtedly influenced the court's decision to convict the Jewish Captain Dreyfus and exonerate the Christian Major Esterhazy.

Colonel Picquart, who had accused Esterhazy, did not die in battle and was then imprisoned to silence him. Many anti-Dreyfusards presented the argument that it was better to preserve the honor of France than to release Dreyfus the Jew from prison. But in January 13, 1898, the eminent novelist, Emile Zola, wrote in the newspaper *L'Aurore* his famous article "J'Accuse." In it he stated that the military had committed fraud against Captain Dreyfus and was responsible for "a high crime against humanity." For Zola, the integrity and honesty o f the individual was more important. National honor had been betrayed by the military and not by Dreyfus.

Emile Zola was arrested, tried, and sentenced to one year in prison. Before he could be incarcerated, Zola fled to England to escape imprisonment. Major Esterhazy later confessed that he was the one who wrote the false document and was the guilty one, not Dreyfus. Zola returned to France, but mysteriously he died of asphyxiation due to being poisoned by a faulty stove pipe while asleep. Some speculate that Zola was assassinated for humiliating the military and the government as well as for defending a

Jew. In 1906 Dreyfus was acquitted, restored to the army, promoted to major, and awarded the French Legion of Honor. Colonel Picquart was released from prison, was made a general, and subsequently became the

Minister of War in France.

The Dreyfus affair clearly showed that even after the Enlightenment had destroyed the political power o f the alliance between the nobility and the church, anti-Semitism and violence against Jews in Europe continued. Several reasons interfered with the rational ideals of liberty, equality, and fraternity from becoming a reality in French society. Europeans generally consisted of nations composed o f homogeneous groups that shared a common tribal history and culture. Nationalism represented a greatly expanded form of tribalism, which continues to exist even today. As nationalism rose, xenophobia flourished in Europe. Jews were still relegated to the position of an outsider and continued to be blamed to preserve national power and honor.

English anti-Semitism that existed in Shakespeare's time has continued through the centuries up to the present. Books against Zionism are written by authors born in England, such as Rose, Hobsbawm, Goldberg, and Judt. They blame the worlds troubles on Zionism. This seems a repetition of blaming Jews for the Black Plague and everything else during the Middle Ages. It is easier to focus blame on a single outside group to feel in control than to delve into trying to understand and deal with the complicated issues involved. Jews became the universal scapegoat throughout Europe because of their small number and vulnerability and because of its history of anti-Semitism.

In the United States xenophobia did occur but less so, since it was pluralistic with immigrants from many countries possessing a number of religions. This was unlike European countries, which were more homogeneous both ethnically and religiously. Also, the United States was formed after the Enlightenment and did not have the baggage from a feudal past where religion and politics had been dominant. The astute founding fathers of the United States created a democratic government separating religion from politics. Checks and balances were established to prevent the abuse of even secular power. They were aware of emotional issues concerning the hunger for power.

The European nations had lived under theocratic rule for generations prior to the Enlightenment. Thus, Europeans had difficulty shaking off their preexisting authoritarian and cultural norms. This was derived from centuries of living under the absolute rule of a king and the church who were endowed with divine rights. As an example of autocratic rule persisting, even after the French Revolution, Napoleon declared himself an emperor and the monarchy was restored.

As mentioned, despite the Enlightenment, anti-Semitism continued to be used by demagogues to gain and sustain political power. The effect of the trial of Captain Alfred Dreyfus, a totally assimilated Jew, had a major influence on history. Theodore Herzl, who in 1895 was a reporter from the Viennese newspaper *Neue Freie Presse,* covered the trial in France. Herzl understood that the conviction was a fraud and only resulted because Captain Dreyfus was a Jew. He felt that European Christianity continued to be intrinsically anti-Semitic, including among liberals and conservatives. People in favor of Dreyfus were labelled traitors of France, and the French mob shouted, "Death to the Jews."

Besides the Dreyfus affair, there were pogroms against Jews in Russia starting from 1880. Thus, Herzl concluded Jews needed to have a homeland of their own; assimilation was not the answer. Herzl wrote, *Der Judenstaat* (The Jewish State), stating that by having their own homeland Jews would not be powerless victims. He advocated Political Zionism and sought support from many countries for a Jewish nation. Herzl organized a Zionist congress in 1897, and the Zionist movement hoped to create a homeland for the Jews in Palestine. However, Ahad Ha'am (the pen name of Asher Ginsberg) advocated Cultural Zionism, feeling pessimistic that other nations would be supportive. He advocated small Jewish settlements in Palestine to create an infrastructure and not to go for a total political Jewish state. He hoped this would support a renaissance of Jewish culture and the use of the Hebrew language. It would also spiritually uplift Jews in the Diaspora, who were being demeaned and violated. Other Jews did not agree with going to Palestine. One was the Jewish Bund, which was a Yiddish-speaking group, that sought to stay and fight back against anti-Semitism. They were the modern-day Zealots. Another group, the Ultra-Orthodox Jews, felt that a return to Israel should not occur until the Messiah comes. However, the Zionists persisted in their efforts, which eventually proved to be the correct course of action.

In 1917, Dr. Chaim Weizmann, a professor of chemistry at the University of Manchester, was helpful to the British war effort by finding a way to synthesize acetone. Dr. Nahum Sokolow and Yehiel Tchlenov were then able to negotiate with England for a Jewish homeland in Palestine. Lord Arthur James Balfour, who was the British foreign secretary, wrote a letter to Lord Rothschild, which agreed to the Zionist wishes. The letter became known as the Balfour Declaration. In 1918 Vladimir Jabotinsky requested the formation of a Jewish Legion in the British Army, recognizing the need for a military power. He created three battalions of the Royal Fusiliers, which fought battles in World War I under the leadership of British General Allenby. Because of the instigation of the Grand Mufti, Haj Amin al-Husseini, Arabs attacked the Jewish settlers in Palestine and murdered many innocent Jewish settlers.

In 1930 one hundred and thirty-three Jews were killed by Arab mobs. The British response was to issue the Passfield "White Paper" curbing Jewish immigration. This was done in the hope of placating and pacifying the Arabs. Since the British were not adequately protecting the settlers and seemed to side with the Arabs, a Jewish Army, the Haganah, was formed. With the rise of Hitler in Germany, many immigrants from Europe began to arrive in Palestine. The Grand Mufi formed an alliance of the Arabs with the Nazis, who provided him with arms and money, resulting in increased violence against the Jews in Palestine.

In 1939, another "White Paper" was issued by the British government, limiting immigration of Jews to only 15,000 a year for five years. The vast number of refugees at this time fleeing Nazism for their lives now could only come into Palestine illegally. The Haganah tried to follow the law and cooperate with the British. On the other hand, Menachem Begin formed the underground Irgun Zvai Leumi whose goal was to drive the British out in order to permit unlimited immigration and save the desperate European refugees. Ships with Jewish refugees were intercepted by the

British Navy and prevented from entering Palestine. The German ship St.

Louis, with 937 Jewish refugees, was not permitted to land in Cuba or the United States. It was sent back to Europe, where many of the Jewish passengers were murdered by the Nazis.

How did Germany, such an advanced and enlightened country, descend into such barbarism? The loss of religious belief in Europe and its rituals after the Enlightenment resulted in a loss of group cohesion and social alienation. To maintain group solidarity, the French Utopians created a secular religion that revived rituals. Germany was ripe for a messianic leader when they suffered rampant inflation and social chaos after the First World War.

How could a despotic leader like Hitler arise in an advanced democratic society, one that had been blessed by the rationality of the Enlightenment and was advanced scientifically? Clearly, a theocratic authoritarian society could arise more easily in ancient times, since peopie had little scientific knowledge of nature. Divine leadership of the nobility and the church had offered group solidarity and protection. Yet what remained was the traditional method of gaining and maintaining political power. It was to create divisiveness and instill fear that threatened survival. Historically, when the Romans dominated Judea, they used fear to sustain their power to prevent rebellion. During the Middle Ages, the fear of hell was employed by the Roman Catholic church. Martin Luther challenged the Catholic church, which sold indulgences to save peoples' souls, yet he created divisiveness between Protestants and Jews.

In the twentieth century, Hitler rose to power in an enlightened German nation, but one that had a collective history of autocracy and admiration for militarism. Economic chaos and conflict with Communists created political instability. To stay in power in 1932, Hitler created a fear of terrorism by probably setting fire to the Reichstag. Germans felt helpless and humiliated, having lost World War I and following the harsh terms of the Versailles Treaty. The military loss was displaced from the military and the Jews were blamed. Rampant inflation existed and legislation that favored the wealthy wiped out the savings of the middle class. The German people regressed emotionally into a tribal society and looked for a savior to rescue and avenge them.

As a child Hitler became a savior o f his mother by absorbing the physical abuse onto himself from his alcoholic father (Stierlin). Later Hitler was primed to be a messiah by Dietrich Eckart, editor of the *Volkisher Beobachgter.* Hitler dedicated the second volume o f *Mein Kampf(* 1927) to Eckart. Hitler established a secular religion, as he assumed political power as the savior of Germany. Hitler claimed he was Germany, blurring the boundaries between himself and the nation, just as he had done with his mother. Even a group, the German Christians, claimed, "Christ has come to us through Adolf H itler" (Lilia). When Hitler invaded Austria in 1938, he took the "lance of destiny" from the Vienna museum. This lance was thought to have been used by a Roman soldier who inflicted the wound on Jesus while on the cross. The lance was supposed to contain magical powers, and it confirmed Hitler's mystical view o f himself as a messiah for the German people.

Hitler promised to restore order, people's pride, and the economy. He would avenge losing World War I and the humiliation of the Versailles Treaty. Anger was displaced onto the traditional scapegoat, the Jews, to create group solidarity. This also entitled Germans to rob Jews of their assets. Hitler employed the totally false pseudoscientific premises advocated in the Social Darwinism of H erbert Spencer (1820-1903). Hitler justi110 fied killing Jews, who he implied were inferior to the superior Aryan race. The Jewish religion he said supported the weak and emasculated the strong, while natural law favored survival of the fittest. He emphasized his anti-Semitic attacks by depicting physical features of Jews that made them look sinister and inferior. Hitler promised to create a nation of supermen and promised a utopian society in Germany. Instead, he devastated Germany, bringing it to its knees and inflicting a great loss of life.

After the rise of Hitler to power in 1933, anti-Semitic restrictions were legislated. This culminated in 1938 with Kristallnacht, when Jewish shops and synagogues were destroyed and Jewish citizens were assaulted. Many Jews were shocked and could not believe what was happening. They identified themselves strongly as Germans of the Mosaic persuasion. German Jews could not believe that an advanced enlightened country, which they had loyally defended by serving in the army in World War I, could betray them. They were rudely awakened when Jews were sent to concentration camps, first in Vienna and then in the rest of Europe where they were systematically murdered in killing factories.

France was overrun by the Germans rapidly in World War II, and the French Vichy government collaborated with the Nazis. Anti-Semitic bigotry, reminiscent of the Dreyfus affair, was alive and well in France. It reemerged with vigor, as some French even fought alongside the Germans. A great number of labor camps for Jews were set up throughout Vichy France. Many Jews in France were rounded up by the French police and sent to Drancy in Paris. This was the assembly place before the Jews were sent to Auschwitz, where they were systematically gassed and their dead bodies burned. Many European nations, including France, Greece, Holland, Hungary, Norway, Poland, and Romania, allowed or actively cooperated with the Nazis in sending large numbers o f Jews to their death in concentration camps. The greatest slaughter occurred in Poland, where half of the six million Jews living there were systematically m urdered. Italy had around 50,000 Jews, and some had lived there for 2,000 years, while others came in 1492 during the Spanish Inquisition. Italy protected its Jewish population, but when Italy surrendered in 1943, the Germans sent 8,000 to be killed in concentration camps. However, Denmark and Bulgaria bravely protected their Jewish citizens. The Dominican Republic did open its gates to a limited number of Jews, but they had to be u nmarried. The invitation was out of self-interest, since the Jews, like animal stock, were expected to intermarry with the indigenous black population and lighten the color of the race. In the Dominican Republic one had more social status by being lighter skinned.

Individually, there were a number of truly moral and courageous persons, from various countries, who risked their lives to rescue Jews. Some important examples were the Swedish diplomat Raoul Wallenberg, who saved a great many Jews in Hungary by giving them Swedish passports. Another was the Japanese diplomat Chiune Sugihara, who saved 6,000

Polish, Lithuanian, and German Jews by giving them Japanese exit visas. Arturo Castellanos issued Salvadorian citizenship to 40,000 Jews, and Guimaraes Rosa of Brazil also saved many Jews by granting them exit visas. A movie was made by Steven Spielberg of the German industrialist, Oskar Schindler, who saved Jews by employing them in his factory during the war.

It is a matter of record that six million Jews were murdered by the Nazis during World War II. In the Polish town o f Jedwabne in 1941, most o f the 1,600 Jews were killed. Most of the Jews there were rounded up by their Polish neighbors and forced into a barn that was then burned down, killing everyone inside. Even after the war, when some Jews returned to their homes, they were assaulted or even killed by the local residents, for fear they would reclaim their possessions.

After World War II, there was an increase in violence by Arabs against Jews and a lack of protection by the British. The Irgun army continued their fight with the British, and in 1946 blew up part of the King David Hotel in Jerusalem where the British had their offices. In 1947 the ship *Exodus* loaded with Jewish refugees tried to go to Palestine. However, the ship was intercepted in international waters by the British Navy, which was illegal. The *Exodus* was forced to return to near Marseilles, France, and then to Hamburg, Germany, where the Jewish refugees were placed in a displaced persons' camp. Around this time the British hanged members of the Irgun, who had tried to smuggle in refugees. In retaliation, two British sergeants were hung by the Irgun. This resulted in attacks on English Jews in Liverpool, Manchester, and London. Since the British could not manage Palestine, its mandate was turned over to the United Nations.

The British tried to disarm the Jewish military before they left, but they were not successful. Had the British been successful, there would have been a massive Jewish genocide, since the Arabs invaded Israel when the United Nations declared Israel to be a state in 1948. The Jewish military defeated the invading Arab armies from the su rro u n d ing countries. With Israel now a sovereign state, the council elected Dr. Chaim Weizmann as president and David Ben-Gurion as prime minister. Israel had to maintain a strong military force to defend itself against Arab armies who attacked repeatedly in subsequent years. After the victorious 1967 War, Israel was able to regain all o f Jerusalem, King David's city.

Many of the Jewish Holocaust survivors suffered from posttraumatic stress disorder, with nightmares, terrors, and fears for the safety of their children. It was noted that when the parents, who were survivors of the holocaust, maintained a veil of silence about their Nazi experiences, it tended to create psychological problems for their children (Slipp 1984). Dr.Shami Davidson studied Holocaust survivors and their children at the University of Tel Aviv's Shalvata Hospital. He had also noted the same negative effects on children when their parents maintained a veil of silence about their Holocaust experience. This finding of the parents remaining silent might be explained as resulting from their not having mourned and worked through their emotional trauma. They were suffering from an unresolved traumatic stress disorder. Those parents who discussed what happened to them in the war had generally gained emotional mastery over their trauma. They openly spoke of their experiences to

their children, and their children did well psychologically. His findings were presented at Grand Rounds at Bellevue Hospital in New York and at the Atlanta meeting of the American Academy of Psychoanalysis. The results were then published in the book, *Object Relations: A Dynamic Bridge Between Individual and Family Treatment* (Slipp 1984). These findings helped to contribute to the establishment of support groups for children of Holocaust survivors. They could talk to other children having similar experiences and could master the effects of the emotional trauma transmitted from their parents.

Anti-Semitism continues, but in another name, such as the United Nations equating Zionism with racism. Anti-Semitism has continued to be used politically by leaders to gain and preserve their authority. One exception in England was Winston Churchill, who was supportive of the Jews and Zionism. In 1908 he informed the English Zionist Federation that he was in "full sympathy" with its desires to establish a Jewish homeland. He respected the integrity of Jews for having maintained their beliefs, despite an England that had traditionally been anti-Semitic. This positive attitude of Churchill toward Jews created problems in his political career. As secretary of state, Churchill bravely refused to go along with others to renegotiate the Balfour Declaration, which had previously declared Palestine as a homeland for the Jews. In addition, he was against the Passfield "White Paper," which restricted immigration of Jews to Israel. This was a cruel and inhumane paper, since Jews were helpless victims and being systematically murdered by the Nazis. The escape of Jewish refugees was blocked, and it contributed to their slaughter. However, Churchill did not open up the gates of Israel to refugees when he was prime minister of England during World War II. He hoped not to antagonize the Arabs and Muslims in order to maintain the British Empire.

9 Freud as Conquistador: Power through Science

As emphasized, when religion and politics are joined, a need is created to assign a scapegoat to protect the illusion of absolute power of the ruler and of society. As Volkan astutely noted, the collective emotional memory of Jews as scapegoats persisted, even after the Enlightenment. Anti-Semitism was preached by demagogues to be elected to political office. Freud (1856-1939) was profoundly affected by political anti-Semitism all of his life. Prior to his birth, laws for the integration of Jews into the Austro-Hungarian Empire were passed. Previously Jewish men had to convert to Christianity to be able to obtain a higher education. But the new laws allowed Freud, a Jew, to enter the University of Vienna without having to convert. But a demagogue, Karl Lueger, won the office of m ajor of Vienna on an anti-Semitic platform. After Freud's graduating from the university, the new government passed laws that limited academic advancement of all Jews. A thumbnail summary is provided here to illustrate the effect of anti-Semitism on the life of Freud:

§ As a child, Freud's father's wool business in Freiberg, Moravia, failed due to Czech nationalism and anti-Semitism, forcing the family to move.

§ After moving to Vienna, Freud's father, like o th e r Jewish im m igrants, could not su p p o rt his family due to political anti-Semitism.

§ After graduating medical school, Freud's academic career was blocked by anti-Semitic laws and he had to enter private practice.

115

§ The academic presentation Freud delivered before his colleagues was called a scientific fairy tale; he was labeled a Jewish pornographer.

§ Freud then presented his papers before the Jewish B'nai B'rith Society.

§ Freud's closest relations were Jewish, including Doctors Breuer, Fleiss, and Ferenczi.

§ Most of the members of the psychoanalytic circle he established were Jewish.

§ In his work *Jokes and Their Relation to the Unconscious* (1905), Freud used Jewish jokes and anecdotes.

§ All of Freud's work was demeaned by the Nazis as a Jewish psychology.

§ The elderly Freud and his family had to be ransomed from the Gestapo in Vienna by Princess Marie Bonaparte, William Bullitt, and Ernest Jones in 1938.

§ He was established in London after being rescued by his Gentile associates, which probably contributed to his writing *Moses and Monotheism* in 1939 and making Moses into an Egyptian. He died in 1939.

This chapter will review Freud's family background, how he experienced political anti-Semitism during his life, and how he fought back.

Freud's father, Jacob, came from an Orthodox Jewish family, yet he seemed to adopt to Reform Judaism. Jacob Freud's family lived in Freiberg, Moravia, which was in the Austro-Hungarian Empire and later became part of Czechoslovakia after World War 1. Jacob was an elderly

widower. His first wife died leaving him with two grown sons. The eldest
son was called Emanuel, who was married and lived close by with his wife
and son. Jacob's younger son was Philipp, who was nineteen years of age
and still lived in the house. Jacob married Freud's mother, Amalie, who
was a vital and attractive twenty-year-old woman.

Why would she pick a man old enough to be her father, and who was
already a grandfather? In addition, by marrying Jacob, she had to move
from the cosmopolitan city of Vienna to the small provincial town of
Freiberg. This was certainly an arranged marriage for financial security.
Jacob had an established business as a wool trader, and he was a tall, gentle, and kindly man with a good sense of humor. They were married in a
Reform Jewish ceremony. The couple did not go to synagogue regularly,
but they did celebrate the High Holidays as well as Purim and Passover
(Krull 1986).

Amalie was more assimilated and less religious, having come from
Vienna. On the other hand, Jacob, who lived in Freiberg, Moravia, continued
to read the Philippson Bible and was more involved in his Jewishness.
A year after the marriage, in 1856, Sigmund was born. Even though Freud
idealized his early childhood, describing himself as his mother's favorite,
others have noted that his preoedipal period, from birth to three years of
age, was emotionally traumatic. He never analyzed his relationship with
his mother, but his later nonverbal behavior toward her reflected a good
deal of ambivalence. His own early childhood influenced his psychoanalytic
theory of child development. Freud ignored the importance of emotional
attachment to the mother and focused on the later oedipal conflict
with the father.

When Freud was eight months old his mother became pregnant. His
brother Julius was born when Freud was one and a half years old.
According to Blum (1983), Freud was jealous and entertained death wishes
toward his baby brother. Unfortunately, six months later, baby Julius
died. Freud suffered guilt because he felt his death wishes had caused
Julius's death. Freud repeatedly played the role of Brutus, in the assassination
of Julius Caesar, with his step-brother Emanuel's son, John. This play
enactment was probably Freud's way of trying to work through his guilt.
In addition, since his brother Julius's death had occurred when Freud was
in the rapprochement period of child development, where separation and
individuation occurs, he continued to suffer insecurity and fears of abandonment
later in life.

Around this time, Amelia, his mother, not only lost her baby, Julius, but
she also heard that her brother had died in Vienna of pulmonary tuberculosis.
Thus, she was in mourning for both her baby and her brother, and she
probably was not emotionally available to Freud. This had to add to Freud's
insecurity. Amelia shortly became pregnant with her third child, and she
now had added worries as well. Jacob's business was gradually failing, due
to anti-Semitism that erupted following the Czech nationalist revolution.
Jews spoke Yiddish, which was taken from German, and this added to their
being discriminated. In addition, the northern railroad bypassed Freiberg,
which had a negative effect on Jacob's wool business. Amalie seemed to be

trapped in a marriage to an older man who was having difficulty providing
her with the economic security she had anticipated. Thus, the prime reason
for the arranged marriage to an older man in a provincial town was rapidly
deteriorating.

To cope with her difficult situation, Amalie employed an elderly
Czech nanny, Resi Wittek (also known as Monika Zajic by other writers),
to raise Freud (Slipp 1993). The nanny regularly took Freud to Catholic
services, where he learned about God, sin, heaven, and hell. He would
come home and preach to the family what he had heard in church, to the
amusement of his mother. It is questionable why his Jewish mother
would allow him to go to Catholic services and also be amused at Freud's
preaching. Was this her wish to assimilate because of the impact of political
anti-Semitism on her husband's business? Assimilation was frequent
among Austrian and German Jews who wished to become part o f the
mainstream of society and not to be discriminated against as outsiders.
Was she angry at her elderly Jewish husband and wished to h u rt him,
since he was more religious? Jacob was failing to provide financial security
and was on the verge of bankruptcy. Or was she so preoccupied with
her pregnancies and loss of her second son and her brother that she was
just not emotionally invested in her oldest son? Freud was originally
called Sigismund Schlomo, but he later changed it to Sigmund, which
was more maistream German.

As a very young child, Freud was confused about having two mothers.
He wondered if his father, Jacob, was married to the elderly nanny, Resi,
and if his young mother, Amelia, was the wife of Jacob's grown son,
Philipp. This was because of the similarity in the ages of the supposed
couples. In addition, Jacob's other son, Emanuel, had two children, John
and Pauline, who were about the same age as Freud. They called Jacob
grandfather, which only added to Freud's confusion.

Freud was attached to Resi, his nanny, who was tender with him, but
she also was sexually seductive. Rezi would bath him in the same water
after she bathed, and she played with his genitals. In a letter to his friend
Fliess, Freud considered her the originator o f his neurosis because of her
seduction (Rizzuto 1998). Freud noted that Resi was his instructress in
sexual matters. Resi informed him about God, heaven, and hell, yet she
also encouraged him to steal *zehners* (coins) for her. This contradiction
of Rezi's sinful action and religious morality created a dilemma for
Freud.

In 1859, Philipp caught Resi stealing money and had her arrested.
Freud knew Philipp was involved in his nanny's disappearance, and Freud
became panicked. He asked Philipp where Resi was. Philipp replied, *"Sie
ist eingekastelt."* This is a colloquial expression for imprisoned, but literally
means put into a chest. Freud cried bitterly and asked Phillip to open
the chest that was in the room. Resi was like a mother to him, and he
feared he had also lost his mother. He feared that his mother would die,
since she was pregnant. Fortunately, his mother walked into the room.
However, Freud had the fantasy that Philipp and his mother had been
together sexually, and another unwelcomed baby would be born. The
family lived in tight quarters and Freud probably witnessed sex, birth, and
death. It is likely that Freud associated the chest with a coffin, since he
probably had witnessed his dead brother Julius lying in a coffin.

As mentioned, Freud's father, Jacob, was forced into bankruptcy
because of anti-Semitism that arose as a result of Czech nationalism and

the railroad bypassing Freiberg. The family then moved first to Leipzig,
Germany, when Freud was about three years of age. On the railroad trip
to Leipzig, Freud saw giant gas jets aflame when the train passed through

Breslau. He associated this with sinful souls burning in hell as punishment. This perception was clearly influenced by what he had learned about heaven and hell in the Catholic church. His nanny, Resi, had fondled his genitals and been seductive and had stolen money. He seems to have connected her disappearance with her banishment and burning in hell for being sinful. Rizzuto (1998) considers that Freud's feeling seduced and abandoned by Resi and her stealing was linked to his loss of faith in God and religion.

Freud's father, who remained religious, read to his young son Sigmund from the Reform Philippson Bible. This Bible had German translations of the Hebrew and also included many vivid pictures. These were tender loving moments between Freud and his father. After a short stay, the family then moved from Leipzig to Vienna in 1859. But Jacob was still unable to financially support his family, which like other immigrant Jews was a result of political anti-Semitism. The family was impoverished and survived on money that was sent by Jacob's sons from his previous marriage, who now lived in Manchester, England. Freud's sisters also worked to support the family. Another factor Rizzuto (1998) feels contributed to Freud's rejecting God was that his father, who was associated with the Jewish Bible and God, was not a strong protective figure. His father seemed to have been emasculated by the virulent anti-Semitism that was rampant in Austria. Freud was unable to idealize Jacob and identify with him as a model of strong masculinity, resulting in disappointment and unconscious anger at his father.

Freud recalled when he was around ten years o f age his father describing an incident in Moravia of his hat being knocked off by a Gentile. He was told, "Get off the pavement, Jew!" Jacob did not fight back but meekly submitted and picked up his hat. Jacob accommodated to anti-Semitism like many other Jews who did not want to stir up more trouble. But he was not the heroic figure who fought back that Freud wanted and needed.

Freud's mother also may have not respected her husband, seeing him as weak, old, and ineffectual. At the request o f his mother, Amalie, Freud and not his father was asked to name her new baby. This seemed to be an expression of her anger, since it subtly demeaned the father. It implied that Freud had the privilege of naming the baby instead of the father. Thus the mother provoked Oedipal competition with the father, as if it were Freud's baby. Freud colluded with his mother's request and named the baby after a heroic figure, Alexander, after Alexander the Great. This name demeaned his passive father, highlighting Jacob's being a passive victim unlike the conquering hero Alexander the Great. In addition, Alexander the Great was tolerant of other cultures and did not impose his religion on the Jewish people. Freud identified with powerful military heros, and as an adult saw himself as a conquistador who would fight back against political anti-Semitism.

Freud received religious instructions in the school system of Vienna, which was mandatory (Hertzberg 1999). Interestingly, Freud received high grades in Jewish studies, and he could read Hebrew. However, when

Freud matriculated in the University of Vienna, he listed himself as an atheist. This may have been another manifestation o f his rejection of his father who was associated with the Jewish religion. After graduating from medical school at thirty-five, his father gave him the same Philippson Bible that they had read together during Freud's childhood. His father wrote a dedication in Hebrew inscriptions, hoping it would reignite Freud's early religious interest. According to Gay (1988), the inscription read "the spirit of God speaking to his seven year old son."

The Philippson Bible was a product of the Haskalah, the Jewish Enlightenment Movement, created by the philosopher Moses Mendelssohn (1729-1786). As mentioned, this liberal movement sought to help Jews assimilate into the general culture without abandoning their Jewish identity. Mendelssohn had published the Pentateuch, the Torah, with both Hebrew and German to enable German Jews to learn to read the German language. Jacob was influenced by the Haskalah, and thus read the Philippson Bible to Freud as a child. However, when Freud received the Bible on graduating medical school, he considered it to be too late and blamed his father for letting him grow up ignorant o f Jewish history.

Because of his excellent performance as a student, when Freud graduated from the Medical School of the University of Vienna, he was granted an appointment with the eminent neurophysiologist Professor Ernst Brucke. In Brucke's laboratory Freud made important contributions to the understanding o f how neurons functioned, and he also studied the use of cocaine. Professor Herman Nothnagel, chief of the Internal Medicine Clinic, impressed with Freud's research work, proposed him for promotion from instructor to assistant professor. However, Freud's promotion was blocked politically by the Ministry of Education, due to laws preventing Jews from advancement in university positions.

These anti-Semitic laws were instituted by Karl Fueger, the mayor of Vienna, who had been voted into political power, as head of the Christian Social Party, on an anti-Semitic platform. As mentioned, Hitler was living in Vienna at the time and learned from Karl Fueger how to use anti-Semitism to gain political power. Emperor Franz Joseph, who was friendly to Jewish citizens, had attempted to block Fueger's confirmation as mayor. But eventually the emperor was forced to submit to pressure from the Vatican in Rome, and Fueger was confirmed as the mayor of Vienna. With his academic advancement completely blocked, Freud quit the u niversity and entered private practice to earn a living. Freud was now able to marry M artha Bernays, who came from a distinguished Jewish family. Her grandfather was the chief rabbi in Hamburg, Germany, and Freud and Martha were married in a Jewish ceremony.

As compensation for having to leave academia, Freud was awarded a scholarship by Professor Brucke to visit the brilliant psychiatrist, Jean Martin Charcot, in Paris. The reason for the trip was that Charcot was able to hypnotize women and temporarily remove their hysterical symptoms. Freud also visited Hippolyte Bernheim in France, another psychiatrist who worked with hysterical women. When Freud began working in p rivate practice, he also started hypnotizing hysterical women patients to eliminate their symptoms. He then tried suggestion, by laying his hands on these patients. However, he stopped both these techniques when he listened

to these women and recognized the importance of the memories they revealed. By their openly bringing up repressed memories of trau matic sexual seduction from childhood into conscious awareness, he hoped to cure hysterical symptoms. Freud noted that cure of physical symptoms occurred when the patient was able to consciously reexperience and talk about the trauma, as well as express the associated emotions. Freud then treated one of the patients of a psychiatric colleague, Joseph Breuer. This was the case of Anna O, who said recalling these memories was like chimney sweeping, and thus Freud named this method his cathartic technique. He then experimented w ith the use of free association with his patients, telling them to say whatever came to mind without censorship. This he hoped would limit conscious censorship and reveal unconscious emotional memories. Frau Cacilie M and Emmy von N were treated by free association and Freud was able to recover their unconscious repressed memories of sexual seduction as a child. After eighteen cases, he and Breuer evolved his Seduction Theory about the genesis and treatment of hysteria in 1895.

Freud compared himself to an archaeologist who dug into the unconscious of his patients. Freud probably compared his exploration of the unconscious to archaeology because many important archaeological discoveries had been made at the time. Heinrich Schliemann (1822-1890) had discovered the site of Troy at Hissarlik, Turkey, and he later found the site of Mycenae in Greece where Agamemnon had been king. Not only Freud but many other Europeans became fascinated by these archaeological findings and began collecting antiquities as a result.

In April 1896 Freud presented his Seduction Theory before the prestigious Vienna Society for Psychiatry and Neurology. Without notes, he told the audience that hysteria resulted from the physical seduction d u ring childhood of a woman by a family member, relative, or servant. He boldly saw himself as a courageous explorer who had discovered the head of the Nile. He claimed he had discovered the root cause of hysteria. The memory of the seduction was repressed into the unconscious. The unconscious pressed for return of the repressed, and the conflict was converted into hysterical symptoms. The audience felt that Freud had made a frontal assault on Christian morality and responded with an "icy reception." Baron Richard von Krafff-Ebing, the prestigious professor of psychiatry at the University of Vienna and chairman of the meeting, responded sarcastically, saying, "It sounds like a scientific fairy tale." Subsequently, Freud received scorn and was isolated in the professional community. Jones (1953) comments that Freud was now condemned as a Jewish pornographer. Due to these anti-Semitic attacks, Freud sought a community that would accept him.

In September 1897, Freud joined the Jewish organization B'nai B'rith and presented many of his early works where he found a receptive audience to his findings. Despite the anti-Semitic attacks on him, he was proud of his ancestry and identified himself strongly as a secular Jew. In one of his B'nai B'rith lectures, he stated,"Because I was a Jew I found myself free from many prejudices which restricted others in the use of their intellect, and as a Jew I was prepared to join the opposition and to do without agreement with the compact majority." He found being Jewish was advantageous, since as an outsider he enjoyed the intellectual

freedom that permitted him to be creative.

In 1902 Freud established his own Wednesday night group, which consisted of mostly Jewish members originally, except for Ernest Jones (Grosskurth 1991). Jones always felt an outsider in this group yet was close to Freud. Jones courted Freud's daughter, Anna, and later married a Jewish woman. Fearing psychoanalysis would be seen as only Jewish and demeaned, Freud invited Carl Jung, a Swiss Christian, into the psychoanalytic circle. Freud designated Jung as his heir in psychoanalysis to prevent the political anti-Semitism in Vienna from discrediting psychoanalysis as a science. Ironically, Jung and Freud parted company because Freud considered Jung himself to be anti-Semitic. Jung later became head of the Nazi journal of psychiatry and what Freud feared most o f all did occur. Psychoanalysis was demeaned by Jung as a Jewish psychology, as opposed to an Aryan psychology. Jung had accepted the Nazi myth of Aryan superiority, which combined religion with politics. Jung eventually quit the Nazi journal and explained his appointment as an attempt to protect German Jewish psychiatrists. While Jung continued to be interested in religions and mysticism, Freud was critical of religion. This split was never healed, and Jung developed his own theory and method of treatment. Throughout this time, Ernest Jones remained a deeply loyal friend to Freud. Jones was one of the three people who rescued Freud and his family from being murdered by the Nazis. He traveled to Vienna in March 1938 but was detained by the Nazis. Jones was arrested but was able to talk his way out of incarceration. He ardently tried to convince Freud to leave Vienna but was not successful. What eventually convinced Freud was that his daughter Anna was called in by the Gestapo for questioning. Freud agreed to leave his beloved Vienna after Jones offered to help not only Freud, but also his immediate family to escape. Princess Marie Bonaparte and U.S. ambassador William Bullitt also helped to ransom and rescue Freud and his family. Jones aided Freud and his family to set up a home in a spacious flat in the Hampstead section o f London. Freud felt comfortable there, since many of his possessions from his Vienna apartment were able to be ransomed out as well. After Freud's death a year later, his daughter Anna continued to live in this apartment for many years. Jones was intimately acquainted with Freud, and he was able to write the first extensive biography about Freud's life, which consisted of three volumes.

Freud expressed his attitude toward religion by writing *The Future o f an Illusion,* which denied the existence of an anthropomorphic God. In *The Future o f an Illusion,* (1927) Freud considered that an anthropomorphic God was a projection of the all-powerful protective father figure from childhood. But, Freud did not have a strong powerful father to offer protection, since his father had been defeated by anti-Semitism. Also his mother was not emotionally available, thus neither of his parents were protective. Freud, who despite his early childhood insecurity and anti-Semitism, did not become a passive victim like his parents. Nietzsche had stated if one is not defeated by adversity, one can become stronger. Freud tried to separate the joining of religion and politics by considering religion to be an illusion. Then politics would only be secular. He considered religion and its rituals were used by people to deny their existential helplessness.

He saw religion as a crutch and saw its rituals to be an obsessional neurosis, where repetitious movements, like handwashing, occurs. However, Freud did recognize the importance of religion in establishing and perpetuating attachment to a community, but he did not elaborate on how this occurred. In the chapter on biological adaptation and survival, I will present a detailed explanation o f why I consider rituals facilitate group attachment and are not pathological. During the first three years of life, the right cerebral hemisphere is dominant. During this time the attunement between mother and infant facilitates attachment, especially their attuned mutual gaze. A physical synchrony develops between mother and infant, which is internalized and regulates the emotional and social development of the child. This childhood synchrony with mother is replicated in adult life when people function simultaneously together. A sense of oneness with the group develops as a result of people moving, singing, or reciting together. But unlike obsessive compulsive repetitive acts that are individual and uncontrolled, religious rituals are engaged in voluntarily and by groups of people. Rituals are not limited to religion but are involved in group formation elsewhere. For example, soldiers moving together with martial music can stir militancy and forge cohesiveness as if one. A nother example of this phenomenon is with American Indians and other tribes. Solidarity evolves as they dance together accompanied by drum beats and simultaneous vocalizing. It is also enjoyable for two people to dance together in rhythm or to watch groups dancing or singing together, as in ballet. Mutual gaze is involved in loving intimate relations as adults. Attempts at reestablishing this merged relationship in certain forms of pathology, which I called the symbiotic survival pattern, were published in a number of my papers. In addition, the hypothesis of the effects of synchronous merging with the mother was partially validated by my tachistoscopic laboratory studies, which are described in the appendix.

Marianne Krull (1986) in her book, *Freud and his Father,* points out that Freud was greatly attached to his archaeological statuary. They were his most prized possession, which he took with him when he was able to escape Austria for England. She proposes that these statuaries represented his memories of a close emotional connection to his father. These statuaries were similar to the pictures in the Philippson Bible that he and his father had read together during Freud's childhood. The Philippson Bible contained over 500 woodcuts of Egyptian and other ancient images. Recalling reading the Bible together were tender memories that Freud shared with his loving father.

Psychologically the statuaries could be called transitional objects, which maintain a symbolic connection to a loved person. His father gave Freud a copy of the Philippson Bible as a thirty-fifth birthday gift with a personal inscription in Hebrew. This Bible and its many illustrations were intimately connected to his father, who though not protective was tender and loving. Although Freud denied the existence of God as a protective father figure, his statuary served a similar purpose, at least connecting him to his tender and loving father.

What evidence do we have that might support this assumption? Freud was deeply distressed at his father's death in 1896, and began his selfanalysis after that time. He also started collecting the archaeological

objects shortly after his father's death and arranged them in his office where he could be close to them and observe them as he worked. Six weeks after his father's death, Freud bought a picture of Michelangelo's dying slave. This purchase can be interpreted as Freud's having experienced his father as a submissive person, like a slave, who had died. The picture and his archaeological objects maintained his emotional connection with his dead father.

Freud's favorite statue was Athena, who, according to Greek mythology, was born from the head of Zeus. Athena remained a virgin, never married, and never became a mother. Freud was ambivalent toward his m o th er and also to women who identified themselves primarily as mothers. Freud's father functioned like a loving surrogate mother, and thus a n u rturing male figure was important even though being weak. Freud was not a misogynist even though his theory of female sexual development placed women into a secondary position. Feminists have criticized him for his theory of female development, which is seen as being influenced by the patriarchal values existing in Austria. As mentioned previously, Freud accepted a number of bright, career-oriented women who became psychoanalysts. He valued his relationship with these bright and educated women, especially Lou Adreas-Salome, who refused to marry the great philosopher Friedrich Nietzsche. Freud's daughter, Anna, became a famous psychoanalyst, a staunch defender of her father's work, and also never married. Most of these women were more interested in a professional career than in motherhood, which made them acceptable to Freud. He was not against women, but he was prejudiced against women who became mothers (Slipp 1993). He had felt abandoned by his mother due to her multiple pregnancies, and her narcissistic inability to be sensitive to his needs.

With his own wife, his romantic attachment to her dimmed after she became a mother, and Freud developed a close relationship with Wilhelm Fleiss (Slipp 1993). This may have been history repeating itself; a recapitulation of Freud's close relationship with his father, which occurred after his mother became preoccupied with her many pregnancies. When his mother died, Freud did not attend her funeral and sent his daughter Anna. Hardin (1988) considers that this was in retaliation for her lack of interest in him as a small child. He sent a mourner-by-proxy just as his mother had hired a Czech nanny, Resi Wittek, as a surrogate mother. In general, Amalie is described as a narcissistic person, unable to be n u rtu rin g and emotionally unavailable to Freud. As mentioned, in a letter written by Freud, when he was sixteen, after visiting the Fluss family in Freiberg, he praised Frau Fluss. Frau Fluss was n u rtu rin g and looked after the emotional needs o f her children. This was unlike his own mother who restricted herself to only his physical needs. On his visits to see his mother, Freud would be late and keep her waiting, which caused his mother anxiety about whether he would come or not. Judith Bernays Heller (1956) wrote that when Freud was seventy years old, he was ambivalent about inviting his mother to his birthday party. Amalie came to the party w ith a basket of eggs. Sigmund was one o f her eggs and she defined herself as the mother o f her golden Sigi. She had laid the golden egg. She exploited his success and used it for her own narcissistic advantage.

Freud unconsciously recapitulated having two mothers during his childhood. There was his biological mother Amalie, and his nanny, Resi Wittek. As an adult, he invited his sister-in-law Minna into his household and proudly referred to his children as having two mothers. The children were insured not to suffer neglect or abandonment. In addition the theme of two mothers appears in his writings on Leonardo da Vinci, Moses, and Oedipus who all had two mothers (Slipp 1993).

Freud's not experiencing his father as a strong protective figure d u ring his childhood probably accounts for his not seeing God as a powerful male protective figure. Also, Freud did not take into account the religious worship of goddesses. For example, there was the Egyptian goddess Isis, who some considered was the model for the Virgin Mary. Both were motherly figures, depicted as seated with their infant on their lap. Isis held Horus tenderly and Mary did the same with Jesus. Suffering people turned to both of these motherly figures for comfort and for help against adversity. This lack of recognition of early female goddesses probably was also due to Freud's ambivalent relationship with his mother. He did not turn to his mother for comfort and solace, since she only attended to his physical needs. Freud also denied the importance of mothers in his theory of child development, and to cap it off he never analyzed his relationship with his mother.

Historically, it is interesting that ambivalent attitudes generally also existed toward the original female deity. There was the great mother goddess, who was like nature, being both nurturing and destructive. She was the giver of life and fertility, but also the weaver of human destiny and death. In Mesopotamia she was called Ishtar, among the Semites Astarte, and in the Hindu religion Kali. In the Greek religion Athena was the goddess of war as well as of wisdom and handicrafts. Even the change o f seasons was attributed to the Greek mythical goddess Demeter (mother earth). She withheld the fertility o f crops and created winter in retaliation for the abduction of her daughter, Persephone, by Pluto, god of the underworld. Persephone returned from the underworld to her mother Demeter each year and brought about spring. But in the underworld Persephone was the cruel goddess who punished the dead in Hades. In most early civilizations religion was integrated with the political structure and provided a mythical understanding of the world. It was an attempt to make some sense and offer a semblance of power and control over life events. Instead o f feeling helpless, by anthropomorphizing a god or goddess, one could plead, pray, offer food, or sacrifice, to influence the god for a semblance of control. But the dark side occurred when religion was joined with politics and used to endow the leader with absolute divine power. Then to protect this illusion of absolute power after defeats and disasters an outside group needed to be blamed and persecuted.

The earliest religion feared women's bodies, who could produce new life, and women's menstruation was connected to the lunar cycle of nature. Babies were thought to come from a mysterious contact with ancestral spirits. Children were believed to be the reincarnated souls of dead ancestors, which entered the mother's body through a spiritual visitation. Female procreation was thus also related to death and rebirth. This

resulted in female goddesses and women who were worshiped as well as feared. Women then needed to be demeaned and controlled, which occurred in many institutionalized religions.

In the book *Oedipus in the Stone Age,* Lidz and Lidz (1988) found that in primitive tribes of Papua New Guinea, men were fearful of women's powerful vaginal emanations. Instead of penis envy there was vagina envy, because of the ability of women to give birth. Adult men lived separately from women, while boys lived with their mother until fifteen years of age. At that time the boys needed to be reborn through men by undergoing bloody initiation rituals. This was similar to male menstruation and mimicked vaginal birth. Religious rituals were integrated with the political structure in primitive societies to offer an illusion of mastery over women and nature.

Also in some native American tribes, when a woman is menstruating, "in her moon," she is considered to be very powerful and is not allowed to touch the tribal drums. The power of women was thought to be greater than the power of the tribal drums. In general, through the ages women were feared because o f their magical power associated with nature. They needed to be demeaned and controlled to feel a sense of mastery resulting in religious societies that were patriarchal and that existed from the stone age up until recent times. Freud's mother was influenced by demeaning attitudes toward women in Vienna, and her response ultimately affected him.

Freud's family and his own professional career suffered because of the flagrant political anti-Semitism existing in Europe and Vienna. Freud not only saw himself as a conquistador but also tried to imbue his children with power. Freud named his own children after family members of his idealized strong father figures. Mathilde was named after Breuer's wife, Martin after Jean Martin Charcot, Oliver after Oliver Cromwell, Ernst after Ernst Brucke, and Sophie and Anna after Professor Paul Hammerschlag's niece and daughter, respectively.

When his father, Jacob, died in 1896, Freud had the illusion he looked like Giuseppe Garibaldi, the courageous military hero who united Italy into a nation. This was clearly wishful thinking, since Freud had wanted his father to be such a heroic figure with w hom he could idealize and identify with as a model. Freud wanted his father to present a strong masculine image, instead of being impotent, a passive victim o f anti-Semitism. His father had practiced the conventional policy of not making too many waves, so as not to provoke the populace of the country.

Freud saw himself as a conquistador, a proud military hero, valiantly fighting back against anti-Semitism. As mentioned, Emperor Franz Joseph held up confirmation of the election of Karl Lueger, who was elected on an anti-Semitic platform to be mayor of Vienna. However, the Vatican in Rome intruded religion into the political process, and the pope pressured the emperor to submit. Karl Lueger was then sworn in as mayor of Vienna in 1897. The next day, Freud had a dream about Hannibal, the Semitic w arrior from Carthage who attacked Rome. This dream was clearly a wish fulfillment of wanting to fight back against anti-Semitism. Since both his father and Emperor Franz Joseph had been defeated by Rome, Freud identified himself in the dream with the Semitic general Hannibal. Hannibal's father, Hamilcar Barca, was the famous general of

Carthage, who in 228 BCE was also defeated and killed by the Romans in the first Punic war. Carthage, in what is present-day Tunisia, had been the other powerful kingdom that existed besides Rome. The war had been fought to establish which nation had supremacy in the region. Hamilcar Barca had his son Hannibal take a vow to avenge his defeat by Rome. Hannibal kept his promise to his father, and in 218 BCE started the second Punic war against Rome. After crossing the Alps with troops, cavalry, and elephants, he defeated a number of Roman legions at Ticinus, Trebia, and Trasimene through superior tactics. At Cannae, in southern Italy, where he was outnumbered by the Romans two to one, Hannibal's army killed a very great number of Roman soldiers and took many prisoners. However, he did not follow up his advantage by sacking Rome, since he did not have siege machines or local support. In 203 BCE Hannibal returned to Carthage, which was being attacked, and he was defeated the following year at Zama by the Roman general Scipio Africanus the elder. Like Hannibal, Freud also wanted to avenge the defeat by Rome of his father as well as Emperor Franz Joseph, who was a friend of the Jews. However, there is an ironic twist to the identification of Freud with Hannibal. At the time of the Punic Wars, Rome had not threatened or invaded Judah but was an ally. Chilton (2000) notes that Judah, under the Jewish Maccabee rulers, allied itself w ith Rome against Carthage. Out of appreciation of this alliance, Rome made the Jewish religion legal, and its worshipers were permitted to practice their religion without being persecuted. Freud must not have been aware of this. He was emotionally responding to not wanting to feel helpless like his father or the emperor. The support from the Vatican in Rome for Lueger legitimized anti-Semitism as a political tool. Hitler was living in Vienna at the time, and he learned to use anti-Semitism to gain political power.

Freud suffered from a phobia about going to Rome. Interestingly, on his way to Rome he unconsciously traveled the same route as Hannibal. His phobia may have been related to his fear of being helpless and not wanting to be cowed by anti-Semitism. He did not want to be like his father or the emperor, who had accommodated themselves and submitted to religious pressure. Freud would not allow the pervasive anti-Semitic prejudice existing in Austria to defeat him. Freud saw himself as a proud Jew, who like a military hero, fought to conquer his adversary. He was proud of his opposition to the Roman Catholic Church, which considered Jews as perfidious and Christ killers. These stereotypes inflamed anti-Semitism among the populace and were used by demagogues to gain and maintain their political power.

Freud's opposition to the pervasive anti-Semitism in Vienna was an important part of his identity. In a letter to his fiancee, Martha Bernays, he wrote, "I have often felt as though I had inherited all the obstinacy and all the passions of our ancestors when they defended the Temple, as though I could throw away my life with joy for a great moment" (Gay 1988). The psychoanalytic circle that Freud later established could be seen as his Jewish troops in the battle against anti-Semitism. He offered his bold ideas in psychoanalysis in direct opposition to existing bourgeois and religious values. His aim was to establish a universal psychology of the mind and behavior that did not segregate Jews from others, but was inclusive. He hoped that through science and reason he could vanquish political

anti-Semitism. But it was not to be; it had limited success.

Freud's efforts for change were not aimed at the culture but at the individual with the hope it would spread upward into the culture. By resolving the internalized prejudiced myths and stereotypes learned in childhood from the family and environment, anti-Semitism might be eliminated. By changing the internal dynamics of individuals, Freud tried to change the way patients perceived others and behaved in the outside world. These internalized stereotypes were projected onto others. He hoped that others would be seen as individuals and not distorted by emotions. Not only would the distortions of childhood perceptions be corrected but also religious biases eliminated as well. He hoped that by recognizing one's internal motives and the effect of perception and behavior, other individuals would be seen through the light of reality. To achieve this Freud developed a psychology that was individualistic, universal, and humanistic.

Despite his fight not to be a helpless victim of political anti-Semitism, Freud like his father became a victim due to the external circumstantial events that occurred. Before the Nazis took over, Austria had around 300,000 Jews, with two thirds o f them living in Vienna. After the Nazi troops entered Austria, Freud and his family were in great danger of being sent to a concentration camp, murdered, and cremated like so many other Jews. As mentioned, his daughter, Anna, had been called into Gestapo headquarters, which was a frightening occurrence. They feared she would be arrested and they would never see her again. But to their relief she was released.

After Freud decided to leave Austria, he needed to obtain an exit visa in 1938 from the Gestapo in Vienna. He was asked to sign a statement by the Gestapo that he had been well treated before he was given the visa. He did sign it, but he used a twist of irony that subtly maintained he was not a powerless victim. He was not defeated even under this coercive circumstance; he still had courage to fight back. He wrote, "I can heartily recommend the Gestapo to anyone." Freud and his immediate family were ransomed out of Austria with some of their possessions. There were about 130,000 Viennese Jews that were able to leave, but about 65,000 Austrian Jewish citizens were murdered in concentration camps.

In England, Freud finished writing *Moses and Monotheism* (1939), which he had begun in 1934. This interest in Moses had occurred a year after Hitler assumed political power in Germany and anti-Semitism became rampant in Germany and Austria. Even Jewish men and women in political power were helpless to affect change. Walter Rathenau, the former foreign minister of Germany, and Rosa Luxemburg, a member of the Reichstag, who were both Jewish, were assassinated. In Austria, Chancellor Dollfuss was murdered by 154 members of the Nazi SS who were dressed in Austrian Army uniforms (Shirer 1960). Hitler was an Austrian, and he had proposed in his book, *Mein Kampf* the unification of Germany and Austria. However, his initial Nazi putsch to take over Austria failed. Austrian forces under Dr. Kurt von Schuschnigg captured many of the rebel Nazis and hung thirteen of them. Freud recognized the danger to Austrian Jews from the violent anti-Semitic policy of the Nazi political party. The Nazis wanted to take over Austria, and Jews would become helpless victims of aggression, like his

father. Although he was not intimately familiar with Jewish history, Freud's interest in his heritage came to the fore.

In February 1938, Hitler gave Dr. Schuschnigg an ultimatum, indicating that the ban against the Nazi party had to be lifted, and all Nazis in jail were to be released, including the murderers of Chancellor Doffuss. Hitler demanded that the Austrian economy was to be assimilated with Germany and the ministers of finance, security, and war were to be Nazi appointees. Dr. Schuschnigg had no choice but to capitulate to these demands under the threat of invasion. But he tried to establish a boundary, saying Austria would never give up its independence voluntarily. In March 1938 Hitler ordered Dr. Schuschnigg to resign, which he was forced to do, but his last words were, "God protect Austria." German troops entered Austria and when Hitler arrived in Vienna on March 14, he received a triumphant and tumultuous welcome, as a returning Austrian hero. The Nazis humiliated the Jews in many ways, including their being forced to scrub the streets and latrines. Then tens of thousands of Jews were jailed, their possessions were stolen, and they were sent to concentration camps, where they were murdered.

In *Moses and Monotheism*, Freud transformed Moses from a Jew into an Egyptian. What may have contributed to his changing Moses into an Egyptian in this work? Freud seems to have identified his father with the Jewish slaves in Egypt who were rescued by Moses. The Jews in Egypt had been helpless slaves for 400 years. Freud also saw his father as a passive slave, which was probably a source of unconscious anger toward him. His father's passivity was the very trait that Freud had so valiantly fought against all his life. Freud could not accept any part of that helplessness as his identity. Freud himself, despite all his efforts to the contrary, became a helpless victim to political anti-Semitism and needed to be rescued from Vienna. Jews had no power to be of any help, so that he and his family could only be rescued by Gentiles. As mentioned, the rescuers included U.S. ambassador William Bullitt, Ernest Jones, and Princess Marie Bonaparte, none of whom were Jewish.

In *Moses and Monotheism,* Freud questioned the biblical version of the Egyptian princess who rescued Moses from the Nile. He proposed this story was a fictional cover-up for her being pregnant, and that Moses was actually her child. Moses was not only raised as an Egyptian prince, but, according to Freud, he was in fact actually an Egyptian prince. This gave Moses the confidence and the power to rescue the Jews from slavery. This speculation seems factually very unlikely, since Moses would not have had to escape after killing an Egyptian taskmaster. Being a prince had its privileges, and taking the life of a commoner had little value then. One wonders if Freud's making Moses into a non-Jewish prince may have been something to do with the fact that his three rescuers were all not Jewish; one was even a princess. One can speculate that changing Moses into an Egyptian prince was a secret tribute to this Gentile rescuers, especially princess Marie Bonaparte.

Freud's speculation about Egyptian history also suffers from another problem. If Moses was an Egyptian, who was the monotheistic God that Moses proclaimed? Freud had to find another explanation for the Jewish God. Freud claimed Moses was a follower of the monotheistic pharaoh Akhenaten (1353-1336 BCE). However, Akhenaten's god, Aten, was physically represented by the external sun disc, which was a merging of Ra, Amun, and Horus. There was no mention of YHWH or Elohim, the Jewish God, in connection with Aten. Even more important, Moses's God was

invisible, not corporeal, not the external sun disc. After Akhenaten's death, Tutankhaten changed his name to Tutankamun when the Amun religion was restored. The Pharoah at the time that Moses lived was Ramses II, and the Exodus occurred around 1263 BCE, when the Amun religion was fully in force. Thus, the speculations Freud made in *Moses and Monotheism* do not fit historical evidence. When Freud wrote this work he was an elderly, terminally ill man yet still fighting against being a helpless victim. Ironically, the death of Jesus almost caused the death of Freud. As Volkan noted, the Catholic church inflamed people with a collective emotional history of virulent anti-Semitism by accusing Jews of being Christ killers. Hitler had learned to use the existing anti-Semitism to achieve political power from George von Schonerer, a member of the Austrian Reichsrat, and Karl Lueger, the mayor of Vienna (Schorske 1981). Despite the prevalence of anti-Semitism, Freud identified himself as an Austrian and loved his homeland. But, Austrians welcomed its native son, Hitler, with open arms and threatened the life of Freud and his family. Freud abhorred being a helpless victim and strove to assert a heroic individualism. This corresponded to his psychoanalytic treatment, where he tried to liberate the patient from the bonds of emotional fears and distortions. However, like a Thomas Hardy novel, external circumstances proved to be of greater power and determined his destiny. Fortunately, Freud and his immediate family were able to be rescued from being murdered, but his four sisters and 65,000 other Austrian Jews were less fortunate.

On a positive note, the relationship between Jews and the Roman Catholic Church have now improved greatly. In October 1965, the Second Vatical Council established the proclamation, "In Our Time." This stated that the Jews could not be blamed for the crucifixion o f Christ in the past or present. Later, Pope John Paul II apologized for the legacy of anti-Semitism that had been preached by the Roman Catholic Church. He visited the synagogue in Rome, the Holocaust Memorial, and the Temple Wall in Jerusalem. He declared Judaism to be the older sibling of Catholicism. Dialogue and mutual understanding between Jews and Catholics continues in the Ecumenical Meetings that are held in Rome.

1 0 Individual Power or Compliance to Power

Religion was used by all tribal and national societies in the past to provide a sense of power over their existential helplessness. It had a positive component by providing hope and meaning to the lives of individuals.

However, it could be used to gain political power over individuals as well. Political leaders claimed divine power, which was complied with by the community since it provided a greater sense of security. Rigid group boundaries were also established as a protection against outside threatening groups. As mentioned, the divine power was an illusion, b ut it needed to be preserved in the face of disasters and defeats. Either the group blamed themselves for sinning and offending their gods or else an outside group needed to be blamed and punished. Scapegoating an outside group also served to enhance group solidarity, since they had a common enemy. The outside group could also be incorporated by forcing its members to accept the gods o f the victorious group. As an example, the Romans forced others to accept their pantheistic gods and rituals. The gods o f the defeated group were taken away and placed in the Pantheon in Rome. Group identity was paramount, since it provided power and security b ut at the expense of individual freedom.

One exception was Alexander the Great, who did not impose his religion on the conquered nations but attempted to assimilate with them.

Another exception were the original Israelites, who did not have a human king who was divinely inspired. According to the Bible, when Moses descended from Mount Sinai with the Ten Commandments, the requirement was that people observe God's laws. A covenant was established between God and the Israelites, which required mutual responsibility between God and individuals. In this Kingdom of God, Israel was not to be governed by a human king claiming divinity. Only God was king and the rule of his law was what prevailed. Thus power was invested in individuals who were responsible for their moral behavior.

In the surrounding countries, human rulers existed who claimed divine power and demanded total obedience. For example, the Egyptian pharaoh was considered to be a supernatural being. His power was so great that his orders were obeyed not only in life but in death. In life the pharaoh was the human form of Horus, Ra, the god of the sky, the sun, and the moon. Building the pyramids as the burial place for the pharaoh required vast numbers of laborers. After death, he was embalmed, put in a sarcophagus, and placed in the tomb's burial chamber. In the early dynasties his wives and many nobles were buried with him to attend to his

needs. Later people were replaced by statues and items that he would need in the afterworld. After death the pharaoh became the god Osiris. His body, the Ba, needed to be preserved by m ummification, and his spirit, the Ka, would be carried over a river on a boat or brought into the sky, where he would live eternally. Egyptians believed in eternal life after death, which stemmed from the myth that Osiris was resurrected from the dead. Similar to the Christian reverence for relics, one city, Busiris, claimed to have the backbone of Osiris.

When the Israelites were fighting the Philistines, they suffered severe defeats and felt the solution was to install a human king. They felt their power was not enough by following God's covenant. The book of Samuel in the Bible states th at the prophet Samuel was against appointing a human king, since it was against God's requirement. Samuel said the rule of law had been ordained as the only governing principal that people were to follow. God was to be their only king. But the people did not feel safe enough, and they believed a powerful human leader could provide greater military organization and strength. Samuel was forced by the Israelites to anoint the first king of Israel, Saul, who was from the tribe of Benjamin.

According to the Bible, Samuel clearly recognized that the very jo in ing of politics and religion created a potentially toxic combination. It made the power of the ruler too strong and the people too weak. First of all, this request by the people was a loss of faith in the power of God, and a loss of individual freedom and responsibility. Subsequently, some Israelite kings did impose their will on the people for their own advantage and were not be responsive to the needs o f the people. Also, some Israelite kings, such as David and Hyrcanus, were involved in wars of conquest of surrounding tribes and forced them to convert.

Both Jesus and Freud were involved in strengthening the individual and opposed to the limitations of freedom by an often corrupt ruling elite. Jesus created a Jewish sect that preached a religion that was egalitarian and not hierarchical. As mentioned, the Jewish religion Jesus taught emphasized the golden rule for personal relations, including the Ten Commandments. Like the prophet Samuel, Jesus preached the reestablishment of an ethical and moral society ruled by God's law. He was against violence and was inclusive of those individuals society considered to be outcasts. Jesus hoped to reverse the decision that Samuel was forced to make under duress, which created a divinely appointed human king. During the time Jesus lived, the secular king of Judea had been appointed by and allied with the Romans. Jesus wanted to restore the just Kingdom of God, with God again being the sole ruler and responsive to the needs of the people.

Freud hoped that by presenting religion as an illusion, it would remove religion from politics. More recently, Dawkins and Hitchens and others similarly have considered that religion has been the fault for a good deal of human suffering. They bring up the cruelty of the Middle Ages, the crusades, the Inquisition, and the holy wars between Protestants and Catholics. Tragically, many innocent people have suffered and been killed in these religious wars, which still exist today.

As mentioned, if we look at the conflict more carefully, it is not the religion itself that is the cause of the disaster. It is the use of religion by demagogues for political power and economic gain. The leader's selfinterest

became paramount and resulted from the installation of power when politics and religion are joined. The ruler's power could not exist in a vacuum but was enabled and maintained by the collusion of the people.

Even though the independence of the people was diminished, as in the case of Israel against the Philistines, it created and sustained an illusion of power and safety.

As the novelist Fyodor Dostoyevsky noted in "The Grand Inquisitor" part of *The Brothers Karamazov,* most people submit to domination, because they prefer security over freedom. Most people complied to the will of the ruler, hoping to be protected, as if by a powerful parent. It was not the religion itself, but how religion was misused for power by the ruling class for their own personal gain. Not only the nobility but the church itself enjoyed political power from the time of Constantine up to the Enlightenment. The church also accumulated wealth and property, appointed kings, and even initiated wars. As mentioned, this combination of religion and politics continued to exist in the twentieth century. A secular religion with a messianic leader occurred that also contributed to an abuse of political power. This occurred in Nazi Germany, Fascist Italy, and Communist Russia, resulting in massive death and destruction.

One of the earliest power conflicts occurred when the Eastern Orthodox church would not accept the authority of the pope and separated. The conflict between Western and Byzantine Christians occurred when the leaders of the fourth crusade sacked the churches and palaces of Constantinople in 1204 CE. This conquest of a Christian city by Christians crusaders was done purely out of economic self-interest. Religious differences had been used as a pretext for conflict, but the reality of the incident was different. The Venetians promised to cancel the debt of the French and Italian crusader nobles if they captured the rich city of Constantinople. This economic deal with the Venetians was consummated when the crusaders sacked the Christian city of Constantinople. The crusaders looted Constantine's great palace and among the valuable items given to the Venetians were the four bronze horses from Constantine's hippodrome. Ironically, the Venetians placed these looted bronze horses above the church in St. Marks Square, where they stand today. Since economics and not religion was the prime motivation, this fourth crusade never reached the Holy Land.

During the thirteenth century, Pope Gregory IX instituted the Papal Inquisition, and inquisitors were appointed to conduct trials of supposed heretics. In 1252, Pope Innocent IV authorized torture to be used to obtain confessions from suspected heretics. The Inquisition was also used at times by political rulers to get rid of their enemies and to acquire property. In 1468, King Ferdinand V and Queen Isabella of Spain enlisted the grand Inquisitor, Tomas de Torquemada, to try heretics. They issued the Edict of Expulsion in 1492 that forced Jews to convert to Christianity or leave Spain.

Many Jews escaped the Inquisition by going to other countries. Those Jews who remained were forced to be baptized into Christianity and were called *conversos.* However, the conversion was often superficial and many Jews continued their Jewish beliefs and practices secretly. Informers would look for these new Christians and denounce them. The telltale signs of Judaizing were wearing their best clothes on the Sabbath, fasting on Yom

Kippur, seeing no smoke from chimneys on Saturday, refusing to eat pork, or circumcising a male child.

These new Christians were called *marranos,* pigs, and accused of being Judaizing heretics. Many of them were arrested and told if they confessed to their and others' Judaizing sins, they would receive amnesty. They were tortured to the point where they would reveal other *marranos,* but then they were convicted of heresy and sentenced to death anyway. Those whose names had been revealed were also arrested, convicted, and killed as heretics. To save their souls, the Inquisition court sentenced them to be burned at the stake. This was termed auto-da-fe, an act of faith, and served as a public display that intimidated and terrified witnesses. It was similar to the crucifixion of the Romans and used to control people through fear. It is estimated that more than 2,000 people were burned at the stake d u ring that time. They were burned alive to save them from eternal punishment in hell. The inquisitors believed that they had the absolute tru th and were being helpful by killing people so that they would not have eternal damnation in hell. In 1542, Pope Paul III used the Inquisition to fight the spread of the Protestant Christian religion. Burning o f heretics at the stake began in 1481 and it lasted for 300 years throughout Europe, and did not end until the nineteenth century. The French philosopher, Montesquieu, commented in 1738 that the Inquisition was proof that the people of Europe during his time were not civilized but were "barbarians."

The authority of the church was challenged in the fourteenth century when the obscure Latin in the Bible was translated into a language that people could read for themselves. More people were becoming literate as a consequence. John Wycliffe (1320-1384), an Englishman who had studied at Oxford and was the Vicar of Lutterworth in Leicestershire England, questioned the authority of the Catholic church. He opposed the selfinterest of the clergy, who owned valuable property that gave them considerable power. He had ideas similar to the Gnostics and felt that individuals could turn directly to God and read the Bible for themselves. Wycliffe translated the Bible into English in 1380, so that people could also think for themselves and not be dependent on the priests' sermons.

There were five bulls issued against him by Pope Gregory XI, since Wycliffe challenged the church authority. Wycliffe died in 1384, but in 1415, he was declared a heretic. His corpse was exhumed and burned, and his ashes scattered in the River Swift. The followers of Wycliffe, called the Lollards, secretly followed his teachings and circulated his English Bible. They opposed the Catholic church, which restricted the Bible to priests. The political authority of the church was threatened even more seriously when Johann Gutenberg (1398-1468) invented the printing press.

For the first time books could be made in large quantities and distributed. Previously books had to be handwritten by scribes and were very expensive. The first printed Bible was published in 1456 and was known as the Gutenberg Bible. It was in Latin and about 200 Bibles were originally printed. Printing spread rapidly throughout Europe and the average persons could now afford to buy the Bible cheaply and learn to read it for themselves.

In 1515, William Tyndale decided to translate a new edition of the

New Testament into English from the Greek. He was a linguist and part of the Lollard group of Wycliffe. He fled England in 1524 and probably went to Germany, where he finished his Bible. He felt the church obscured the true teachings of Jesus, and he was against the power of the church hierarchy. He went to Cologne, where in 1526 his New Testament was p rin ted. However, in England, his Bible was burned and those reading it were arrested. He was arrested in Brussels by the Inquisition, strangled, and burned at the stake. Thus, fear and execution was used to maintain the political power of the church and state.

The political authority of the Catholic church was then further threatened by the Protestant Reformation, which was started by Martin Luther (1483-1546). Luther was an ordained Catholic priest who studied at the University of Wittenberg. He was made doctor of theology in 1512. As a lecturer at the university, he noted that God's love itself forgave men's sins, and he opposed the selling of indulgences by the church to forgive sins. The Catholic church had created an atmosphere of fear, in that people would be sent to hell after death and suffer horrible punishments for their sins. The church used the sale of indulgences to forgive sins, which would avoid a person going to hell after death. The sale of indulgences brought in considerable money for the Catholic church and was used to enhance its power. The Pope Leo X is said to have used the money to build St. Peters and other churches, to fight wars, and to keep mistresses for himself. Luther considered that the Catholic church was selling indulgences solely in the self-interest of the church and extorted money for its own use. In 1517, he posted ninety-five reasons about the abuse of indulgences on the door of the Wittenberg Castle Church. He directly challenged the power o f the Catholic church by stating the study o f the scriptures was the only real authority. In 1520, the pope declared him a heretic and a bull of excommunication was issued in January 1521. But Luther burned this papal bull and considered the pope the anti-Christ. In April 1521, Luther was tried at the Diet of Worms and the Edict of Worms found him to be a heretic and a criminal.

Luther preached that people could be near God by living a lifetime that expressed love and doing good works. However, his ideology did not find expression in his actual deeds. Even though his religious ideology matched that of the Jews, in doing good deeds and studying the Bible, he oppressed the Jews. He even wanted to burn down their synagogues, confiscate their property, and force them into work camps. However, the nobility did not carry through his vindictive wishes. In 1522, Luther made a translation of the New Testament into German and had religious services conducted in German. Luther aligned himself with the local German princes who supported and protected him generally. In 1525, he sided with the nobility against the peasants' revolt and gave the nobility assurance that sanctioned the killing o f the opposing peasant men, women, and children. Luther spent the rest of his life teaching and preaching in Wittenberg. He was in constant demand in Germany, supported the Protestant Reformation, and established the Lutheran church.

King Henry XIII (1491-1547) of England broke away from the Vatican in Rome and established the Church of England. Rome would not dissolve his marriage to Catherine of Aragon which he requested, since she could not conceive a male heir for the throne. The Archbishop of

Canterbury, Thomas Cranmer, then wanted a new Bible, since England was now Protestant. Cranmer authorized the Matthew Bible to be written in English and distributed it in each church. However, when Mary (called

Bloody Mary) became queen after Henry's death, she placed Cranmer on trial. Cranmer had directly challenged the power o f the pope and was convicted and sentenced to death. Cranmer labeled the pope the anti-Christ and was summarily burned at the stake. When Queen Elizabeth I assumed the throne of England, she restored Protestantism. She maintained the Protestant religion when her fleet defeated the large armada of ships sent by the king of Spain in an effort to restore England to Catholicism.

After Queen Elizabeth's death in 1603, her reign was followed by King James I of Scotland (1566-1625). King James brought together the best scholars and linguists and authorized an English translation of the New Testament. The King James Version of the Bible was beautifully written, became universally accepted, and is still read today. It contains the Old Testament, Paul's Epistles, Acts, Letters, the Apostles' Gospels, and John's Revelations.

Church dogma was further questioned by the scientific revolution that was occurring in Europe, and the church fought back to preserve its authority. In 1555, Pope Paul IV attacked the University of Padua, which had not been created by the church, because of its scientific interests and books. In addition he attacked the teachings o f Jews as a false theology and reversed years of religious tolerance. Previously, Pope Alexander VI had welcomed around 6,000 Jews, who had escaped the Spanish Inquisition around 1492. He considered their coming as financially beneficial for Italy, since Jews were able to establish businesses and commerce. However, Pope Paul IV walled the Jews into the ghetto, which was locked at night, forced them to wear distinctive clothing and hats, and burned all the issues of the Talmud he could find. But scientific discoveries were challenging the church's power, and like being attacked by a swarm of bees change could not be controlled and stifled.

The findings of Galileo Galilei (1564-1642) confirmed the theory of Copernicus that the earth was not the center of the universe as depicted in the Bible. Using his telescope he saw that the earth went around the sun. He also discovered that the moon derived its light from the sun. In 1613 he published his work in *Letters on the Solar Spots.* But the work came to the attention of the pope, who ordered Galileo in 1616 to not teach his discoveries that opposed absolute religious beliefs.

Galileo was a devout Catholic and his intentions were not meant as an attack against the church. However, his findings were experienced as a direct assault upon the foundation of the authority o f the Catholic church. The next more liberal pope allowed Galileo to present his views alongside those held by the Catholic religion. In 1632, Galileo published a book on the theories of the universe, but he had a simpleton present the religious view. When this work was discovered, he was made to reappear before the Inquisition court at the Minerva church in Rome. Here the power of the church came down upon his head, since his scientific findings did not confirm religious belief. To avoid being burned at the stake, Galileo was forced to renounce his scientific discoveries. However rumor has it that as he left the church he whispered to a friend that his discoveries were really true. He was placed under house arrest and spent the last nine years of his life in isolation so that he could not spread his findings. His name was not mentioned by a Pope for the next 300 years, as if he never existed. It is interesting that now the Vatican has established a telescopic observatory in Arizona staffed by Jesuit scientists that study the solar system.

When Napoleon invaded Italy in 1796, he declared edicts to demolish the Jewish ghetto and to bring the Inquisition to a halt. He introduced the rational thinking o f the Enlightenment into Italy and opposed the political power of religion over the state. In 1808, Napoleon conquered Spain and abolished the Inquisition there as well. It is estimated that about 15,000 people had been burned at the stake by then in Spain, supposedly

an act to save their souls. The famous artist Goya had painted
some of the cruelty that had been practiced by the Inquisitors. In 1815
after Napoleon had been defeated, the Inquisition was reconstituted.

Goya was brought before the Inquisition court, because of the paintings
he had made about its brutal punishments. Fortunately he was able to
escape to France to avoid being burnt at the stake. In Italy, the Inquisition
was also restored, and Jews were forced again to live in the ghetto as virtual
prisoners. This imprisonment lasted for another forty years, until the
Italian nationalist revolution.

In the Jewish religion, similar conflict over authority resulted in the
subsequent death and suffering of many people. Conflict among Jews
occurred in the revolt against Rome by the Zealots in 66 CE. The
Sadducees were the established Jewish authority, but to maintain their
power they had collaborated with the Romans. Because of their subservience
to Roman authority, the Zealots saw them as traitors and killed
many of them during the rebellion.

It is interesting that recently the tomb o f King Flerod (37-4 BCE)
was discovered by Professor Ehud Netzer, head o f a Hebrew University
archaeological team. The tomb had been described by the ancient historian
Josephus as being in Herodium, near the town of Hebron in
Israel. Indeed, it was discovered there. The sarcophagus was made of
pink Jerusalem limestone and was expertly inscribed with royal
rosettes. Herod was a half Jew, coming from the Idominean tribe conquered
by King David, which was forced to convert to Judaism. Herod
had been appointed the king over the Jews by the Romans, since they
trusted he would be loyal to them. He was described by Matthew as a
brutal monarch, ordering the "slaughter of the innocents." All Jewish
males under two years of age in Bethlehem were ordered to be killed.
He also had his two sons strangled, and he killed his wife, who was a
descendent of the Hasmonian Jewish kings. He also assassinated many
of his in-laws and had his eldest son beheaded. His sarcophagus had
been violently smashed to pieces. The speculation was th at the Zealots
had destroyed Herod's sarcophagus, since he was a brutal puppet king,
who had been appointed by and collaborated with the Romans against
the Jews.

Violence also occurred between Jews in the later revolt by bar-Kochba
(132-135 CE) against the Romans. Many opposed the Jewish military
attack against the more powerful Roman army. Those Jews opposing the
revolt did not believe victory was possible. They rationally knew that it
would only lead to defeat and devastation, since Rome had the most powerful
army at the time. Ideology won over reason, and war ensued. Bar-
Kockba initially was victorious but was ultimately defeated when a large
Roman army was sent to Judea, and terrible consequences resulted.

Another instance of conflict in the Jewish religion occurred in the
nineteenth century. When Theodore Herzl wanted to establish Israel as a
national homeland for the Jews, he met with considerable conflict over his

authority. A number of very Orthodox Jews claimed that this should not
occur until the Messiah came. These Orthodox claimed that they had the
true authority and Herzl and the Zionists were breaking the law. Conflict

still remains even today. Orthodox Jews in Israel do not serve in the army out of religious reasons, and they had stoned cars in Israel that traveled during the Sabbath. It is a characteristic of all fundamentalist religions that they feel they have the absolute truth. Ideology triumphs here over external reality, and Herzl's predictions became a reality.

In the twentieth century, the rise to power of Adolph Hitler in many respects is similar to that of Emperor Constantine in the fourth century. Both were militaristic leaders who used their semireligious positions for their political gain to enhance their power. Constantine used the Christian cross, which he placed on the shields of his army, and Hitler used the swastika, the twisted cross, on the armbands and banners of his army. The swastika is a religious symbol used by nature worshipers of the Aryan races, from Scandinavia to Persia and India. It is a Greek cross with extended arms folded backward and is enclosed in a circle. Interestingly, the swastika was also the symbol of the Sun god, Apollo, which Constantine worshiped. As mentioned, Hitler had been the savior of his mother by becoming the family lightening rod. He then saw himself as the messiah of Germany. As mentioned, he had been primed to believe he was the messiah to save Germany by Dietrich Eckart. Rudolph Hess, one of the closest associates of Hitler, also openly declared that he saw Hitler as a messiah. Indeed most of the German people also saw him as their savior. Hitler promised a heavenly utopian third Reich for Germany that would last 1,000 years.

What else contributed to Germany falling under the sway of such a fanatic leader as Hitler? After World War I, the terms of the Versailles treaty imposed devastating terms on the economy o f Germany. This treaty was essentially written by Clemenceau of France and Lloyd George of England out of vengeance, to punish Germany for the war. Interestingly, Freud and Bullitt (1967) wrote an applied psychoanalytic study about Woodrow Wilson's very ineffective efforts to influence the Versailles treaty. Freud and Bullitt wrote that Wilson had repressed his hatred of his father, Reverend Joseph R. Wilson, but consciously idealized him as a god. Wilson felt he was like Christ, and his own life was divine. He would be a "savior of the world." But Freud and Bullitt considered that unconsciously Woodrow Wilson wanted also to be a martyr like Jesus. Wilson believed that God ordained that he become president of the United States; his naive religious belief also told him that the "noble intentions" of people would triumph over the vengeful proclamations in Versailles. This was not to be the case, and he was defeated there and in the United States.

Freud and Bullitt wrote, "I do not know how to avoid the conclusion that a man, who is capable of taking the illusions of religion so literally and is so sure of a special personal intimacy with the Almighty, is unfitted for relations with ordinary children of men." Thus Freud was critical of Wilson combining religion and politics. Freud and Bullitt commented that the German Kaiser also felt he was "a chosen darling of providence." Wilson was so blinded by his religious idealism concerning his fourteen points, that he could not see the vengeful motivations that drove the decisions of the French and English diplomats at Versailles. The Wilson book

was written between 1930 and 1932, but it was not published until 1967, out of respect for the widow of Woodrow Wilson.

Unfortunately, the French and English diplomats did not see the consequences of the punitive Versailles Treaty. The German populace suffered humiliation and helplessness and endured runaway inflation. In 1925 currency reform was enacted to stabilize the fortunes for the upper class, but it wiped out the savings of the middle class. This created the soil for the basic assumption group of pairing and looking for a messiah, as described by the psychoanalyst Bion. It also created a collective emotional memory of being defeated and stimulated a desire for revenge as described by Volkan. The German people were carried away by the shared emotional fantasy and rage. They wished to be saved by a messiah who would avenge their defeat. Hitler was able to assume this role as a secular messiah, by his charismatic speeches, political manipulations, and ability to choreograph huge demonstrations. He was able to create group solidarity by visually having elaborate ceremonies and parades where people shouted and acted together in synchrony.

Both Hitler and Constantine used political anti-Semitism to scapegoat the Jews, which diverted blame and enhanced group cohesion. Hitler had learned to used political anti-Semitism from Karl Lueger and Georg von Schonerer when he lived in Vienna. Lueger, a Christian Socialist, was able to sway public opinion on an anti-Semitic plank to insure his election as mayor of Vienna. Hitler learned from Georg von Schonerer, of the Pan-Germans, to use street brawlers to attack and intimidate opponents. Schonerer considered himself the knight redeemer of the German folk and evolved into a raucous anti-Semitic demagogue as a member of the Reichsrat (Schorske 1981). Instead of feeling inferior, Germans were made to feel superior to Jews, who were demeaned.

What are some of the factors that made Hitler the most evil man in the twentieth century? There was mental illness in a branch of his family; a niece was schizophrenic and required hospitalization. She was later killed on Hitler's orders to destroy her and all the mentally and emotionally impaired Germans. By generalizing the killing of these challenged individuals, it covered up the defect in his own family. Apparently Hitler himself had suffered a breakdown as a soldier during World War I. In a personal communication to me, Dr. Ruth Lidz, who was an eminent psychoanalyst at Yale, told me that her father, a psychiatrist in Germany, had diagnosed Hitler who had suffered a breakdown in the German army d u ring World War I. Hitler was diagnosed as suffering from major hysteria, which probably now would be called a borderline personality. The father of Ruth Lidz had to escape Germany to avoid being killed. Hitler tried to cover up and silence anything negative about his family background.

How did Hitler assume power in Germany? Germany had a long history of autocratic military rule. In 1871, William I of Prussia became emperor of Germany. The militaristic nature of the nation he established was continued by his successor William II. But after the defeat of Germany in World War I, William II abdicated. The unstable Weimar Republic that was established suffered economic chaos and revolts by Communists and Nazis. After an unsuccessful attempt to seize power by Hitler in 1923 and imprisonment, he was appointed Chancellor of Germany in 1933 by

President Hindenburg. However, Hindenburg died in 1934, and Hitler did away with the constitutional political system and assumed supreme power. Hitler became the absolute ruler and saw himself as the messiah who would save Germany. As mentioned, when Hitler invaded Austria, he took the lance of destiny from the Vienna museum, which supposedly was used by a Roman soldier to w ound Jesus. Hitler's assuming the role o f savior was enabled by the German population who felt helpless and humiliated.

The biographical book about Hitler and his family by Helm Stierlin (1976) sheds light on the genesis of how Hitler assumed the role of a messiah who would save Germany. Hitler's mother, Klara, had been brought into the house by Hitler's father, Alois, to care for his first wife who was dying. During that time, Klara had a sexual affair with Alois. After the wife's death, Alois married Klara. However, Klara lost a number of her children, which she considered as punishment by God for committing the sin of adultery. When Adolph was born and survived, she distanced herself from Alois and became overly close to her son. Adolph then sided with his mother and became her "bound delegate" and savior. His father's anger was displaced from his wife on to Hitler. Hitler became the lightening rod of the family, diverting anger away from his mother, and suffered repeated beating from his tyrannical and alcoholic father.

Hitler continued the same identity he had with his mother, but now he became the savior of a helpless Germany against the abuse of a powerful father, now France and England. The ego boundary o f Adolph Hitler was never fully formed between he and his mother and was reflected in his later saying that he was Germany, and Germany was Hitler. He would now rescue Germany from the harsh beating delivered by the allies after World War I. Understanding the personal and family dynamics o f such an evil demagogue does not excuse his destructive actions. The amount of human suffering he inflicted was enormous, with more than fifty million people killed in World War II. The combination of political power and religion again proved to be a toxic mixture.

A beginning effort to resolve conflict and avoid war by mediation has been conducted by Vamik Volkan, who has used his knowledge of psychoanalysis to help prevent the outbreak of violence. Volkan's mediating efforts began following a comment by the former president of Egypt, Anwar Sadat, in 1977. Sadat stated that 70 percent of the problems between Israelis and Arabs were psychological. The American Psychiatric Association sponsored a committee to mediate a dialogue between Egyptians and Israelis. Volkan was in this committee, and he later continued his efforts to understand other international conflicts. These included those in Albania, Estonia, Georgia, Turkey, as well as other counties. Volkan has published books describing his work. These include *Bloodlines: From Ethnic Pride to Ethnic Terrorism* (1997), *Blind Trust: Large Groups and Their Leaders in Times o f Crisis and Terror* (2004), and *Killing in the Name o f Identity: A Study o f Bloody Conflict* (2006).

As mentioned, many people condemn religion as the source of conflict. Yet it is not religion itself that causes conflict. Rather, it is how under chaotic social conditions some politicians have used religion to gain political power. These politicians are demagogues and are able to assume the role of savior, which ultimately can lead to violence against another group. We live in an age of anxiety due to the rapid advances of science, which

has aroused strong opposition to change in many quarters. The tribal nature of society is conflicted with the process of globalization. The very existence of the earth is even threatened. A nuclear winter would follow if an atomic war occurred between nations. Transportation, heating, and energy that use fossil fuels have become a problem in polluting the atmos146 phere and creating global warming. The bottom line is that the discoveries of science need to be used for the benefit of all of humanity and need to be regulated. For this purpose, psychological knowledge can serve as a safeguard to understand leadership and political decisions. The behavioral sciences and the moral values of religion can be employed to mediate political conflict between nations. People can retain their national and religious identities, but they can also embrace the universal interests of all of humanity. Hopefully, some day the United Nations will become less a field of competing national self-interests, so that members can work together to be an effective force for peace and development on our planet. The excellent work of Vamik Volkan to mediate conflict between nations needs to be expanded greatly. Possibly some day national leaders in the United Nations, religious leaders, and the scientific community can work together in a combined effort, respect differences, and focus on the needs of all humanity.

1 1 Biological Adaptation and Cultural Survival

Religion, especially in ancient civilizations, offered an understanding of how nature functioned and people's role in it. Even if their beliefs were not correct by modern scientific standards, it provided a sense security and mastery. Instead of feeling totally helpless and overwhelmed, ancient cultures created anthropomorphic gods, who they believed could be placated by prayer, gifts, or sacrifice. Religion was a form of cultural adaptation to environment that offered hope, courage, and facilitated survival. Adaptation and survival was the central focus of Charles Darwin's research, but it was biological and not cultural. The physical changes in birds and animals that enabled a species to adapt best to their environment were then most fit to survive and reproduce. We now know that Darwin's findings about the different changes in the physical characteristics of the surviving birds and animals that he studied were the result of genetic mutations occurring over a great many generations. With the environment of the earth changing, the question o f adaptation and survival of humans also becomes a central issue. However, we can scientifically study what produces a threat to survival in our environment, and then work out ways to correct these conditions.

Also, human beings are less instinctually driven than animals, and we can influence and change our culture, making us more adaptive to the environment. Humans do not solely rely on the slow process of genetic mutations to adapt. The Nobel award winner Eric Kandel (1983) has been able to experimentally verify that our behavioral responses are not simply driven by our genetic endowment. He found that at a molecular level, genes interact with the environment, which changes their chemical gene expression. It is the interaction of the genetic endowment interacting with what is taken in from the environment that makes human beings especially adaptive. Thus, we are not simply at the mercy of our genes. Also, the brain has been shown to be plastic and changeable in response to its environment. Social interaction has been shown to be essential for brain fitness and beneficial for emotional and physical health. Thus, genes are not destiny, and the culture that we establish can be viewed as essential for human adaptation and survival.

As mentioned, Freud had been a neurophysiologist in Professor Ernst Brucke's laboratory for six years. Brucke admired and strongly influenced

Freud, even securing the scholarship for Freud to visit Charcot in Paris. Charcot was able to relieve hysterical symptoms such as blindness and paralysis through hypnosis. Thus, an environmental input could influence actual physical symptoms. Brucke was a member, along with Hermann Helmholtz, in a group called the Logical Positivists. They believed it was necessary to apply the laws of physics and chemistry to understand human beings. In accord with Brucke's ideas of Logical Positivism, Freud wrote *Project for a Scientific Psychology* (1895), which involved a neuron theory. Because it was severely criticized, Freud hesitated publishing it, yet his later libido theory reflected Logical Positivist thinking.

Freud tried to explain how the individual interacted with the environment, but he focused on the investment of libido, a supposed force, within the individual. He created a one person psychology based on the conservation of energy derived from Newtonian physics. His libido theory considered that the personality was a closed system with a fixed amount o f libidinous energy, which was based on the principle of constancy. According to the first law of thermodynamics, this fixed amount of libido energy could be invested in the self or others. If one area was invested, which he called cathected, with libidinous energy the other area was depleted. He also felt that intracerebral excitation had to remain constant, and that excess energy needed to be liberated through sensory, motor, or ideational activity. If the energy could not be discharged, Freud felt it resulted in a "hypnoid" state and could be diverted and be expressed through physical symptoms. Freud's libido theory attempted to retain a biological basis, and was linear, deterministic, and mechanistic. However, he did recognize that this metapsychology theory was his weakest contribution. Not having the means to study the brain, and unsure of his concepts, he had to focus on the mind. We now have the tools to come up with a more scientific understanding of the functioning of the brain. Despite this limitation, Freud was aware of the importance of child development, even if his focus was intrapsychic. The child internalizes attitudes from the parents and the environment that have a lasting impact on personality development and on neurosis. He recognized that children were not simply small adults, and he tied child development to biology. Freud postulated that the child sequentially went through oral, anal, phallic, and genital phases of development. Here his focus was a one person psychology and did not include the relationship with the mother or the culture. Freud depicted the mother as only an object for oral gratification or of sexual desire and focused on the later Oedipal phase.

As mentioned, a two person psychology was later developed by British psychoanalysts, who were more aware of the impact of the environment and interpersonal relations. Melanie Klein (1948) emphasized the infant's relationship to the mother, which Freud had omitted. Bowlby (1969), Fairbairn (1954), and Winnicott (1965) studied and elaborated on the effect of infant-mother attachment during development.

Freud deduced his hypotheses retrospectively from clinical material obtained from adult patients. However, we now have direct child developmental studies that have validated or refuted some of Freud's theory. In addition, we now know from neuroimaging studies where old traumas from childhood are stored as emotional memory. This is in the limbic part

of the brain, especially the amygdala. These internalized old relationships from childhood and their associated feelings are displaced onto current relationships without conscious awareness. This provides empirical evidence for Freud's theory of the unconscious influence of childhood emotional trauma expressed by the adult and projected onto others.

These old emotional memories from childhood color and shape our perception and reasoning as adults. In the process of psychoanalysis, these childhood relationships are also projected onto the analyst in what is called the transference. When the transference is interpreted and recognized consciously, the patients then can rationally work through their old emotionally driven memories. Then, as Freud stated, ego will be in place of id. This can be explained neurologically. The prefrontal cortex can restrain the unconscious effects of old memories stored in the amygdala. They can then see others not by the unconscious emotional distortions that are automatically projected, but they can differentiate and recognize others more realistically. In addition, the patient then can recognize the connection of how their behavior affected others, and not view the world solely from an egocentric position.

Winnicott (1965) noted that the mother was also intimately involved and not only the child in their relationship. He found a mutually interactive relationship between mother and infant. She showed a "primary maternal preoccupation" according to Winnicott, and attachment was facilitated by visual mirroring. This was characterized by an intense m u tu al gaze between the mother and infant. Winnicott commented that the mother-infant relationship only needed to be "good enough," not perfect. This provided a safe holding environment and security for the infant.

Stern (1985) and Emde (1987), based on direct infant observation, further elaborated on the pre-verbal dyadic attunement between the mother and infant. This mother-child relationship then becomes internalized in the infant's mind. This attunement of infant and mother, as if they are one, persists into adulthood. The tachistoscopic research of this area we performed is described in the appendix.

Now, we are not limited to retrospective clinical material or direct observational studies of child development, since neuroimaging can demonstrate the areas of the brain that are involved. The human adaptive process develops sequentially in several ways during infancy. Both of these ways are related to the interaction of the brain and the environment. Clinically, Freud recognized that the first foundation of the child's personality occurred during the first three years of life. However, he focused more on the infant's instinctual gratification and did not give sufficient import to the mutual relationship with the mother. We now know the brain is plastic and constantly changing in response to its environment, and thus the culture is extremely important to understand adaptation and survival. Essentially, biological endowment, intrapsychic dynamics, as well as interpersonal family and culture interact and are all important in understanding human behavior, health, and survival.

Besides advances in genetics and biology, neuroscience can now provide knowledge about the functioning of the brain. We know from clinical experience that the talking cure in psychotherapy and psychoanalysis helps treat psychiatric disorders. However, as mentioned, there is now empirical evidence that the talking cure actually changes brain circuitry.

Glenn Gabbard reported at the 2001 meeting of the American Psychiatric Association that neuroimaging studies of patients suffering obsessive compulsive disorder who received either psychotherapy or fluoxetine

medication actually showed changes in the brain with either approach.
There was decreased metabolism in the right caudate nucleus, which is
responsible for memory and emotion.

Gabbard also mentioned a study in Finland conducted with patients
suffering borderline personality disorder. On neuroimaging, it was found
that there was a low uptake of the neural transmitter serotonin in the
medial prefrontal area and the thalamus, which are responsible for judgment,
planning, and reasoning. After a year of psychotherapy the patients
were clinically improved and the uptake of serotonin was found to be n o rmal.
In the control group there was neither clinical improvement nor
changes in the brain.

We now know from neuroimaging that the mutual attunement of the
mother-infant relationship is essential for emotional awareness of self and
others and is the basis for attachment (Schore 2003). This attachment
develops because the right orbitofrontal cortex and the subcortical limbic
system of the infant's brain are dominant for the first three years of life.
The intense mutual gaze between the mother and infant, which is synchronous,
regulates the emotional communication between both of them.

The right orbitofrontal-limbic system becomes myelinated between
seven and fifteen months and is completed by two years of age. The limbic
system, the so-called reptilian brain or fear center, includes an almond
shaped structure, the amygdala, which is involved in rapid automatic
emotional response. It is a rough and ready emergency system that operates
instantly and is out of conscious awareness. The amygdala insures
survival against danger, and its perception can be more refined by the
frontal lobe (LeDoux 1996). For example, one may immediately be startled
by what appears to be a snake, but on further observation it may turn
out simply to be a stick. The amygdala also stores emotional memories.
Attachment involves the anterior cingulate part o f the limbic system and
the right temporal cortex of the brain. Environmental experiences are
internalized here, which facilitates the social and emotional development
of the child. These memories are carried onto later adult life and influence
relationships. Allan Schore (2003) comments that as a consequence of
normal attachment, the mother and infant's homeostatic systems resonate
together in synchrony to form a feedback system. The infant's right brain
that is involved eventually enables the infant to self-regulate. This emotional
attunement between mother and infant is internalized and enables
the infant to self organize its emotional experiences.

This early synchrony between mother and infant had been noted clinically
by Margaret Mahler (1975), which she called the symbiotic phase of
development. Clinically, when the attunement between mother and infant
is not synchronized, the child as an adult later suffers from a condition
called alexithymia. In this condition there is a lack of awareness of its own
and others feelings, a focus on concrete events or bodily symptoms, as well
as a paucity of dreams and fantasies.

Recent brain research has also revealed that neurobiologically there is
a cellular basis for empathy, attachment, and socialization with the environment.
(This was reported in the Science section of the *New York Times*

on January 10, 2006.) Giacomo Rizzolatti, a neuroscientist at the
University of Parma, Italy, noted that certain brain cells fired when a mo n key
watched others put food in their mouths. The same cells fired when

the monkey brought food into its own mouth. He labeled these special class of cells, mirror cells. On examination, humans were also discovered to have these mirror cells, which were smarter, more flexible, and more evolved than in monkeys. These more complex cells are different from ordinary brain cells, and they are located in the premotor cortex, the posterior parietal lobe, the superior temporal sulcus, and the insula. The mirror cells enable people to understand the actions of others, their intentions, social meaning, and emotions. In small children, these cells facilitated socialization through observation and imitation.

Dr. Christian Keysers at the University o f Groningen in the Netherlands also found that the mirror cells enabled an individual to share emotions; thus, these cells were involved in empathy. Dr. Keysers noted that people who ranked high on a scale of empathy had more active mirror neuron systems on brain scans. Social emotions such as guilt, shame, pride, disgust, and pain of rejection were found in the mirror cells of the insula. Thus people are hard wired to become socially and emotionally understanding of others, enabling the establishment o f communities. These are survival mechanisms that have been genetically hard wired into individuals. However, their activation is also determined by the quality of interpersonal relations with the mother.

In summary, the limbic system and the right hemisphere are the predominant areas of brain that function during the first three years of life.

It is the beginning of attachment, socialization, and relating to others, which is pleasurable and essential for survival. The preoedipal synchrony between the mother and infant is encoded in the right cortex and limbic system, and this activity is termed implicit (or nondeclarative) memory. This memory is distinct from the explicit (or declarative) memory recorded in the left cerebral cortex, which evolves after three years of age. The left cerebral cortex is involved with language, sequencing, and cognition. It is interesting that Freud from clinical material was able to appreciate that from birth to three years of age the preoedipal development was crucial in child development. The importance of this early period has now been acknowledged empirically. Other parts of the brain, the basal ganglia and cerebellum, are involved in recording memories of skills and habits, which also functions unconsciously.

When Freud called religious ritual an obsessional neurosis, it was too simplistic and individualistic. He compared the repetitious movements of people performing religious rituals to individuals suffering obsessional neurosis. But there are distinct differences between obsessional neurosis and religious rituals. In obsessional neurosis a single person is compelled to perform repetitious actions, such as repeated hand washing. This is done automatically and without any sense o f control. However in religious rituals the repetitious actions are voluntary, also performed together in a group, and are part of a cultural setting. Freud did acknowledge that religion helped to form and perpetuate communities, but he did not understand that it was the religious rituals that facilitated group cohesion, enabling people to feel as if they were one.

As mentioned, one of the first person to investigate and to understand

the social role of rituals was Susan Langer, In her book, *Philosophy in a New Key* (1942), she made the point that people respond on two levels of functioning. One was rational, using language and reason, and the other was emotional, responding to images, metaphors, and rituals. On an emotional level for example, babies are soothed by lullabies and rhythmic rocking. As adults, music and rhythm can influence people to sing, tap, or move in synchrony. Langer noted that in response to different types of music, people can experience different emotions. They can feel sad, devotional, stirred, or happy. Music also can influence group cohesion and facilitate group action. For example, martial music can inflame patriotism and a fighting spirits in a group of soldiers marching together. Essentially, rituals foster a sense of group belonging when people simultaneous speak, sing, or act together in synchrony. Even the content of the repetitious prayers may not be understood, but the shared rhythm of people performing them together facilitates group cohesion.

Oliver Sacks (at the American Psychiatric Association National Convention in 2008) presented his finding that music is registered in the sensory, emotional, and motor areas of the brain, which explains the power of music to influence feelings, behavior, and actions. In addition, mothers usually hold their baby's head over their left breast, where the baby can hear the rhythmic heartbeat. Interestingly, American Indians consider their drum beating to be the heartbeat of their nation and of the earth, and this act is significant in their rituals.

I have proposed that the synchronous actions o f individuals performing together in dance, singing, sports, and religious rituals are the adult manifestations of the pre-oedipal synchrony that initially produced attachment of the infant to the mother. The mother's attunement to the infant's verbal, visual, and physical cues facilitated merging, as if they were one person. This synchrony becomes encoded in the right brain and limbic system of the infant, and serves as the template for later connections as an adult. This is a neurological explanation for the observations of Susan Langer concerning the importance of synchronous singing, talking, or moving together.

As mentioned, the right brain is involved during the first three years o f life when attachment occurs. I hypothesized that the attunement established at that time between mother and infant is replicated between adults to foster attachment when they behave in synchrony. The religious rituals o f communal prayer, singing, moving, and eating together establishes a secure emotional attachment that bonds people in a group together as if one. This may have been instinctively perceived by Jesus, when he substituted the communal meal for individual baptismal immersion. Thus, religious rituals are not as Freud stated a form o f obsessional neurosis because of their repetitious nature. The repetitious synchrony of gaze, movement, and sound between infant and mother insured survival. Similarly, the synchronous rituals between people provides the security to help attachment and form a shared group identity. On an individual level, more intimate or loving connection between two adults is also manifested by their mutual gaze, as they look deeply into each other's eyes. Thus, Freud's ideas about the importance of early child development and its influence on adult behavior can be extended further than he thought. In summary, I hypothesized that the synchronous movement between adults is a repetition o f the early attachment of mother and infant to provide a

sense of safety in the culture.

Activating the maternal attunement of oneness between the self and mother can be achieved experimentally in the laboratory. Through the use of an instrument called a tachistoscope, subliminal image and verbal messages can be simultaneously flashed so fast as to be out of conscious awareness. Neuroimaging studies of the brain have shown that this subliminal stimulation directly activates the limbic system, especially the amygdala (Rauch et al 1996). Based on the clinical work of Mahler, who noted this symbiosis between mother and infant, Silverman (1971) and others found that the subliminal message o f "Mommy and I are One" had beneficial effects in a number of neurotic and behavioral problems. This subliminal message of "Mommy and 1 are One" taps into the original synchronous relationship of oneness that was established between mother and infant (Slipp 2000). This synchronized relationship with the mother becomes permanently internalized in the child, but it is not fixed in the brain and can be influenced by outside events. In the studies my staff and I performed, this subliminal maternal merging message was only effective when the relationship of the mother and the child was originally or is currently attuned. Thus, we realized that this synchronized internalization of self with the mother can change and is not fixed. We considered that it can change following a corrective emotional experience, or after psychotherapy. The relationship between the parent and child needed to be appropriate to the child's needs and not simply used for the mother's narcissistic needs. When there was a discrepancy between their needs and a lack of attunement, this subliminal message did not work beneficially. As mentioned, several of my experimental studies are described in the appendix.

The brain is hard wired to become attached to others empathically through the right cortex, as well as later through learning cultural information via the left cortex. Religion has played an important role, involving both the right and left cortex. From the subcortical right brain, amygdala, and basal ganglia, rituals facilitate attachment and help becoming part of a community. During a life span, rituals also have strong emotional significance, marking the major life stages, such as birth, initiating adulthood, marriage, achievements, and death. Socially and emotionally, rituals serve to provide group support and dignity for the individual traversing these landmarks of life. It also can stir a m artial spirit among soldiers to help achieve military victory if war occurs.

On the rational left brain level, all religions instill ethical values, essentially teaching the golden rule that facilitates trusting interpersonal and social relations.

As Rabbi Hillel stated the essence of his religion is, "W hat is hateful to you do not do unto your fellow man: that is the whole Law, the rest is commentary." This golden rule restrains the egocentric orientation that was originally essential for survival of the infant and is taught by the culture. Treating others as one would want to be treated fosters group affiliation by establishing trusting social relationships. The chances for survival on this earth are enhanced by embracing and being embraced by the

156 *The Quest for Power*

family, tribe, one's ethnic and religious group, and hopefully someday by all of humanity working together.

What more specifically have we found out about the neurological process of attachment? Darwin's work, *The Expression o f the Emotion in*

Man and Animals, reported that facial expressions of emotions are inborn in humans and are universal. Facial expressions are not learned from the culture. This would make sense, since all infants gaze at the face of their mothers, especially their eyes, during the process o f attachment. The infant's imprinting of the mother's face, whether it is loving or fearful, influences the infant's self-regulation. One of the few areas of the brain specifically hard wired and devoted to faces was found by Kanwisher (2004) on neuroimaging studies to be in the right fusiform gyrus. Damage to this area resulted in an inability to recognize the self or others. Thus, adaptation to the environment is hard wired in the brain.

The fact that face recognition is hard wired in the brain and that facial expressions of emotions are universal was used in subliminal stimulation studies. Breiter et al (1996) noted the amygdala lighted up on neuroimaging studies when subjects were exposed to a rapid exposure of fearful or happy faces, but not to neutral faces. However, Whalen et al (1998) also noted that subliminal stimulation exposure of fearful faces caused a signal increase in the amygdala, while happy faces caused a decreased signal in the amygdala. If the fearful face proved inconsequential, habituation occurred, but the happy face response persisted, indicating a condition of safety. The emotional network in the brain is thought by others to be more extensive. For example, the anterior cingulate gyrus is involved in attachment and separation anxiety. Damasio (2003) also includes the somatosensory cortex and Panksepp (1999) the periaqueductal gray and ventral tegmental area.

Gabbard (2004) noted that early childhood trauma may adversely affect the integration of the right and left cortical hemispheres. Abused children use the left hemisphere when thinking of neutral memories and use the right hemisphere for frightening memories. In normally developed children, he found both hemispheres are used regardless of the content of the memory. Gabbard stated that failure to integrate the hemispheres is found in patients with borderline personality disorder, which he considers may reflect the borderline patient's use of the defense of splitting into all good or all bad. People with insecure attachment he also found have difficulty in reading another's face and knowing what another is feeling. There also seems to be an intergenerational transmission of care giving that affects mental functioning. When the caregiver is insecure, it can also be passed on to the infant and then to later generations.

Schore (2003) noted that stress due to unattuned attachment may first produce hyperarousal, activating the sympathetic nervous system and an increase in the release of adrenalin, dopamine, catecholamines, and the excitatory neurotransmitter glutamate. With chronic stress, there may also be a release of opiates and cortisol. Under this latter circumstance, damage to neurons in the right orbitofrontal-limbic system and hippocampus may occur. Main (1996) found that insecure attachment in infancy continues to make adult individuals less able to recover after loss of an attachment and often precipitates psychopathology. Thus, we are now able to start developing a map of the brain to understand the functioning of the mind. This ability to integrate the mind and the brain had been Freud's greatest hope and is now being fulfilled.

Freud had noted that emotions in the unconscious had a great impact on the conscious. Besides Freud, Schopenhauer and Nietzsche as well

challenged the primacy o f rationality th at had existed since the Enlightenment. Freud noted that the unconscious played a powerful role in rational thinking. Modern neuroimaging of the brain seems to be able to validate or refute some of Freud's clinical observations. We also have become aware of the importance of nonlexical communication, such as facial expression, voice tone, body tension, etc., in relationships.

Under normal circumstances, a complementary interaction exists between the right cortex and left cortex of the brain. They create a dialectic between emotions/attachment and reason/autonomy as well as between nonlexical and verbal content o f spoken communication. However, interpersonal and cultural input can strongly tip the balance. For example, death of a loved one can precipitate severe emotional or physical problems. On the cultural level, when an individual is overwhelmed by circumstances in society and survival is threatened, the right orbitofrontal and limbic system of the brain may take over and serve as a rough and ready emergency survival system. People then may respond emotionally as a mob, overshadowing their rational left brain and behave immorally as barbarians. Religion, on the other hand, may provide hope and act as an antidote.

In summary, subcortical dominance of the reptilian brain seems to occur when a group of individuals feels powerless and cannot reasonably cope with external circumstances in their society. The group members may resort to the basic assumption group of pairing, as described by the British psychoanalyst Wilfred Bion. This results in a shared group fantasy of being rescued by a messiah. Groups of people can revert to a more primitive emotional state that is alien to their normal rational self. This involves magical wishful thinking and is an effort at dispelling despair and facilitating survival. However, during this process group boundaries are reinforced, and they can see themselves as good and other groups as bad. Under normal environmental circumstances, the universality of facial expressions is significant in close individual relations, since one can sense the emotional state of the other. However, when people's survival is threatened by a chaotic environment, they may become blind to individuals in the other group and only see them in terms of negative emotional group stereotypes. The group can then behave like an animal or a mob, and commit violence against other groups that they would not do ordinarily as moral individuals. This provides further information to explanation of the work of LeBon and Freud on mass group psychology.

The Zionist movement faced the reality that the dispersion of Jews in the Diaspora by the Romans made Jews powerless and vulnerable to persecution. Dispersion was the Roman vengeance against the Jews for daring to rebel several times against them. Jews became the minority outside group and was subjected to persecution by the majority Christian group. Under stress Christian individuals regressed and tended to coalesce into an unreasonable mass group. Jews became the traditional scapegoats, since they existed in small scattered settlements and did not have the power to fight back. Theodore Herzl recognized during the Dreyfus trial in France that assimilation was not the answer, since all of Europe became more and more nationalistic and antagonistic to those having another heritage. The unjust trial and conviction of Captain Dreyfus in France was

an eye opener to Herzl of the pervasive anti-Semitism that existed in Europe. He concluded that Jews had to rescue themselves by their own actions. Jews needed to reestablish a Jewish national state in Palestine, where they would be a majority and have power to defend themselves. This conclusion was based on reason, since the Zionists recognized that they needed to return to their biblical homeland. There they could again reestablish a government and a military force for self-defense. On an emotional level, however, the Zionists were opposed by the Jewish Bundists, who wished to stay and fight back, and by the fundamentalist Orthodox Jews who wanted to wait for the Messiah. The Zionists did reestablish a homeland in Palestine, despite these objections. The Zionists revived the use of the ancient Hebrew language, which had been used prior to Jewish dispersal by the Romans. The homeland was called Israel, which became a nation in 1948, when the United Nations voted it into existence. In Israel, Jews again became a strong nation, developed a democratic government, a modern army, and economic independence. They would no longer be the helpless scapegoat to preserve another group's illusion of power.

We still live in a rather primitive tribal world where often compassion and tolerance is not extended to other individuals or groups. There are ethnic, religious, and national episodes of genocide in Africa, the Middle East, and in Asia. It is a difficult task, but the golden rule needs to become universal, so that compassion for human beings is not limited to one's own group. Pope John Paul II made strides in this direction by emphasizing the brotherhood of humaniy. Rome established ecumenical meetings to help integrate the world's religions. The efforts to create political dialogue between conflicted groups instead of war and violence is a giant step forward to creating world peace.

1 2 Power from the Bottom Up or from the Top Down

Both Sigmund Freud and Karl Marx (1818-1883) repudiated the combination of religion and politics that had been said to dominate individuals. Freud considered religion to be an illusion, while Marx saw religion as an opiate used to continue the exploitation of the workers, the proletariat. Although their methods were different, both of their aims were to empower people. Freud hoped to change society from the bottom up through the individual, while Marx advocated change from the top down, to topple the powerful bosses through group action. Freud tried to heal individual patients, which would gradually spread upward into society. Karl Marx, the father of Communism, advocated social class revolution, which he hoped would equalize the structure of society.

Marx was born of Jewish parents in Treves, Prussia, a part of Germany. He was baptized as a Protestant at six years of age, when his parents converted. As a Christian he was able to be educated at the University of Bonn, and he received his Ph.D. in philosophy from the University of Berlin in 1841. He moved to Paris in 1843, where he met Friedrich Engels, and they became lifelong close friends. Moving to Brussels, they published the *Communist Manifesto.* Their philosophy was based on dialectical materialism, which was derived from Hegel. Hegel postulated that there was a basic interconnection of opposing elements or forces (thesis and antithesis) that synthesized into something new. Hegel also considered the state more important then the individual.

After moving to London, Marx published *Das Kapital,* which recognized and focused on the existence of a class struggle between the poor and rich groups. He observed that the workers, including children, were exploited by the English factory owners. The workers labored in factories and mills during the industrial revolution. He wrote that the working class, the proletariat, were like slaves without rights. He commented that the proletariat received little pay compensation for their labor and lived marginally from a hand to mouth existence. On the other hand he noted that the owners of the factories and mills, the capitalists, greatly profited from the workers' labor. Essentially, the capitalists had replaced the powerful nobility when the industrial revolution developed after the

Enlightenment. The same hierarchical class structure had persisted from the feudal society. He noted that the poor were still exploited and remained powerless victims under the heel of the new bourgeois ruling class that had evolved.

Marx proposed that a class war was necessary to overthrow capitalism, since the capitalists would not give up their power voluntarily. Change would not occur peacefully in this rigid class system but could only occur through force. He advocated revolution, since the workers had nothing to lose but their chains. After the class war, he thought the poor would achieve power, a classless society would evolve, and the lives of the formerly poor would improve. According to this rational ideology, he predicted that capitalism would decay everywhere and a dictatorship of the proletariat in a Communist society would evolve throughout the world. To accomplish this revolution, Marx condemned and sought to eliminate all religions as an obstacle to change . He commented that religions perpetuated capitalism, by its forming an alliance with the capitalists who were now in power. This was not dissimilar to the alliance previously of religion with the nobility to maintain their power and to exploit the serfs. Although this was not the obvious goal of Marx, by eliminating all religions, anti-Semitism might no longer exist. Marx called religion the opiate of the people, which he felt provided a false rationale to cover up the pain and suffering inflicted by the capitalist system. Religion he felt made the poor endure their victimization, as well as perpetuated the power of the ruling class. He stated that religion promised that a miserable life on earth would be rewarded after death by a good afterlife in heaven. Marx commented that religion thus perpetuated passivity of the working class and stood in the way of class revolution. He wrote that capitalists would not give up power voluntarily, and that only by class revolution could the poor achieve power.

However, despite having been converted to Christianity as a child, Marx unknowingly followed the Jewish responsibility o f trying to improve the world; the Hebrew phrase for it is *tikkun olam.* He was also like Jesus, in being concerned for the welfare of the poor and wretched of the earth. Jesus stated that the poor would inherit the earth, but for Jesus it would be achieved through religion and not by revolution. Marx was opposed to institutionalized religion, which promised a utopia in heaven for the poor after they died. But Marx stated that the poor did not have to die to enjoy a better life. Marx promised a utopia on earth for the poor, and that after the revolution they would have power and their lives would improve. Using Hegelian dialectic, he assumed a new egalitarian society would evolve after the clashing of the opposing social classes. But this solution of Marx for change was ideological, and limited to politics and economic determinism.

Marx thought in group terms and hoped that the class revolution would trickle from the top down to the individual. Rationally he thought getting rid of the capitalists was the answer. His theory was intellectually idealistic, but it basically was flawed, since it failed to recognize the emotional factors of individuals. He did not account for the personal grab for power by the leaders of the revolution. Marx developed his theory in England, which had gone through the industrial revolution and had gained a parliamentary democracy, where power was more distributed.

But the revolution started in Russia, which had not gone through the industrial revolution and was still a feudal society and under the autocratic rule of a Tsar. There was very little middle class to speak of in Russia. Practically all the population were peasants who were illiterate and tribal.

Like other illiterate societies, they continued to uncritically internalize
and accept the authoritarian power structure that evolved after the revolution.
The Tsar was replaced by the leaders of the revolution.

After the Soviet revolution in 1917, a new power elite came into
being, but they failed to share power with the people or improve conditions
for the serfs. The poor expected to be protected by a powerful ruling
class as had previously existed, and they accepted a centralized
authority. However, after the revolution the condition of the serfs was
made even worse than had existed during the monarchy. Large numbers
o f Kulaks, wealthy peasant farmers, and others died of starvation, were
killed, or sent off to Gulag prisons in Siberia. Also many of the original
revolutionary leaders were killed. This included Leon Trotsky, the chief
lieutenant of Lenin and former head of the Red Army. Trotsky was exiled
and later assassinated in Mexico. These killings were similar to the "terror"
of the French revolution, which also saw many o f its own revolutionary
leaders killed in addition to the nobility. The Tsar and his entire family
were shot and killed just as the French king, Louis XVI, and his wife
were guillotined.

Joseph Stalin set himself up as a messianic leader and changed his
name from Joseph Vissarionovich (also called Dzhugashvili) to Stalin,
meaning "man of steel." His new name proclaimed his absolute power, as
he became the head of a secular religion. Changing his name may also have
been due to his effort to dissociate himself from his father. Like Hitler,
Stalin had been a helpless victim of abuse during his childhood, also suffering
repeated beatings from his brutal alcoholic father. Organized religion
was repressed, while Stalin was worshiped like a savior who would
protect the populace and establish a utopian society. As the autocratic
head, Stalin formed a powerful central elite and set up a totalitarian state.
All the means of production, all personal property, farms, and transportation
were not owned by the serfs but by the central government.

The ultimate objective of the philosophy of Marx, to empower the
poor, did not materialize in the Soviet Union. Power did not flow from the
top down to the serfs and workers. Instead, the lives of the poor were not
made sweeter; their lives were made more bitter. Also Jewish anti-
Semitism, which had been promulgated in the time o f the tsars, continued
to remain as virulent, despite the suppression of all religions. Top down
change resulted in a totalitarian society, power remained in an elite class,
and anger again was drained off by institutionalizing divisiveness. The
frustration and anger of the people resulted in scapegoating the Jews, dissidents,
and other nations. Like the authoritarian society under the tsars,
political dissenters were imprisoned, executed, or sent off to Gulag prisons
in Siberia.

Jesus, Freud, and Marx all strongly impacted society, and they
have been the objects o f considerable controversy. However, there are
distinct differences that differentiate and separate Jesus and Freud
from Marx. Jesus and Freud were humanistic leaders, who were not
involved in politics. They were healers, trying to relieve the emotional

suffering and oppression o f individuals directly. Marx had an in te llectual
theory, based on the philosopher Hegel, for improving the life
o f the poor that was group-class oriented and political. He advocated
a military revolution, in which bo th the existing religious and p o litical
authorities would be destroyed and a classless society could evolve.

The group ideology employed by Marx did n o t look at the in d iv id u als involved in the revolution. To Marx, the ends justified the means. This meant that to achieve the uto p ian goal for the pro leta rian society, individuals might have to suffer and be sacrificed for the revolution. Unfortunately, the means instead became the end, and b ru tality was institutionalized.

In summary, Marx's solution was based on an ideology that was top down and deductive. He advocated a revolutionary group movement, which he thought would allow power to trickle down to the individual serfs. Due to the Soviet leaders' hunger for power, a new ruling elite arose, supported by a secular religion. The leaders of the Russian revolution did not relinquish their power, and they did not empower the serfs. They evolved a secular religion with Stalin and his image worshiped as a messiah having absolute power. Both Jesus and Freud used a bottom up, inductive approach. They empathically tried to improve and enrich the lives of each individual, which they hoped would extend upward and outward to encompass society. Their empowering individuals directly was similar to democratic ideals.

The ideology of Marxism failed, partly because Russia was still feudal and had not gone through the industrial revolution and created an educated middle class. But more significantly the poor were illiterate. They enabled or were intimidated to support a powerful political au th o rity. As the Russian novelist Dostoyevsky noted, people preferred security to freedom. Those that sought freedom could be intimidated and arrested by the secret police. The revolution did not take into account emotional motivations of the revolutionary leaders, their self-interest, and their hunger for power.

The utopian ideals of Marx were highjacked by the leaders of the revolution. As a result, Communism left a history of profound human misery and death for the serfs and workers. Like the banned church and the tsars, Communism demanded conformity and stifled creativity in the arts and science. Marx had predicted that capitalism would self-destruct and fail. However, Communism and not capitalism failed, being abandoned in recent years. In contrast, the humanistic contributions of Jesus and Freud have continued to have a positive worldwide effect that has continued to benefit all human beings.

As mentioned, several current writers have also been antireligious and have suggested a utopian ideology in some ways similar to Marx. They advocated a return to the rational thinking o f the Enlightenment, but, unlike Marx, they focused on the individual and not on a social group revolution. Hitchens recounted many incidents of inhumanity and violence associated with religion throughout history, and he presented a thesis that eliminating religion would be the cure all. Hitchens mentions that the Catholic church, under Pope Pius XII, capitulated to the Fascists and Nazis. However, Hitchens does not explore the underlying political motivation for this move. The motivation for this capitulation was probably driven by fear and was done to protect the survival of the Vatican in

Rome. The Nazis could easily have eliminated the Roman Catholic church, since the Nazis revived the ancient Aryan religion with Hitler as its messiah. Apparently Pope Pius XII did secretly help many Jews, although many claim this was not enough. The extent of his help will not be known until his papers are revealed.

Catholic priests and Lutheran pastors, such as Dietrich Bonhoeffer, who were anti-Nazi, were imprisoned and killed. In addition, many Catholic schools and orphanages hid Jewish children, which saved their lives. There are a number of these hidden Jewish children who tell o f the care and kindness they received during the war. Some Protestant and Catholic individuals courageously helped Jewish adults escape at the risk o f their own lives if they were caught. Pope John Paul II was anti-Nazi during World War II, and later helped emancipate Poland from the totalitarian grip of Communism. Thus, many religious individuals sought to protect the freedom and lives of the Jews.

Hitchens makes the statement that human decency is innate and is not derived from religious ethics. His self-righteous statement does not make it true, since innate morality may result from religious ethics being integrated into society. Hitchens is also critical of the Jewish community in Holland that excommunicated the famous philosopher Benedict Spinoza. Spinoza's writings questioned the existence of an anthropomorphic God who was concerned about people's daily lives, and he denied an afterlife. Most of the Jews in Holland had recently escaped from the Inquisition in Spain and Portugal and were insecure about their safe haven. They did not wish to offend the Christian community that had offered them refuge. Hitchens would have done better listening to the Jewish sage Hillel, who said do not condemn, you do not know what you would do in their place.

Being critical of all religions, Hitchens advocates a renewal of the Enlightenment as the answer. Despite elevating reason in the Enlightenment, the collective emotional memory o f anti-Semitism preached by the Church persisted, as exemplified in the writings of Voltaire. Despite the revolt against the church and the nobility in the French revolution, anti-Semitism remained rampant in France. This was demonstrated in the Dreyfus affair, when the crowd shouted, "Kill the Jews." The elevation of reason and science was an important advance, but preexisting emotional factors continued to influence behavior. But even more devastating was the historical antagonism between enlightened nations that persisted. Many European wars occurred, in which more people were killed because of scientific advances in weaponry. It is the interaction of a number of factors that is important and not simply blaming one issue. It is inaccurate to polarize reason as good and religion as bad, which is like the religious persecution of groups seen as bad.

Hitchens does not acknowledge that it is the interaction of reason and emotion as well as the joining of religion and politics that contributed to a history of injustice and violence. Anti-Semitism was p romulgated by the church and nobility, since this divisiveness displaced aggression and protected their political power. It is not religion alone that is at fault, and it is not reason alone that is the answer. It is not a simple linear cause and effect, but the interaction of emotions and reason, and it is the use of religion for political power that needs to be recognized as

the cause of violence.

As mentioned, it was the Roman emperor Constantine who initiated the divine right of kings to rule, and kings used religion to claim absolute power. The church and the nobility both benefitted from this alliance up until the Enlightenment. The Enlightenment brought an end to this powerful alliance of the nobility and the church, but it did not change the collective emotional memory that resulted in violence as Volkan noted.

The other antireligious writer, Dawkins (2006), also recounts the great many incidents of inhumanity in history that are associated with religion. However, he also only blames religion and does not elaborate on its misuse when religion is joined with politics. His simple solution is to eliminate religion and all will be well. He is like a reverse Dr. Pangloss from Voltaire's novel *Candide.* Pangloss justified violence by idealizing religion. Dawkins idealizes atheism and implies that this will be the best of all possible worlds because of rationality.

As mentioned, Dawkins claims religion holds no monopoly on moral values but that there is a "zeitgeist" that makes society moral. This "Zeitgeist" is not a scientific fact but an absolute ideological belief. Herbert Spencer's Social Darwinism is similar to the belief used by Dawkins about a progressive improvement in society. This is inaccurate, since Darwin did not apply it to society. Darwin only noted that those physical changes in a species that facilitated biological adaptation to the environment enabled survival. Social Darwinism has been widely disputed as totally unscientific and a misuse of Darwinian theory.

The hypothesis of an innate social morality, a "zeitgeist," is also contradicted by the psychological research of Milgram (1974). Milgram showed that 65 percent of people conform to the power of authority, even though their actions might inflict damage to another human being. In Milgram's experiment, each subject was instructed to shock a learner (an actor who was not actually shocked) with progressively increasing voltage every time the learner gave an incorrect answer. The subjects proceeded to shock the learners to the maximum listed as 450 volts, even though this voltage was clearly labeled as very dangerous to life. This experiment confirmed Nietzsche's observations about conformity, a herd mentality, of people so as not to be an outsider. Where was this innate morality, a "Zeitgeist," when subjects conformed to authority even when they m ight inflict life threatening damage to another person. Morality gave way to conformity to the group.

Dawkins's claim for a "zeitgeist," a progressive improvement in society, is much like the generalized utopian ideas of Marx, who believed that capitalism would self-destruct and that an ideal Communist state would evolve. This progression did not occur, and in addition there are static cultures existing today that still maintain the brutal values that existed in biblical times. People are still being stoned to death, hands are being cut off for crimes, and violence between tribes continues. Progress in moral values in society is not universal. Another example is the postsecular movement of wishing to return to a theocratic society. This is demonstrated by religious fundamentalists and radical Islamists. In addition, even people who experience a threat to their survival may regress to a basic assumption group and look to a messiah to save them. When this occurs they

behave like amoral barbarians and can commit violence against others. As mentioned, this occurred in a highly advanced country like Germany, which descended into unspeakable brutality. Hitler became the messiah, who promised to create a utopian Nazi third Reich on earth that was to last 1,000 years.

To emphasize a point made earlier, Dawkins claims he does not rely on philosophy or social theory alone, but claims there is "scientific" proof for an innate altruism that is independent of religion. He proposes that altruism is genetic and innately makes people moral. Although Dawkins acknowledges that there is probably no single gene but a combination, he then proceeds to label a single gene as responsible for morality. He mentions a so-called selfish gene that enables survival of the individual. Then he speculates about the existence of a gene for kin altruism, that is responsible for the care of children and one's group. In addition, he considers a reciprocal altruistic gene, where a profitable symbiotic relationship can exist between different species. But as mentioned, we are not at the mercy o f our genes, since genes interact with the environment. Finally Dawkins states that morality can be transmitted through language. This is an exam-

pie of simple determinism and linear thinking that does not hold up under psychological, developmental, and neurobiological research. People's moral decisions are often influenced by the immediate situation (Appiah 2007). In addition, on a biological level en v iro n mental learning triggers gene expression o f different proteins that determine behavior (Kandel 1983). Genes alone do n ot determine social-emotional development. Instead it is the neurobiological in te raction with the mo th er and the environment th a t facilitates social and emotional development.

Genes are responsible for a number of factors, which are both positive and negative. These include intelligence, bodily characteristics, talents in music, mathematics, science, and art. But genes also increase susceptibility to certain diseases such as amyotrophic lateral sclerosis, cancer, diabetes, fibrocystic disease of the lungs, mental illnesses, developmental abnormalities, etc. The one genetic factor that is important is the need to make an attachment to a mothering figure. To facilitate attachment o f the infant, women are genetically m ore sensitive to emotions, eye contact, and social interaction. However, many genes need to be triggered by the environment to turn them on. This has been discovered to be the case in early child development. There are critical periods before four years of age, where interaction with the environment is essential. However, later in life genes interact with the environment to facilitate adaptation and survival. Another area not covered by Dawkins or Hitchens is ethology, which further illustrates the interaction of genes with the environment. Konrad Lorenz noted that geese imprinted with the first moving object they see in the first twenty-four hours after being hatched. This was usually the mother, but could be a human being. When Lorenz placed himself before these newly hatched geese, they imprinted on him. Then they followed him around and also were later sexually attracted to him. Neurological imprinting made the geese more adaptive to their environment, since if their mother died in childbirth, they could attach to another female goose for mothering.

For his discovery o f imprinting, Lorenz received the Nobel Prize in 1973. Dawkins has ignored the work o f ethologists. Another example that altruistic socialization is not innate is the discovery of feral children, who raised themselves in the wilderness. They remained primitive

and asocial. Further evidence shows that disturbed attachment and
social learning occurs during child development when mothering is not
good enough. As mentioned, u nattuned mothering can create later emotional
problems, such as alexithymia. Here individuals are unaware of
their own and others emotions. Dawkins does not recognize that in teraction
with the environment is crucial, which includes the moral values
o f religion in the culture.

There are biologically built-in factors that facilitate socialization, but
they are influenced by social learning. People are born temperamentally
different, and thus they may react differently to social experiences, but
these differences are not major. Dawkins then attempts to invalidate the
importance of social learning. He points to a psychological experiment by
Hauser that exposed atheists and religious people to a dilemma, but they
both had the same results. However, religious ethical values are so integrated
into the environment that no matter whether one is an atheist or a
believer the results would be the same. There was no valid control group,
such as people from different cultures with different values.

Several scientific studies with animals show the strength of the
impact of society. Monkeys who are naturally ferocious that are brought
up in a peaceful community o f monkeys become peaceful. Another
example is of goats raised among sheep, who prefer to have sex with
sheep. Sheep raised among goats prefer to have sex with goats. But also
great novelists offer us insight into how humans are influenced socially
by their environment. In his novel *The Heart o f Darkness*, Joseph Conrad
dramatically points out the thin veneer of civilization. The ivory trader
Kurtz, who had been a civilized European man, goes native after living
for a period of time among "savages" in the Congo wilderness. He not
only becomes like one of the savages, but he leads hunting raids with the
savages for ivory. After conquering and killing other tribe members, their
severed heads are stuck up on poles. Before dying, Kurtz cries out on
what his life had become saying, "The horror. The horror." Scientists and
perceptive novelists have noted the strong effect o f the community to
influence identity and behavior.

Religion cannot be relegated to the dust heap as recommended by
Dawkins and Hitchens. Instead of only seeing religion as provoking violence,
religion has also contributed to bringing about freedom and equality
for the people and avoiding violence. It is not religion itself, but how it is
used, for political power or for freedom. The prime example o f religion's use
for freedom was Moses, who had been a model for Jesus, Freud, and many
religious leaders. Moses was the religious leader who liberated the Jewish
people from Egyptian slavery. His words, "Let my people go," have been
resounded by other religious leaders, especially in the black community.
Another religious leader was Mohandas Gandhi (1869-1948), also
called Mahatma, meaning "great soul," as well as Bapu, the father of India.
The British had dominated India, and Gandhi was able to form a nonviolent
movement to confront them. From the bottom up Gandhi brought
about the transfer of political power from the English to the people of India.

The English authorities felt superior and discriminated against the
Hindu and Muslim population of India. Gandhi recognized the limitations
of intellect but not the emotional heart, which enabled him to gather
people to his cause. One of the deadly sins he proclaimed was science

without humanity. His confidence came from what he called soul power and his religious belief in the ultimate triumph of good over evil. He p ro claimed God was in each human being. Truth (*satya*) is God, and nonviolence (*ahimsa*) was his means of achieving truth. These sentiments resonated with the English, who were influenced by the Christian sense of morality and justice. Against an authoritarian state like Communist Russia, nonviolent resistence would not have been effective.

The economic exploitation o f the people of India by the English was in conflict with these shared religious moral values. When the English imposed a salt tax, Gandhi lead a Salt March of 248 miles to the sea. People made their own salt and also spun and made their own clothing. He was able to achieve Indian independence after World War II, as the power of England declined. He hoped to eliminate the hierarchical class structure and poverty and to liberate women. When asked if he was a Hindu, Gandhi replied, "Yes, I am. I am also a Christian, a Muslim, a Buddhist, and a Jew." He respected his own religion but was pluralistic and against religious intolerance. He emphasized the golden rule that was the universal basis of each religion.

Originally Christianity emphasized that belief alone was necessary for salvation, and yet actions often did not comply with beliefs. Gandhi showed that complying to religious values was necessary but not sufficient. He actively practiced his religious values by enlisting others to bring about change from the bottom up. A great number of people have been inspired by Gandhi's use of his religious beliefs to achieve freedom and equality in India. Gandhi's nonviolent actions provided a model for Reverend Martin Luther King, Jr., Nelson Mandela, and Archbishop Desmond Tutu. The Reverend Martin Luther King, Jr. (1929-1968) used Gandhi's method of nonviolent resistance to bring about change in racial bigotry and violence against blacks in the United States. Reverend King formed a movement that confronted many southern Christians who were opposed to both the integration of schools and eliminating segregation of blacks. Many o f the freedom riders and civil rights lawyers who joined his movement were Jewish.

Other individuals have been able to change society through nonviolence. One was Nelson Mandela, who after many years of imprisonment, prevented a bloody civil war in South Africa by teaching nonviolence and acceptance of past injustice. He was elected president but did not seek power, giving up leadership after his first term. Another was Archbishop Desmond Tutu, who preached forgiveness in South Africa and who considered the average people to be the real stars.

In the United States there was an individual who emerged as a prophetic soul. He was Rabbi Abraham Joshua Heschel (1907-1972). Many years ago I was so intrigued by the title o f his book, *God in Search o f Man: A Philosophy o f Judaism* (1959), that I attended his lecture. He spoke about God being in need of man to be an active partner to help redeem other human beings. Actually performing good acts, compassion for others, represented the expression of the divine within each person. He stressed the importance of social action, which had been the call of the

Hebrew prophets. Just belief and performing rituals to feel righteous and superior, or to serve as a personal insurance policy for salvation in an afterlife, was not enough. The universal spirit of religion, the concern for others was the fundamental human impulse of all religions.

Rabbi Heschel preached that religion must remain separate from politics (S. Heschel 1996). He despaired over the fact that many politicians were opportunistic and Machiavellian. They used religion to advance their personal power and did not speak with honesty and the truth. He compared these deceptive demagogues to the biblical characters in Genesis, especially the snake, Adam, and Eve. They were expelled from the Garden of Eden by God for being deceptive. Rabbi Heschel emphasized the importance and power of words that make up the Bible. When people speak falsehoods, they desecrate the Bible and destroy what he called the "fortress of the spirit."

Rabbi Heschel spoke of Jesus as a profound Jewish teacher, who expounded the Torah, the prophets, and the Ten Commandments. Many Christians only see the Jewish Bible as a preparation for and being succeeded by the Christian Bible. Jesus saw and valued only the Jewish Bible, from which he preached. Rabbi Heschel noted that the Kingdom of God that Jesus hoped to reestablish was mentioned in the Jewish Bible in Exodus 19:6. It states that after the Israelites were freed from Egyptian slavery and arrived in the Sinai, the Lord God said, "You shall be to me a kingdom of priests and a holy nation." Heschel mentioned, it was many years later, only after being defeated by the Philistines, that the people of Israel demanded that Samuel change their political structure. Instead of the Kingdom of God, the Israelites pressured Samuel for a human king and Saul was anointed. But later, Jesus sought to bring back the Kingdom of God, with God as the sole ruler.

Rabbi Heschel spoke about our living in an age of pluralism, where Judaism and Christianity need to respect each other's divergence and to help each other to understand the meaning of God. To condemn Jews, who had divergent views about the divinity of Jesus, does not follow in the footsteps and the inclusive beliefs of Jesus himself. Rabbi Heschel stated that to tu rn a disagreement about Jesus into an act of apostasy from God seemed neither logical nor charitable.

The concern for human freedom and equality was expressed in Rabbi Heschel's efforts to help Soviet Jewry leave Russia, where they were being persecuted. In 1965, Rabbi Heschel joined Martin Luther King, Jr. on the walk from Selma to Montgomery Alabama to protest discrimination and violence against blacks. Rabbi Heschel and Reverend King not only talked the talk but literally walked the walk that demonstrated compassion, morality, and justice for all.

Chosen by American Jewish organizations to negotiate with the leaders of the Second Vatican Council (1962-1965), Rabbi Heschel was able to influence Pope Paul VI. This had a profoundly positive effect on Catholic-Jewish relations. In the Second Vatican Council, the Roman Catholic church would no longer seek to convert Jews to Catholicism. Christians and Jews shared the same patrimony, and anti-Semitism was decried. In the Nostra Aetate section, the Vatican announced that all

Jews were not responsible for the death o f Jesus then or now. Pope John Paul II asked for forgiveness for the many years o f past sins by Catholics against the Jews. He went to Israel, visited the Holocaust Museum and the Western Wall in Jerusalem. One o f the most important books written on the relationships between Christians and Jews was by James

Carroll. As a former priest, Carroll had been influenced by Rabbi Heschel, which resulted in his writing the superb book, *Constantine's Sword: The Church and the Jews, A History.* Rabbi Jack Bemporad has continued to be part of this ecumenical movement and teaches at the Angelicum College o f the Vatican.

Essentially all religions emphasize ethical values, which include moral values for individuals and society. Pope John Paul II also reiterated the sentiments that all religions were brothers. Buddha emphasized acting ethically toward others and against seeking personal power, greed, hatred, and callousness. The Koran also teaches the golden rule and preaches tolerance. We live in a global world that needs to become more pluralistic and accept the diversity of beliefs of humankind. There is no absolute truth, and thus there should not be efforts to coerce others to accept one's belief system. During a television interview with Frank Reynolds in the program *Directions* in 1971, Rabbi Heschel made the following statements. He said he was an optimist, even against his better judgement. But, his ability to be surprised kept him alive, and the need to care for other people was the measure of our humanity.

Our Constitution begins with, "We the people," which spells out the basis of our democratic government, which is based on the will of its individual citizens. It arose as a result of the Enlightenment and is dedicated to the wishes and aspirations of all individuals in the United States. It is against a top down form of government which had existed in Europe prior to the Enlightenment, which was authoritarian and in the interests of the ruling elite. Our creative founding fathers achieved a compromise that helped establish our representative ordered democracy. The people elected their leaders, who in turn were responsible to the wishes of their electorate. The founding fathers of the United States in their wisdom also addressed emotional issues, which they recognized would arise even in a secular government. To prevent one branch of government becoming too powerful, they created checks and balances to prevent the abuse of power. Thus, neither the president, the legislature, or the court would exercise absolute power.

With the advance of science and rationality in the Enlightenment, people felt more empowered and did not need to comply to the illusion of the divine right of kings to rule. Thus, the founding fathers of the United States separated religion and politics, which had enabled kings to have the power to dominate their people. The founding fathers of the United States were moderates and did not see faith as the mortal enemy of reason. Faith and reason could coexist separately along side each other. They created a secular government, with no national religion, b ut established freedom of religion in the First Amendment. People could freely practice their own religion, but it prevented one group from seeking political power by imposing their beliefs on others. They created a representative democracy responsive to the group and individual needs of all its citizens. Citizens could freely practice their religious or nonreligious beliefs. They could maintain their ethnic or national identities while also

being American citizens. In the United States religious and racial discrimination has been diminishing as individual ability is recognized more and more. Yet, the outside world still cannot accept a world that is pluralistic, due to existing tribalism, nationalism, and fundamental reli174 gious groups. Hopefully some day, despite past emotional beliefs, ethnic and religious conflict, people can respect diversity and address the needs of all individuals to make the world a place where we can all cooperate and live in peace.

Appendix

Historical Background

According to Stephen Jay Gould (2001), reductionist thinking has existed since the seventeenth century and was responsible for the isolation and rigid boundaries between each scientific discipline. The result was a lack o f interdisciplinary collaboration to investigate complex systems, especially in biology and psychology. Historically, Descartes and the British empirical philosophers had divided the mind from the body and the self from the world. However, in 1905 Einstein published his special relativity theory in which space and time were not separate but were together as space-time. In his later general relativity theory, Einstein revised Newton's theory of gravity. Instead of being pulled, gravity was pushed and resulted from the warping of space-time around the sun. This was later verified by measurements during a total eclipse by the astronomers Eddington and Campbell. Despite these changes in physics, in the social sciences a single explanation for phenomena limited to one branch has generally persisted.

Psychology

Freud, who worked in Brucke's laboratory, was influenced by Brucke's involvement with the Logical Positivists. Thus, Freud tried to link psychology to the principle of conservation of energy, based on Newtonian physics. Freud limited his understanding of behavior to one single factor, intrapsychic dynamics w ithin the individual. He speculated that a conceptual force, libido, operated in a closed system and if invested in one area was depleted in another area. He saw behavior as influenced by the biological instincts of sex and aggression. However, Freud recognized that his metapsychology was the weakest part of his contribution.

Freud's one person psychology was later extended by Melanie Klein and other British object relations psychoanalysts. These British psychoanalysts were influenced by Darwinian theory concerning adaptation to the environment, and they noted the interaction between mother and infant. They introduced attachment theory into psychoanalysis. Winnicott (1965), a major theorist of attachment theory, noted a transitional space between mother and infant, and that not only did the infant seek attachment but the mother experienced maternal preoccupation.

Margaret Mahler (1964), a noted child clinician, then considered there were distinct stages of infant development leading to separation and individuation. In her symbiotic stage, the infant and mother were not differentiated and functioned as if they were one. Direct infant observations studies by Emde (1987), Stern (1985), and others noted there was no initial

autistic stage, as Mahler had claimed, but that attachment and attunement between the mother and infant occurred shortly after birth. Further knowledge of the interaction of the mind, the brain, and the environment came from observations of infants with visual or auditory defects, patients with brain lesions, brain surgery, animal studies, and dream laboratories.

The proof of the interaction between mother and infant came from simultaneous brain imaging studies of infant and mother.

Vamik Volkan extended psychoanalysis by noting the importance of collective emotional memories on large group behavior. In summary, psychoanalysts noted that behavior may result from individual dynamics, interaction between individuals, or collective emotional memories in large groups. My work was to study the psychoanalytic family system's effect on behavior.

The Bellevue Experimental Study

As head of the Family and Group Therapy Department at New York University Bellevue Medical Center, we were able to work with a large number of dysfunctional families. I was able to develop a clinical theory, which I termed the symbiotic survival pattern (Slipp 1984). These families demonstrated a persistent lack of differentiation, somewhat like Mahler's symbiotic developmental stage, that eliminated individual boundaries between its members. This symbiosis was seen as evolving from projective identification of either the internalized self or object representation between parent(s) and child.Families suffering different forms of pathology in their child who showed distinct family projective identification patterns. A family typology was devised that involved a dialectic between indi178

Appendix

vidual and interactional dynamics in the family group. There was some validating evidence in studying families with a schizophrenic young adult by David Reiss (1971), Theodore Lidz et al (1965), and Lyman Wynne et al (1958), in antisocial behavior by Jurgen Ruesch (1957), and in depression by Silvano Arieti (1962) and Jules Bemporad (1971). However, the family structure we found of the neurotic depressive child seemed most evident and easiest to test empirically with a laboratory study.

A double bind theory of depression was postulated in which one or both parents pressure the child for performance and vicariously live through the child's achievement. However, they do not reward the child for achievement, take it for granted, or deem it as never good enough. But the parent threatens rejection if the child does not achieve. Not validating achievement and threatening rejection for nonachievement prevents the child from owning and growing confident. It interferes with separation and individuation. An empirical method to validate this hypothesis was needed and the laboratory procedure of subliminal stimulation was found. This laboratory procedure could study the interaction of the environment on the unconscious mind, especially the internalized object relations and ego boundaries of the child.

The procedure of subliminal stimulation dates back to Otto Peotzl (1917) and to Charles Fisher (1954), who found that visual stimuli that were offered below the level of perceptual awareness influenced the content of dreams. Lloyd Silverman's seminal research (1971) showed how subliminal stimuli, flashed through a machine called a tachistoscope, influenced the unconscious and produced emotional and behavioral effects that could be measured psychologically. To eliminate observer bias, Silverman's research was experimentally controlled. He used controlled

messages and a double blind procedure, where the experimenter did not know what was being flashed. He found that only subliminal messages produced specific effects and that they had no effect when consciously perceived. One message, "Mommy and I are One," was noted to be ameliorative for a large number o f conditions for a brief period of time. It reduced the level of pathology in differentiated schizophrenics, phobic patients, and alcoholics, and helped in weight reduction and counseling. This mommy message replicated the infant's need to bond with their mother, as if one, in order to survive and had a beneficial effect. But, the mommy message actually increased pathology in poorly differentiated schizophrenic patients, since it seemed to lead to too great a merging with the mother and obliteration o f the self. Also increased pathology occurred in schizophrenic patients by sending a subliminal message of "I am Mommy" or "Destroy Mommy." This negative effect in schizophrenic patients apparently resulted again from obliteration of the internal boundaries of self and mother.

In two of our research studies (Slipp 1984), it was found that the "Mommy and I are One" subliminal message was not ameliorative with neurotically depressed women or underachieving high school students when one or both of their parents continued to impinge on their autonomy. The current ongoing relationship with their mother (or both parents) was measured on a pretest questionnaire to see if it was intrusive, pressuring for achievement, and nongratifying. This theory of depression does not encompass all forms of depression, which may be of genetic origin or due to organic pathology or loss of a relationship, job, or status. The form of neurotic depression we studied occurs in a child when one or both of the parents felt unfulfilled in their lives and become dependent on living vicariously through the child's achievements. The parent then impinges on the child's autonomy, interfering with the establishment of normal boundaries of the self, and thus prevents separation. The depressed young adults we studied were exposed to explicit pressure to achieve, but there was an accompanying implicit threat of rejection for failure to achieve. To keep the child from gaining strength from the achievement and separating, the parent(s) did not validate the achievement. The parent(s) owned it and not the child. The result was a no-win dilemma that robbed the child of empowerment. Neither success nor failure would result in enhanced self-esteem and independence. This interpersonal family relationship becomes internalized by the child. As an adult failure is devastating, and no achievement is ever felt to be good enough. Thus the theory was termed the double bind on achievement. This theory is similar to Seligman and Maier's (1967) learned helplessness in animals, who could not win, being shocked whichever path they took, which resulted in depression. It also corresponds to the theory of the dominant other as noted in depressives by Bemporad (1982).

In one study (Slipp and Nissenfeld 1981), my double bind theory on achievement was tested on depressed adult women and the following psychological tests were used. The double bind theory on achievement was operationalized into a Succeed-Fail questionnaire. It was given before testing to assess parental as well as self-pressure and gratification for achievement. In addition the Burdock and Hardesty Structural Clinical Interview, and the Beck Depression Inventory were administered. Before and after each subliminal stimulation the following tests were given: the Multiple

Affect Adjective Checklist, the Thematic Apperception Test, and Silverman's Adjective Rating Scale of self-object differentiation. The sample included forty-eight matched neurotically depressed adult women. The design was double blind, so that neither the testers nor the subjects were aware of the message being flashed subliminally. Both written and pictorial image subliminal messages were used in the tachistoscope to stimulate the left and right sides of the brain. The subliminal messages were "Mommy and I are One," "Destroy Mother," and "Succeed for Yourself," while the control neutral message was "People are Walking." The "Destroy Mother" message was used to examine the role o f hostility in depression as proposed in traditional psychoanalytic theory.

Only the "Mommy and I are One" message reduced depression, but only in those women having a currently gratifying relationship with their mother. Their depression may have been due to other causes. But if the mother was found to be pressuring and nongratifying on the Succeed-Fail questionnaire, this message was not ameliorative. Also the "Destroy Mother" did not increase depression. Thus hostility was not validated as a prime cause for depression, as considered in psychoanalytic theory. The "Succeed for Yourself" was also not ameliorative, since separation was probably associated with loss and rejection by the parent(s). These women remained dependently attached hoping for approval and feeling too inadequate to be unable to separate as an individual. This experiment seemed to validate our clinical hypothesis concerning one form of neurotic depression. It also confirmed the clinical finding o f Bemporad (1982), who noted that neurotically depressed adults transferred their dependency onto another "dominant other," and feared abandonment if they did not achieve or if they tried to be autonomous.

A second study was done with 108 underachieving high school students of both sexes to find out if therapeutic improvement over a longer time could be achieved through repeated exposures to subliminal stimulation (Greenberg 1980, Slipp 1984, 2000). In addition to the above tests used, the Tennessee Self-Concept and Cohen's Fear of Success Scales (1974) were used. The subliminal messages used were "Mommy and I are One" and "My Success is OK," along with a control message of "People are Walking." The "My Success is OK" seemed less threatening of abandonment and sanctioned permission for success. Subliminal stimulation was administered four times a week for six weeks to these underachieving young adults.

The "Mommy and I are One" message improved school performance in most of the boys, but was not effective if they experienced their mothers as pressuring and nongratifying of achievement. This latter group of boys also suffered a high fear o f success, lower self-concept, and lower selfmother and self-father differentiation on post testing. The "Mommy and I are One" message did not improve the school performance of girls. Instead it caused higher anxiety, hostility, depression, and a lowering of the need to achieve. These girls came from a suburban community, where their mothers were housewives, and presented the model of a female cultural stereotype. Achieving beyond their mother may have threatened disruption of the daughter's relationship with her, or perhaps created competition with or envy by the mother. Another possibility is that these high school girls feared they would not be attractive to boys if they outshined them. Interestingly, those girls who had a mother who pressured but did

not gratify achievement suffered the greatest. The mothers may have been frustrated with their role as a housewife and may have wanted to live vicariously through their daughters' achievements. These girls scored high on the fear of success scale, and showed a lower self-concept and lower self-mother differentiation on post testing.

These findings are supported by psychological testing by Carnovan-Gumpert, Garner and Gumpert (1978), Cohen (1974), and Miller (1978), who found that fear of success is related to negative reinforcement by one or both parents to the child's movement toward self-expression and mastery. Separation, individuation, and independent success are experienced as a threat of abandonment. In summary, both these studies validated my double bind on achievement theory of a form of depression in which the parental relationship is internalized by the child. A toxic relationship with the mother can precipitate a form of neurotic depression, poor performance out of opposition, or difficulty having a mature relationship with intact boundaries. More extensive studies on a larger number of individuals would be helpful. In conclusion, a relationship that is sensitive to the needs of the infant and the child and that validates achievement and does not block separation serves as a model for normal adult attachment and is beneficial to healthy functioning. Without other external traumas or collective emotional group memories, the adult can function as an autonomous individual and sustain a healthy attachment to others.

Bibliography

Appiah, K. A. (2007). *Experiments in Ethics.* Cambridge, MA: Harvard University Press.

Arieti, S. (1962). The psychotherapeutic approach to depression. *American Journal of Psychotherapy* 16:397^106.

Asch, S. E. (1956). Studies of independence and submission to group pressure: 1. A minority of one against a unanimous majority. *Psychology Monograph* 70:416, 147-212.

Ausubel, N. (1961). *Pictorial History of the Jewish People.* New York, NY: Crown, p.81.

Bemporad, J. (1971). New views on the psychodynamics of the depressive character. In *World Biennial of Psychiatry and Psychotherapy* 1, ed. S. Arieti. New York, NY: Basic Books.

Bemporad, J. (1982). Change factors in the treatment of depression. In *Curative Factors in Dynamic Psychotherapy,* ed. S. Slipp. New York, NY: McGraw Hill, pp.280-297.

Bion, W. R. (1959). *Experiences in Groups.* New York, NY: Basic Books.

Blum, H. P. (1983). The prototype of preoedipal reconstruction. In *Freud and his Self-Analysis,* ed. M. Kanzer and Jules Glenn. New York, NY: Jason Aronson, chap. 9.

Bowlby, J. (1969). *Attachment and Loss* 1. New York, NY: Basic Books.

Breiter, H. C., Etcoff, N. L., Whalen, P. J., Kennedy, W. A., Rauch, S. L., Buckner, R. L., Strauss, M. M., Hyman, S. E., and B. R. Rosen. (1996). Response and habituation of the human amygdala during visual processing of facial expression. *Neuron* 17:875-887.

Carnovan-Gumpert, D,, K. Garner, and P. Gumpert. (1978). *The Success-Fearing Personality: Theory and Research with Implications for the Social Psychology of Achievement.* Lexington, MA: D.C. Heath.

Carroll, J. (2001). *Constantine's Sword: The Church and the Jews, A History.* New York, NY: Houghton Mifflin Co.

Chilton, B. (2000). *Rabbi Jesus: An Intimate Biography.* New York, NY: Doubleday.

Cohen, N. (1974). The effects of four subliminally introduced merging stimuli on the psychopathology of schizophrenic women. Ph.D. dissertation, Columbia University.

Cohen, N. (1974). Explorations in the fear of success. Unpublished Ph.D. dissertation, Columbia University.

Cohen, S. f. D. (1987). *From the Maccabees to the Mishnah.* Louisville, KY: Westminster John Knox Press.

Damasio, A. (1999). *The Feeling of What Happens: Body and Emotion in the Making of Consciousness.* New York, NY: Harcourt.

Damasio, A. (2003). *Looking for Spinoza: Joy, Sorrow, and the Feeling Brain.* New York, NY: Harcourt.

Darlington, C. D. (1969). *Evolution of Man and Society.* London: Allen Unwin.

Dawkins, R. (2006). *The God Delusion.* New York, NY: Bantom Books.

de Beauvoir, S. (1961) *The Second Sex.* New York, NY: Bantom Books.

Ehrman, B. D. (1999). *Jesus: Apocalyptic Prophet of the New Millennium.* Oxford University Press, New York, NY, pp. 186, 220-222.

Ehrman, B. D. (2005). *Misquoting Jesus: The Story Behind Who Changed the Bible and Why.* San Francisco, CA: Harper Collins.

Emde, R. N. (1987). The role of positive emotions on development. Paper presented at Conference on Beyond the Pleasure Principle, Columbia University Center for Psychoanalytic Training and Research, New York, NY.

Fairbairn, W. R. D. (1954). *An Object Relations Theory on Personality.* New York: Basic Books.

Fisher, C. (1954). Dreams and perception. *Journal of the American Psychoanalytic Association* 2:389-445.

Friedan, B. (1963). *The Feminine Mystique.* New York, NY: Norton.

Freud, S. (1895). A project for a scientific psychology. *Standard Edition* 1.

Freud, S. (1927). The future of an illusion. *Standard Edition* 21.

Freud, S. (1939). Moses and monotheism. *Standard Edition* 23.

Freud, S. and W. C. Bullitt. (1967). *Thomas Woodrow Wilson, Twenty-Eighth President of the United States: A Psychological Study.* Boston, MA: Houghton Mifflin.

Gabbard, G. (2004). *Mind, brain, and personality disorders.* Adolf Meyer Lecture, American Psychiatric Association Annual Meeting, New York, NY. May 3.

Galambush, J. (2005).The *Reluctant Parting: How the New Testament's Jewish Writers Created a Christian Book.* Harper Collins, San Francisco, CA, pp.1-11.

Gay, P. (1988). *Freud: A Life for Our Time.* New York, NY: W. W. Norton.

Gould, S. J. (2001). Humbled by the genome's mysteries. *New York Times,* Op-Ed, A15, Monday, February 19.

Greenberg, S. (1980). An experimental study of underachievement: The effects of subliminal merging and success-related stimuli on the academic performance of bright underachieving high school students. Ph.D. dissertation, New York University.

Greenblatt, S. (2004). *Will in the World: How Shakespeare Became Shakespeare.* New York, NY: Norton.

Grosskurth, P. (1991). *The Secret Ring: Freud's Inner Circle and the Politics of Psychoanalysis.* New York, NY: Addison-Wesley.

Hardin, H. T. (1988). On the vicissitudes of Freud's early mothering: Alienation from his biological mother. *Psychoanalytic Quarterly* 57:72-86.

Heller, J. B. (1956). *Freud's mother and father: A memoir. Commentary* 21:418-421.

Hertzberg, A. (1999). *Jews: The Essence and Character of a People.* San Francisco, CA: Harper Collins.

Heschel, A. J. (1959). *God in Search of Man: A Philosophy of Judaism.* New York, NY: Farrar, Straus, and Cudahy.

Heschel, S. (1996). *Moral Grandeur and Spiritual Audacity: Essays of Abraham Joshua Heschel.* New York, NY: Farrar, Straus, and Giroux.

Hitchens, C. (2007). *God Is Not Great: How Religion Poisons Everything.* New York, NY: Warner Books.

Hitler, A. (1927, 1939). *Mein Kampf.* Boston, MA: Houghton Mifflin.

Holy Bible. Revised Standard Edition, 1974. New York, NY: New American Library.

Horney, K. (1950). *Neurosis and Human Growth.* New York, NY: Norton.

Jacoby, S. (2008). *The Age of American Unreason.* New York, NY: Pantheon Books.

Jones, E. (1953). *The Life and Work of Sigmund Freud.* New York, NY: Basic Books.

Kandel, E. (1983). *From metapsychology to molecular biology.* American Journal of Psychiatry, 140:277-293.

Kanwisher, N. (2004), fMRI Investigations of human extrastraite cortex: People, places and things. Presentation at Columbia University, 250 Conference: Brain and Mind. May 14.

Kirsch, A. (2008). *Benjamin Disraeli.* New York, NY: Schocken/Random House.

Klein, M. (1948). *Contributions to Psychoanalysis, 1921-1945.* London: Hogarth Press and the Institute of Psychoanalysis.

Klinghoffer, D. (2006). *Why the Jews Rejected Jesus.* New York, NY: Doubleday.

Krull, M. (1986). *Freud and His Father.* New York, NY: W. W. Norton.

Langer, S. K. (1942). *Philosophy in a New Key.* Penguin Books, chap 8.

LeDoux, J. E. (1996). *The Emotional Brain: The Mysterious Underpinnings of Emotional Life.* New York, NY: Simon and Schuster.

Lidz, T., S. Fleck and A. R. Cornelison. (1965). *Schizophrenia and the Family.* New York, NY: International Universities Press.

Lidz, T. and R. Lidz. (1988). *Oedipus in the Stone Age.* New York, NY: International Universities Press.

Lilia, M. (2007). *The Stillborn God.* New York, NY: Vintage, Random House.

Mahler, M. S. (1964). On the significance of the normal separation-individuation phase. In *Drives, Affects, and Behavior* 2, ed. M. Schur. New York, NY: International Universities Press.

Mahler, M. S. and M. Furer. (1968). *On Human Symbiosis and the Vicissitudes of Individuation* 1, New York, NY: International Universities Press.

Mahler, M. S., F. Pine and A Bergman. *The Psychological Birth of the Human Infant: Symbiosis and Individuation.* New York, NY: Basic Books.

Main, M. (1996). Introduction to the special section on attachment and psychopathology: 2, Overview of the field of attachment. *Journal of Consulting and Clinical Psychology* 64:237-243.

Milgram, S. (1974). *Obedience to Authority.* New York, NY: Harper and Row.

Miller, J. R. (1978). The relationship of fear of success to perceived parental attitudes toward success and autonomy. Unpublished Ph.D. dissertation, Columbia University.

Neusner, J. (1993). *A Rabbi Talks to Jesus: An Intermillennial Interfaith Exchange.* New York, NY: Doubleday.

Pagels, E. (1989). *The Gnostic Gospels.* Vintage. New York, NY: Random House.

Panksepp, J. (1999). Emotions as viewed by psychoanalysis and neuroscience: An exercise in concilience. *Neuro-Psychoanalysis* 1:15-38.

Poetzl, O. (1917). The relationship between experimentally induced dream images and indirect vision. *Psychological Issues* 2:41-120.

Rauch, S.L., van der Kolk, B. A., Fisler, R. E,, Alpert, N. M., Orr, S. P., Savage, C. R., Fischman, A. J., Jenike, M. A., and R. K. Pitman. (1996). A symptom provocation study of posttraumatic stress disorder using positron emission tomography and script-driven images. *Archives of General Psychiatry* 53:380-387.

Reiss, D. (1971). Varieties of consenual experience, III. Contrasts between families of normals, delinquents, and schizophrenics. *Journal of Nervous and Mental Disease* 152:73-95.

Reusch, J. (1957). *Disturbed Communication: The Social Matrix of Psychiatry.* New York, NY: Norton.

Rivkin, E. (1918). *What Crucified Jesus?* New York, NY: UAHC Press.

Rizzuto, A. (1998). *Why Did Freud Reject God?: A Psychodynamic Interpretation.* New Haven, CT: Yale University Press.

Runes, D. D. (1942). *The Dictionary of Philosophy.* New York, NY: Philosophical Library.

Schore, A. N. (2003). *Affect Dysregulation and Disorders of the Self.* New York, NY: Norton.

Schorske, C. E. (1981). *Fin de Siecle Vienna.* New York, NY: Vintage, Random House.

Schweitzer, A. (1948). *The Psychiatric Study of Jesus: Exposition and Criticism,* Boston, MA: Beacon Press, pp.51-52.

Schweitzer, A. (1948). *The Quest for the Historical Jesus.* New York, NY: MacMillan.

Seligman, M. E. P. and S. F. (1967). Failure to escape traumatic shock, *journal of Experimental Psychology* 744:1-9.

Shirer, W. L. (1960). *The Rise and Fall of the Third Reich: A History of Nazi Germany.* New York, NY: Simon and Schuster.

Silverman, L. (1971). An experimental technique for the study of unconscious conflict. *British Journal of Medical Psychology* 44:17-25.

Slipp, S., and S. Nissenfeld. (1981). An experimental study of psychoanalytic theories of depression. *Journal of the American Academy of Psychoanalysis* 9:583-600.

Slipp, S. (1984). *Object Relations: A Dynamic Bridge Between Individual and Family Treatment.* New York, NY: Jason Aronson, pp.140-141.

Slipp, S. (1993). *The Freudian Mystique: Freud, Women, and Feminism.* New York, NY: New York University.

Slipp, S. (2000). Subliminal stimulation research and its implications for psychoanalytic theory and treatment. *Journal of the American Academy of Psychoanalysis* 28:305-320.

Stern, D. N. (1985). *The Interpersonal World of the Infant: A View from Psychoanalysis and Developmental Psychology.* New York, NY: Basic Books.

Stierlin, H. (1976). *Adolf Hitler: A Family Perspective.* New York, NY: Psychohistory Press.

Volkan, V. (1997). *Bloodlines: From Ethnic Pride to Ethnic Terrorism.* New York, NY: Farrar, Straus and Giroux.

Volkan, V. (2004). *Blind Trust: Large Groups and Their Leaders in Times of Terror.* Charlottesville, VA: Pitchstone Publishing.

Volkan, V. (2006). *Killing in the Name of Identity: A Study of Bloody Conflicts.* Charlottesville, VA: Pitchstone Publishing.

Whalen, P. J., Rauch, S. I., Etcoff, N. L., McInerney, S. C., Lee, M. B,, and M. A. Jenike. (1998). Masked presentations of emotional facial expressions modulate amygdala activity without explicit knowledge. *Journal of Neuroscience* 18:411-418.

Wills, G. (2007). *Head and Heart: American Christianities, How the Tension Between Reason and Emotion has Shaped Christianity in America.* New York, NY: Penguin.

Wilson, E. O. (1998). *Consilience: Unity of Knowledge.* New York: Knopf.

Winnicott, D. W. (1965). *The Maturational Process and the Facilitating Environment.* New York, NY: International Universities Press.

Winnicott, D. W. (1971). *Playing and Reality.* London: Tavistock.

Wynne, L. C., Ryckoff, I.M., Day, J., and S. Hirsch. (1958). Pseudomutuality in the family relations of schizophrenics. *Psychiatry* 21:205-220.

www.ingramcontent.com/pod-product-compliance
Lightning Source LLC
Chambersburg PA
CBHW081828280526
45789CB00007B/2380